Everything is Pickrick

Everything is Pickrick
The Life of Lester Maddox

by
Bob Short

MERCER UNIVERSITY PRESS
1979-1999
Twenty years of Publishing Excellence

ISBN 0-86554-662-2
MUP/H491

© 1999 Mercer University Press
6316 Peake Road
Macon, Georgia 31210-3960

First Edition.

Jacket Photograph: Georgia Dept. of Archives
Cover design: Jim Burt
Book design: Jay Polk

∞The paper used in this publication meets the minimum requirements of American National Standard for Information Sciences—Permanence of Paper for Printed Library Materials, ANSI Z39.48-1984.

Library of Congress Cataloging-in-Publication Data

CIP is available from the Library of Congress

Table of Contents

Acknowledgments

I received cooperation from a number of people during the years of research and interviews for this book. While I cannot thank them all, I can express my appreciation to Lester Maddox himself, who has shared with me many hours of quality time discussing his life and times; to his beloved wife, Virginia; to my wife, Diana, who has been an invaluable ally who helped with research and much-needed encouragement; to John I. Jones, without whose help the contents probably would make little sense; to Governor Zell Miller, Agriculture Commissioner Tommy Irvin; former Pardon and Parole Board Chairman J. O. Partain; the late Steve Polk, former director of the Georgia Building Authority; House Speaker Tom Murphy; former Maddox campaign aide, Ned Young; countless friends of Maddox and untold numbers of Georgia legislators, past and present. Thank you.

Introduction

During the summer of 1966, I was the campaign manager for then State Senator Jimmy Carter who was a candidate for the Democratic nomination for governor of Georgia. In that capacity, my duties included speaking on Carter's behalf—explaining his platform and political goals—when he could not be present. While I made numerous speeches for him that summer, the most memorable was as a political rally in late July at an Eastman, Georgia, high school football field.

As the candidates gathered on the podium—a flatbed trailer located on the fifty-yard line—huge gray thunderheads began to form in the eastern skies. It was sure to rain. Despite the ominous weather, I seated myself on the podium. To my right, in order of seating, were candidates Garland Byrd, Hoke O'Kelley and a young man who was to speak for candidate Ellis Arnall. To my left and seated next to me was Lester Maddox.

I had never met Lester Maddox personally, although I had eaten many times in his Atlanta restaurant, the Pickrick. Once I was seated, Maddox stuck out his hand and said, "I'm Lester Maddox and I'm going to be your next governor."

"Sure," I mockingly said to myself as I shook his hand. Moments later, the moderator introduced the speakers and the rally was underway. Each participant had drawn a number from the moderator's hat to determine the order of speaking. Maddox drew number one and was the first to address the crowd. When Maddox stood and approached the microphone, the clouds overhead began to break up, the sun peeped through and the crowd became silent and attentive. As he began to speak, I watched in disbelief as audience members applauded and voiced loud cat-calls as he damned the federal government for forced school integration, violation of citizens' private property rights, busing of children and wasting their money on social programs that were not working. When he was finished, Maddox waved a miniature American flag at the crowd. There was thunderous applause. It was clear that this man's message had hit home.

At the conclusion of Maddox's speech, people began leaving the bleachers although there were other speakers, including myself, waiting to be heard. Apparently, Lester Maddox was their man and they had heard what they came for. Finally, my turn came, I made my speech for Carter and the moderator announced that the rally was over.

As the candidates started to leave the platform, Maddox tapped my shoulder. I turned. "You're a good speaker," he said.

"Thanks," I replied.

Maddox smiled. "You know," he continued, "you're going to be on my side before this thing is over."

I smiled, politely shook his hand again and started out to the parking lot.

On the way back to campaign headquarters in Atlanta, I asked Jerry Franks, a Carter volunteer, about Maddox.

"Could this guy really get elected?" I asked. "Could an outsider with no experience, no money and no political connections do what several well-known, well-financed candidates are trying to do?"

"I don't see how," Jerry commented. "You have to have it all—money, experience, connections—to win the governor's race in Georgia. Most of the time you can have it all and still lose."

As Jerry and I flew back to Atlanta in silence, I remembered Maddox's comment that I "would be on his side before this thing is over." I chuckled at the man's audacity. "He has too little going for him and too far to go," I thought to myself.

Six weeks later, Maddox accomplished what some observers felt would happen but did not want to admit it. He placed a close second behind heavily favored Ellis Arnall in the primary and was set to face the former governor in a runoff. This meant that my candidate, President-to-be Jimmy Carter, was out of the contest all together. Two weeks later, in the runoff, Maddox clobbered Arnall and was headed for the general election in November.

Having Lester Maddox as the party's nominee for governor posed some very serious problems for the state's Democratic Party. Most loyal party members looked forward to a race between Arnall, a true Roosevelt Democrat, and the Republican nominee, Bo Callaway. Here was Maddox, a tenth grade dropout with no government experience pitted against Callaway, who had all the credentials for which a candidate could ask. Heir to a South Georgia textile fortune, Callaway was a West Point graduate, a Korean War combat veteran and a popular sitting congressman. Few Democrats could foresee Maddox retaining the governorship for the party.

Nobody realized this more than State Comptroller General Jimmy Bentley, a long-time Talmadge ally and prime mover in an alliance of state constitutional officers known as the "clique," composed of Agriculture Commissioner Phil Campbell, State Treasurer Jack Ray and Public Service Commissioners Crawford Pilcher and Alpha Fowler Jr. Since Maddox hardly knew these people and vice versa, it would be very difficult for them to provide direct assistance since Maddox would probably spurn their efforts. But Maddox needed help and Bentley and his clique could provide some.

On Thursday, 17 September 1966, I had finished last minute details at Carter's headquarters and was headed home to St. Simons Island to take up where I left off before joining the Carter campaign. As I started out the door, the Jimmy Bentley called and asked me to pay him a visit. I said I was headed home, but finally agreed.

Over a meal at his home, Jimmy and I talked about Maddox. I told him that Maddox was popular among average Georgians, that he had completely out-campaigned the other Democrats and that, with a little luck, he could become governor. Bentley countered that he needed help from the "big mules" in the party. He could start, Bentley pointed out, by attempting to unite the supporters of other Democratic candidates. Since I had been deeply involved with Carter and knew the other candidates and their key backers, Bentley thought I could help Maddox put together a more cohesive campaign effort.

"But Jimmy," I responded, "from what I have been able to determine he's a one-man show. He has no campaign organization, no consultant, no media advisor, no staff, except family, and, worst of all, no financial backing." Jimmy smiled and nodded in agreement. "An appointment has already been made," Bentley said. "He'll see you as soon as you get there in the morning."

On the way home, I thought again about Lester Maddox. He was a jovial and humorous man who had an optimism that was absolutely contagious. Everybody seemed to like him, even if they didn't share his political views. He had little support among the state's political leadership, but he had proven that he did not need it. There was something intriguing about him. On one hand, he had a childlike honesty and sincerity that I found very appealing. On the other hand, he had home-spun humor that one did not usually find in successful politicians. I knew that any experience with Lester Maddox would be interesting.

So I met with Maddox and, after he listened very carefully to what I had to say, Maddox explained that he knew about me and would be glad to have me onboard. After we talked for a few minutes, Maddox rose from behind his desk, clasped my hand and smiled from ear-to-ear. "Brother Short," he said, "we're going to win this election because God's on our side."

Over the next three months, I got a close, personal look at Lester Maddox. He had unbelievable energy and political savvy. As a campaigner, he was indefatigable. On the campaign trail, at campaign strategy meetings and in private, he was honest to a fault. He worked harder than any politician I had ever seen and he was a firm believer in getting votes the old-fashioned way: out in the streets, walking up to people, shaking their hands and asking for their votes.

Maddox's campaign structure was simple. His brother Wesley was his campaign manager. His sisters served as campaign aides. He had no consultant. No media aid. No secretary. But he had what Ellis Arnall, Jim Gray, Jimmy Carter and the others coveted. He possessed the Democratic nomination for governor. Also, he had his old Pontiac station wagon, its driver J. L. Allen Jr., plenty of "Maddox Country" signs, a hammer and a lifetime supply of nails.

It was obvious that attempting to change the Maddox style would be foolish. It fit the man perfectly. Early on, I could see that my job was to bring other people into the campaign without upsetting the existing structure. Thus, we sought our support from every imaginable source—Democratic congressmen, local officeholders, known "yellow dogs" (voters who would vote Democratic even if a yellow dog were the candidate), state officials, former Maddox opponents—in short, anyone who could add strength to his candidacy. It wasn't easy. We hit one brick wall after another. Slowly, we realized that the only people who wanted to support Maddox were the voters.

Meanwhile, Maddox himself basked in his success. He truly enjoyed campaigning and seldom interfered with the goings-on in the headquarters. We responded to queries from the media, answered mail, coordinated his schedule as best we could, took his calls and performed normal campaign duties while he continued to travel the state and spread his peculiar brand of politics. It was Lester Maddox's show. He was the star and he was good. It was Lester Maddox against the world.

On 8 November 1966, Georgians went to the polls to cast their ballots in the general election. A week later, after all the ballots had been painstakingly counted, Callaway had 453,665 votes; Maddox had 450,626; and the WIGS (a write-in effort for Ellis Arnall), 52,831. Throughout the campaigning, everyone was aware that a write-in effort was on-going, but its effect on the ultimate outcome was considered negligible. Now, this renegade effort had thrown a wrench into the election process and prevented either Callaway or Maddox from reaching the majority required by law.

In such cases, most observers assumed that the state legislature would decide the election's outcome. The state's constitution clearly stated that, if a candidate failed to receive a majority of the votes cast in the general election, the legislature would choose between the two candidates with the highest number of votes. Meanwhile, Callaway supporters John Barton and Nancy Jones, with the help of Callaway lawyers, filed suit asking that the election-by-legislature section of the constitution be declared invalid. They knew that, if the outcome were left up to the legislature, the Democratic majority would overwhelmingly elect Maddox.

Finally, after more than six weeks of speculation and legal wrangling, the United States Supreme Court upheld the state constitution and declared that the state legislature could, indeed, decide the election's outcome. Thus, on 10 January 1997, as expected, the legislature elected

Lester Maddox Georgia's seventy-fifth governor. It was nothing short of a miracle. The high school dropout with no previous government experience now held the highest office in the state.

Once Maddox thanked the legislature for its decision and was sworn in, I and several other close aides and friends accompanied the new governor to his new office in the capitol. Shortly after we arrived there, Maddox pulled me aside. "Brother Bob," he said, " I need to swear you in."

I looked at him. "To what?!" I asked.

"I don't know," he shrugged. "We'll figure that out tomorrow."

I laughed, knowing that my role was defined. Like it or not, I would be a handy man and his press secretary. He needed both—someone with experience to help him navigate state government and a seasoned hand at working with the media. The next day he would deliver his inaugural address and become front page news all over the world. Both he and I knew that his speech would capture the attention of people everywhere and make him an overnight media target.

He quickly recovered the Bible used to swear him in, ordered me to place my right hand on it and began reciting the oath he had taken only a few minutes earlier. "Do you, Bob Short, swear to uphold the laws of the state of Georgia......?" Maddox began. As I stood there repeating the words after him, I suddenly remembered his prediction several months earlier when he said: "you're going to be on my side before this thing's over." Suddenly, one part of me wanted to laugh at the bizarre truth of Maddox's prediction. Another part of me wanted to cry. I had scoffed and considered the forecast a little more than pure silliness. Now it had come true in the most amazing way imaginable! Maddox never mentioned that he had predicted this, but for me, the whole episode had been a valuable personal lesson.

Over the next fifteen months, I served as Governor Maddox's administrative aide and press secretary. I traveled with him, wrote his speeches, listened to his problems and shared his misery. After I left the administration to direct a federal agency, I remained friends with Maddox and talked with him often. During his 1970 campaign for lieutenant governor and later in his 1974 and 1990 bids for governor, he consulted me many times. Today, I am proud to say that Lester Maddox remains a close personal and valued friend.

In writing this book, I want to give testimony to a man for whom I have enormous respect. Few have accused Lester Maddox of being a suave, sophisticated man of culture. Yet, despite his lack of education, his poverty-stricken childhood and his unpolished personal style, he rose higher that most of his contemporaries who had those qualities. In my opinion, history will record Lester Maddox as one of Georgia's finest governors. While he never silenced his critics, his tenure brought progress and his devotion to his "little people" restored their faith in government.

Lester Maddox taught me a valuable lesson—that no person is greater than any other and that there is ample opportunity in America for anyone and everyone who feel that their reach should exceed their grasp. He is a man of great compassion who handled his popularity with humility. He never forgot who he was or where he came from. He was the most honest politician I have ever known. Most political creatures weigh the consequences of every statement before they make it. Maddox didn't. He told the truth, as he saw it, regardless of the consequences.

Secondly, I am writing this book to preserve the truth about the life and times of Lester Maddox for future generations. If my great-grandchildren have no choice but to depend upon media for an account of his life and his place in history, I fear they will be sorely deluded with half-truths and criticism of a man who contributed much to Georgia.

In August 1964, Maddox came to the attention of the world when he, armed with a pistol and backed by a band of pick handle-wielding supporters, chased civil rights demonstrators away from his restaurant. At the time, Maddox tried to explain that he had nothing against blacks, he simply felt that he had the right to say who could and who could not enter his restaurant. Whatever the case, the media and others never let Maddox live the incident down and forever branded him a "racist bigot." While the episode would win Maddox thousands of votes because of racial differences and attitudes of that day, it would also be an albatross around his neck for the rest of his life.

This book has been several years in the making. I have always regretted the treatment Lester Maddox received from the media and his relentless political critics and felt that an accurate accounting of his life and times would, perhaps, help to set the record straight. Although most governors have written, or have been the subject of, books recording their "legacy," a true historical perspective on the life and times of Lester Maddox was never recorded.

This is a book about Lester Maddox, the man. While it is impossible to write about Maddox and not discuss his politics, I have tried to keep political interpretation to a minimum and concentrate on the many facets of Lester Maddox, the individual. I believe that the real Lester Maddox lies within the man, not the politician. That is the story I want to present, the life and times of Lester Maddox, warts and all.

Chapter 1

Home Park

"I felt it was almost hopeless and useless to try to continue in school under those conditions."

—Maddox on his early hardships

Born Lester Garfield Maddox on 30 September 1915, the second child and second son to Dean and Flonnie Maddox, the infant would soon discover that his life ahead would be a dirt-poor, blue collar existence in which survival depended on toughness, self-reliance and sheer determination.

A native of rural Rockmart, Georgia, Dean Maddox had only three years of formal schooling, but he was a skilled machinist who made $40 a week as a roll-turner at Atlantic Steel. Although hard-working and industrious, he liked to drink corn liquor and if his wife did not intercept him when he got his pay at Saturday noon, there might not be food for the family table the following week. Despite his drinking, however, he was also a loving and strict father who did not hesitate to use a hickory switch on his children if he felt they had stepped out of line. "[H]e was a good father and very industrious and worked day and night to try to provide the best for his family," Maddox recalled. He not only worked fifty-five hours a week at Atlantic steel, but he also traded cows and cars and whatever he could. It was this hard work and dedication which made a great impression on me. Dad was anything but lazy and for the benefit of me and my brothers and sisters, he would not tolerate any of us doing less than our best."

While Lester learned his work ethic—and his teetotaler attitude toward alcohol—from his father, the source of his heart-felt religious beliefs was his mother. Flonnie Maddox was born on Piedmont Street in Atlanta in 1894. After her father's death when she was seven, the church and religion became the mainstays of her inner life. "As a bitty child," she would say later, "I learned to go to the Lord. When trouble was so deep, the Bible was my only comfort. I learned to depend on the Lord for what I needed."

When she was 12 and had a nervous condition that caused convulsions, she prayed and she was healed. Shortly afterward, when her family was in dire financial straits, she prayed for a job and, the following week, she was hired for fifty cents a day in the Nunnally Candy plant.

At the age of 16, she met Dean Maddox one Sunday after services at the North Atlanta Baptist Church. After a short courtship, they were married and moved into a house on Grove Street in a quiet, blue-collar neighborhood near Georgia Tech. Flonnie and Dean's first four children were all born within five years and the demands of the burgeoning family took its toll on the young mother. "I was really strict with my children," she recalled later, "And probably spanked them more than I should. There was so many of them hollering at me that I'd say 'Lord, why can't I be six or seven mothers instead of one?'"

Of his mother, Maddox once said, "I really don't believe I have ever known a person with faith in God and a love for and trust in Jesus Christ that equaled my mother's.... Her Christian life and service to God is what impressed me the most because she kept all us kids in church and Sunday School. In fact, I been going to North Atlanta Baptist Church since 1917 and my mother was the reason I attended there all these years."

During the late teens and twenties, the Tech Flats area west of the Georgia School of Technology was a typical southern "mill village" which had grown up in the shadow of the Atlantic Steel company. Most of the residents were from rural, agricultural backgrounds who came to the big city with hopes of getting jobs at the steel mill so they could better themselves. Local churches were the primary centers of social gathering and, at the nearby Bellwood Theater, children could see a movie for a nickel or, for the same amount, ride a trolley car to downtown Atlanta two miles away.

Most of the homes were weathered, woodframe structures without indoor plumbing and, true to their origins, the vast majority of the families had small farming operations in their backyards with cows, chickens and pigs to supplement their incomes. Black families lived in the alleys between bigger streets and it was not uncommon for black and white children to engage in Saturday children's games in a vacant lot. The daily routines of the Maddox family, like that of most other residents, were determined by the shrill sound of the steel mill whistle which announced the beginnings and ends of each work shift.

As a first grader at Home Park Elementary School, young Lester's teachers soon realized that he had an unspecified learning problem but, in spite of it, he was promoted to the second grade. One morning as a new second grader eager to get to school, Lester rushed out of the house and suddenly tripped over his raincoat. His forehead struck a heavy, iron footwiper. The fall resulted in a gash across the top of his head that required several stitches. After that, his school work grew worse. Then a routine school eye exam revealed that Maddox was extremely nearsighted, the cause of his learning difficulties.

After the eye exam, school authorities recommended to Maddox's mother that her son be put in a special class where children with learning problems could receive the individual attention they needed. When his mother took the seven-year-old to the special school, however, and he saw the books with large print, Lester quickly realized he was being set aside as different from other children. He felt abandoned and depressed, so he begged his mother to let him go back to Home Park Elementary. "I pleaded with my mother and promised I would try harder and do better," Maddox said, recalling the painful incident. "I had already been examined for glasses, so she talked to school officials and it was decided I could have another chance."

The following Saturday, Mrs. Maddox took her son to an optometrist on Whitehall Street in downtown Atlanta where he was fitted with glasses. When Maddox and his mother walked out of the shop that afternoon around dusk, the seven-year-old was taken aback by what he saw. "I was amazed at how different the world looked," Maddox recalled. "Since I had not had normal vision before, I had no reason to believe that the blurred images I was seeing were not as they should be. Now suddenly buildings, signs, lights, people and everything up and down the street stood out clearly and made sense to me."

Despite the new glasses, Maddox's performance did not improve much at school. From the first, he was a largely indifferent student and, outside of the required reading for school work, he did no other reading. His mother, busy attending to the needs of his siblings, had no time to help him with his school work.

In school, he liked arithmetic, typing and mechanical and accounting subjects. Social subjects such as English and history held little interest for the young Maddox. Regarding civics and current political events, Lester showed minimal interest in these as a young child.

Although formal education held little more than a passing interest for young Maddox, he loved business undertakings and demonstrated a sure talent for using a small investment to turn a healthy profit early in life. In the fall of 1925, a circus came to Atlanta and ten-year-old Lester got a job bagging peanuts at three cents an hour. Seeing that the peanuts sold well to the circus-goers, he realized that he was in the wrong end of the business working for someone else, so he decided to go into business for himself. "I would go to the farmer's market and buy a ten-pound bag of raw peanuts for fifty cents," Maddox recalled, "Then I would walk back home, build a fire in mom's stove and roast the peanuts. If I didn't burn them, which I rarely did, I would bag them, then walk back to Atlanta the following day and sell thirty small bags of peanuts at five cents each, giving me a total of $1.50. After deducting fifty cents for the cost of the peanuts and five cents for fifty paper bags, I had a profit of ninety-five cents for two days work. That was big money!"

By the time Lester was eleven years old, he discovered he had a natural talent for salesmanship and he spent hours trying to sell live chickens to his neighbors. After chasing down several broilers in the Maddox family's backyard, he tied them together on a string, slung them over his shoulder and took them door-to-door. Once the lady of the house responded to Lester's knock at her door, he launched into his sales pitch: "Yes, ma'am! I've got six of the finest fryers that were ever grown and I'm going to sell all six of 'em to you for one dollar and twenty cents. That's right, just twenty cents apiece for these fine..." Though undaunted, Maddox would often be chased away from the door with a broom and an admonishment.

During his final year at Home Park Elementary, when Lester was 12, his mother fell ill with a goiter and almost died. As a result, he quit school for several weeks to help at home, washing diapers, cooking meals, cleaning house and caring for the family's livestock while his mother was in the hospital. Though Lester's mother recovered, his extended absence from class cost him promotion to the seventh grade.

Like thousands of other youngsters of the time, the enterprising young Maddox would set up a soft drink stand in front of his house during the summer months and sell ice-cold Coca-Colas. "The Coca-Cola Company would furnish you with a stand and a wooden tub to ice the cokes in, provided you bought a case of cokes from them for eighty cents," Maddox recalled.

One day when Lester was 12 years old, he had sold all of his Coca-Colas and was standing in the family's front yard on Fourteenth Street when a man driving a 1925 Chevrolet coupe stopped and made what appeared to be a business proposition. He told young Lester he needed someone to help him nail up some signs out in the country and would like to hire Maddox to help him. He said he would pay him fifty cents if Maddox would go with him and help him with the signs. Lester wasted little time in accepting the man's offer. Despite his youth, Maddox was always interested in making money.

After obtaining permission from his mother, an eager Lester got into the Chevy coupe with the man. After they had driven several miles however, Lester got suspicious. At a rural road near Buckhead, he looked around inside the car for the signs and a hammer to nail them up with. After he saw neither, he turned to the man.

"Mister," the twelve-year-old asked, "where are the signs we're going to nail up?"

"Son," the man replied. "I didn't tell the truth. I don't have any signs to put up. I like the company of young gentlemen like you."

"I hit the door screaming," Maddox recalled. "Never had I been so frightened in all my life."

Once the man saw that Maddox was about to jump out of the moving car, he started to slow the vehicle. When the car had slowed enough, Lester jumped out and began to run toward a open field, where he thought he would be safe.

"Hey son!" the man called from the car to the frightened youngster. "I don't mean you any harm! I won't hurt you. Come on, I'll take you back home."

Lester, knowing he would have to walk some five miles back home, finally consented, but refused to get back inside the car. He rode outside on the running board all the way back to Atlanta. At Peachtree Street near Buckhead, he jumped off the car. Without a word to the man, he caught the first trolley and, an hour later, made it safely back to Home Park.

"That was my first and only experience with homosexuality," Maddox said many years later. "I thank God that was the only man that ever propositioned me."

Summer days were fun in Home Park. There was no school and neighborhood youngsters had time to play when their chores were finished. With time to spare, businessman Maddox would turn his Coca-Cola stand over to his younger brother Wesley and walk the two miles to the nine-hole golf course at Piedmont Park where he could earn thirty-five cents a round as a caddy.

Although he could hardly see without his glasses, Maddox was reluctant to wear them unless it was absolutely necessary. When other boys saw him wearing glasses, they would often taunt him. As a result, he seldom wore his glasses while working as a caddy.

One summer day he was unable to find a caddy job. "My eyesight was so poor," Maddox recalled, "When I caddied for the golfers at Piedmont Park, I was unable to see the golf ball in the air and had to follow the golfer rather than the ball. Finally, it got to where the golfers wouldn't hire me." Maddox started walking back home. As he passed the tee of the second hole, he saw a caddyless golfer preparing to tee up his ball.

"Mister," Maddox offered, "I'll caddy the rest of the way for you for a quarter."

"Okay, son," the golfer answered. "It's a deal. Take my bag and move on down the fairway so you can see where my drive goes."

With that, Lester picked up the bag and lugged it down the fairway. Then he turned to watch the golfer as he teed up a ball and took a couple of practice swings. With a mighty whack, the man hit his tee shot. Instantly, at the sound of the clubhead smacking the ball, Lester heard the man yell, "Fore!"

At the golfer's warning, Lester looked up but, since he was not wearing his glasses, he saw nothing. Instantly, the powerful tee shot slammed the youngster in the side of the head and he fell to the ground in a daze. The next thing Lester recalled was the man kneeling over him and wiping his forehead with a wet handkerchief.

Shortly after impact, the man drove young Maddox to Henry Grady Hospital where he remembers being surrounded by an x-ray machine and several people in white jackets. After two days at the hospital, Maddox left with several stitches and a headache that lasted a week. It would be the last time he hired himself out as a caddy.

In the spring of 1927, Maddox applied for work as a delivery boy with both the *Atlanta Journal* and the *Atlanta Constitution*, but was turned down. Still determined to have a paper route, he went to the *Journal's* and *Constitution's* competition, the Heart newspaper, *The Georgian-American*, and, after some wrangling, was given a route that nobody else wanted. Not only did the route have a mere nineteen customers, but it was long and circuitous, covering almost three miles over much of Hemphill Avenue and Tenth, State and Fourteenth Streets.

Despite these difficulties, Lester undertook the challenge. First, he would walk the two miles from his home to downtown Atlanta in order to save the nickel trolley fare. After collecting his papers, he would sell a few downtown, then lug the others back to his route and deliver them to regular customers. He soon realized that he was walking about five miles a day, seven days a week, for about $1.20 a week.

It was while he wandered in and out of Atlanta retail stores selling the Georgian-American that Maddox became fascinated with the idea of owning his own business. "I got hung up on the fact that the owners and operators were in business for themselves. I could see the satisfaction in their faces. They were very real participants in the American free enterprise system. I determined then that some day I too would become a successful business person."

At the end of each day, however, Lester was exhausted after walking the paper route and he soon began asking himself if the rewards were worth the effort. Again, he decided to draw upon his natural salesmanship abilities and build up the paper route. Realizing that most families could only afford one newspaper, Lester started canvassing each and every house on the route, arguing that the *Georgian-American* was a better paper than the evening's *Journal* or the morning's *Constitution*. Although he was often turned away, he managed to win some converts and after eight weeks of hard work, he built his business up to a total of seventy-nine customers and was grossing an impressive $4.74 a week.

As a result, it was not long before a representative of the *Journal-Constitution*'s circulation department came calling on the enterprising twelve-year-old to offer him a paper route near his home. Maddox declined, quite content with the route and money he was earning at the time. Finally, after more coaxing, the Journal-Constitution representative left, unable to convince the young Maddox to take the new route.

Years later, when Maddox became a candidate for political office, both the *Journal* and the *Constitution* lambasted him unmercifully for his views. He found humor in accusing the newspapers of trying to exact revenge upon him for his refusal to take their delivery route.

In early 1929, a weary Maddox was still delivering the *Georgian-American* and living in the family home on Fourteenth Street when one of the major rubber companies decided to buy the house and acreage to build a plant. After some legal wrangling, Lester's father finally sold the acreage for $5,000 and moved the house—which he had constructed—to a lot he owned on State Street. Feeling better about his fate, the father decided it was time for the Maddoxes to move up in the world so he used the $5,000 to buy a new Model A Ford and make a down payment on a home on Collier road.

Once the Maddox family had moved into their spacious new dwelling on Collier Road, however, their happiness was short-lived. In October, the stock market crashed and economic gloom set in. There was word of massive lay-offs at Atlantic Steel and the elder Maddox's drinking became worse. Again and again, he leveled the charge at his superiors that they were giving preferential treatment to younger and less-experienced roll-turners. Finally, the combination of the elder Maddox's drinking and feuding with his bosses resulted in his termination.

Suddenly, the family—which had high hopes of a brighter future only four months earlier—was plunged into the depths of the Great Depression. Without an income, Lester's father was now faced with monthly car notes, a hefty mortgage payment and eight mouths to feed. Shortly afterward, he lost the house on Collier Road and the family moved back into the old home on State Street.

Once they were back in the old neighborhood, the elder Maddox took whatever job he could find. For a while, he hauled concrete blocks and bricks. Later, he found employment as a night laborer at Link-Belt Company for $10.00 a week. When that job had played out, he worked as a laborer in a foundry for a dollar a week less. Times were hard and jobs were not easy to find.

Of those days, Maddox recalled that, as his father struggled harder and harder to provide for his family, his drinking increased proportionately and, out of his meager paydays, he managed to allot more and more for liquor. "We got hungry in '31 and '32. One Christmas, me and my older brother Howard went to the Salvation Army's Christmas party so we would have Christmas. It got so bad that mother and daddy had to go to the Community Chest and try to get us something to eat, but they wouldn't help and we started taking in laundry."

During the brief period the Maddox family lived in the Collier Road home, Lester had attended North Fulton High. Once they were back on State Street, however, Lester enrolled at Tech High, a public school for boys. Due to family finances, however, attendance was an emotional drain on Lester and he often felt embarrassed in class. His hand-me-down clothes were patched and he seldom had socks. Many days, he did not have lunch money. Most of the time, he put cardboard in his shoes to cover up the holes. When it rained, his feet got wet in spite of the cardboard and in winter, with snow and icy sludge, his feet would get icy cold. "I didn't mind that I had to put cardboard in the bottom of my shoes to get back and forth from Tech High in the wintertime," Maddox said years later. "However it finally got to where the holes in my shoes were so big the cardboard wouldn't work."

As a result, he started playing hooky. After leaving home each morning, instead of going to school, he would walk for miles down Ponce de Leon Avenue to downtown Atlanta taking odd jobs wherever he could find them. In one store, he would earn two cents for sweeping. From another store owner, he would earn a nickel for making a delivery.

One day, while walking down Spring Street, Lester ran into his father who was working his laundry route. The elder Maddox demanded an explanation for the younger's absence from school. Lester could not tell his father the real reason, so he blurted out: "Just playing hooky, dad!"

The father look disapprovingly at his son.

"You know I've always tried to teach you how important an education is," he said. "I got to punish you for this."

The Maddox's father ushered his young son into the car and drove back to their home on State Street. Once he was out of the car, Lester obediently went straight into the bathroom, the customary place for whippings. Moments later, when his father entered with the hickory switches, Lester bent over, closed his eyes tightly and waited for the sting of the switches. He waited. Several moments passed, but there was no sting. Then Lester looked back at his father who stood expressionless, the switches hanging idly at his side. For a moment, the father looked at his son, then he turned and left the bathroom without saying a word. "I always believed that he realized the conditions we were in…without food and without good clothes, maybe that had something to do with me not being in school. I know that was the one and only time he ever started to whip me and didn't," remembers Maddox.

Finally the embarrassment and futility of trying to attend school and help his family simultaneously took its final toll on Lester. In the late spring of 1932, in the middle of the tenth grade, Lester dropped out of Tech High completely and took a job with the Atlanta Wholesale Jewelry Company as a delivery boy for $4 a week. "I felt it was almost hopeless and useless to try to continue in school under those conditions."

Two months later, while riding his bicycle to the new job, the sixteen-year-old Maddox had an experience which he would later describe as "the greatest lesson of my life."

On a hot July morning in 1932, Lester was riding his bicycle to his job at the Atlanta Wholesale Jewelry Company. Tied on the back of the bicycle was his lunch box containing a fried egg and a peanut butter and jelly sandwich. Lester was well aware that he had a lunch, but he did not have anything to drink.

As he neared the corner of Forsyth and Poplar Streets, Lester saw a Coca-Cola truck parked in front of a grocery store. Keeping a wary eye out for the driver, he made his way alongside the truck, quickly grabbed a bottled Coca-Cola, then pedaled furiously away. After he was reached a safe distance from the crime scene, he stopped, placed the soft drink in the lunch box, then pedaled off on his way again.

After he had ridden several more blocks however, he heard a sudden loud explosion inside the lunch box. "The Coca-Cola had exploded and filled the box with broken glass and thick, syrupy liquid. My lunch had been ruined because of my thievery. I had to go without lunch that day, but I saw that as my just punishment for stealing the Coca-Cola. It would be a lesson I would always remember."

Two months later, Lester felt that he was bettering himself when he took a job with a pharmacy on Sixth street. His new duties called for him to make deliveries, work at the soda fountain, stock shelves and sweep up the store at closing time. Although the pay was the same, Lester took the job because there was more variety to the work. Again, the new situation did not last. Only days before Lester had gone to work at the drug store, the owner had been shot in a robbery attempt. As a result, his deteriorating physical condition and the slowly-encroaching effects of the Depression forced him to close. He was so financially strapped that he could not pay Lester his last week's salary. Feeling guilty, the owner gave young Maddox the delivery bicycle in lieu of his wages and wished him well.

But a determined Maddox was not to be denied. Two weeks later, he found himself working again at a $4.50-a-week job as a dental technician apprentice in the offices of Dr. Dean Chandler. His supervisor was a black man, but Lester had no problem with that. As a youngster growing up in Home Park, he had often played with black youngsters and had, in fact, several close friends among them. Thus, Lester happily set about the task of learning how to make false teeth, crowns and caps under the African American's supervision.

After working at his new job only a few days, he noticed that a strange-looking man appeared at the dental lab each day and, after a brief discussion with Lester's supervisor, the African American man handed the stranger money. Puzzled by his boss's action, Lester asked him why he gave the man money.

"That's the 'bug' man, Lester," the African American said.

Young Maddox looked quizzical.

"You pick three numbers and you make a bet with him," the African American explained. "If they're the same three numbers on the stock market page in the afternoon paper, then you win."

That day, Lester realized that an open illegal numbers racket was operating in Atlanta, apparently under the noses of the city's fathers. In later years, Maddox would call attention to this social menace again and again as a politician.

Meanwhile, back at home, his father's drinking had worsened. After the elder Maddox opened a small grocery operation near the Maddox home, the business began to decline because of the owner's tendency to drink and insult his customers.

One day in September 1933, while Lester was coming home from the dental lab, he met an old friend who said he was leaving his job at Atlantic Steel operating a stamping machine to enroll at Georgia Tech. The job paid $10.00 a week and was supervised by a friend of Lester's father, Edgar Schukraft.

An eager Maddox lost no time in applying for the job. Early the next morning, Lester went to the mill to meet with Schukraft. After a short interview, Schukraft offered Lester the job.

Back at home that night, Lester was ecstatic. His brothers and sisters rushed to congratulate him on his good fortune. His mother gave him a congratulative hug and his father had no false pride about his son working at his old place of employment. "I'll always remember that $10 a week," Maddox recalled. "I gave five to my mother, four to the bank and had a dollar left to buy something for me. That was the first time in my life I had spending money.

Several months later, however, President Franklin Delano Roosevelt's Work Progress Administration (WPA) went into effect and Maddox, still seeking his fortune, decided to change jobs again. The WPA would pay him $12.00 a week—two dollars more than he was currently making— for a forty hour week. Maddox, thinking he was going to greener pastures, left the steel plant and joined the government work program.

"The WPA job was ditch-digging," Maddox remembered. "It was leveling and grading the ground for future roadways, curbing and sidewalks. They did not have tractors and heavy equipment because the idea was to provide work for as many unemployed people as possible."

After only four days, however, Maddox was totally disgusted with the government job. "Out of the four days I worked," Maddox said, "It rained for two days and I had to go without pay for those two."

The next day, a grateful Maddox leapt back into his old job at the stamping machine with every intention of working at Atlantic Steel for the rest of his life. At age 18, Lester Maddox had learned his formative lessons well. He now knew that hard work and determination will pay off. With good business and sales skills, almost anyone could invest a small amount and reap great rewards. A belief in God and faith in the American system of free enterprise was an important part of being successful. Most of all, Lester had proven to himself that a poor, blue collar youngster from the wrong side of the tracks could go as far in the world as their knowledge and energy would allow them. Better to shoot for the stars and hit the gate post, he learned, than to aim at the gate post and hit the ground.

Chapter 2
Virginia

"What a pretty girl! She's the girl I would like to have as my wife."
—Maddox on how Virginia stole his heart

In late July 1932, sixteen-year-old Lester Maddox was operating a small novelty shop on McMillan Street. The building was a 12 feet by 12 feet frame structure his father purchased from the city for $25.00 to operate a small grocery. After the business failed, young Lester used the building for a while to raise pigeons. Finally, after growing tired of the pigeons, he sold the birds and cleaned out the building. Then, using his life savings of $4.00, Maddox opened his first real business with two cases of Coca-Cola, one case of NuGrape, and two boxes of candy. Each morning and night, he walked the half-mile between his shop and the family home.

One afternoon while walking home down McMillan Street, Maddox spotted a pretty, brown-haired girl sitting on a bicycle in front of an ice cream parlor. She was eating a ice cream. For a moment, he stopped and gazed at her. Then, afraid she might notice his staring at her, he walked closer and, while pretending to be reading a sign in the ice cream parlor window, Maddox continuing observing her out of the corner of his eye. "I was stopped cold," Maddox recalled later. "I had always taken for granted that I would be married and have my own family some day, but I had never seen a girl that gave me more than a passing interest. When I saw Virginia that day, I was stopped dead in my tracks."

For several minutes, he watched as the young girl finished her ice cream, then finally pedaled away. She was barely out of sight when Lester turned to several friends seated at a nearby table and asked about the girl.

Having discovered her name and address, a smiling Maddox turned and started walking back down McMillan Street. As he walked, he could not get the image of the young girl out of his mind. He was totally consumed by the sight. "What a pretty girl!" Lester said to himself as he walked. "She's the girl I would like to have as my wife."

During the days ahead, as Maddox walked between his novelty store and the family home, he invariably slowed down as he neared Virginia's house and scanned the premises hoping to get another glimpse of the girl of his dreams or, better yet, happen into her.

Some three weeks later, Maddox the merchant was taken by surprise when several young girls on bicycles stopped at his novelty store. One of them was Virginia Cox. After they had purchased Coca-Colas, one of the girls giggled and introduced Lester to Virginia. He shyly looked at her, then turned to admire her bicycle, eventually asking to take it for a ride.

With her agreement, his big chance to make an impression on her had finally arrived. So, instead of sitting on the seat of the bicycle, he turned around, sat on the handle bars and started riding the bicycle backwards down McMillan street as Virginia and the other girls watched with delight.

At the bottom of the hill, Lester, still riding the bicycle backwards, tried to turn in the street and suddenly lost his balance. Instantly, he toppled off the bike and crashed into the concrete curb, landing painfully on the back of his head. Despite the embarrassment, the incident had served its purpose. It would be difficult, indeed, for Virginia Cox to forget Lester Maddox.

Several weeks later, love-struck Maddox learned that Virginia would be attending a party at a friend's house on Atlantic Drive. Another chance to see her! He must be there. "At the party," Maddox recalled, "She treated me like I was the last person on earth. I didn't know if there was another boy she liked or if she just wasn't interested in me." Broken-hearted, Maddox left the party and rushed back home.

In his pursuit, Virginia's suitor learned everything he could about her from friends. Several months later, someone told him that Virginia attended Sunday night youth services at the Center Street Methodist Church. With that knowledge, Lester discontinued his attendance at North Atlanta Baptist and started showing up at Center Street Methodist on Sunday nights. It was there that Lester and Virginia became close friends and started dating.

During the months ahead, the couple became an item among the locals. They were seen sitting together in the pews at Center Street Methodist. They visited with mutual friends in the neighborhood. When Lester could afford it, they attended movies at the nearby Bellwood Theater. Lester was hopelessly in love. He had found his dream girl and was making her his very own. Some ten months after the courtship began, Lester, who was working at Atlantic Steel, proposed.

A delighted Virginia agreed, but insisted Lester's income be equal to a foreman's before they married. As he returned home that night, realized the difficulty in reaching such a lofty goal. A foreman at Atlantic made $33.50 a week, an income far greater than his salary of only $12.50 a week. The task seemed impossible, but Maddox was determined to get a better job. He knew he wanted Virginia for his wife.

As time passed, Lester moved rapidly up the ranks at the steel mill. By the spring of 1935, Atlantic Steel had opened a new operation, the Hoop Mill Galvanizing Plant, which manufactured galvanized steel. When the new facility opened, Maddox's old friend Edgar Schukraft could see that the nineteen-year-old had leadership potential despite his youth and inexperience. Schucraft moved him into the new galvanizing plant as an assistant foreman at $16.00 a week. The promotion gave young Maddox several new responsibilities, including the duties of hiring and firing, overseeing shipping, schedule shifts and employees and even setting prices to customers.

While the new foreman's job took advantage of Maddox's managerial abilities, its most long-lasting rewards would be the technical metallurgical skills he would learn. In the job, Maddox worked side-by-side with Dr. Sandelin, the company's chief metallurgist and former Georgia Tech professor. In that capacity, Maddox learned first-hand the technical side of steel making as well as steel and iron processing and finishing techniques. The experience would prove invaluable in later years.

Meanwhile, Maddox always made time for Virginia. Although he was drawing a salary of $19.75 a week by late spring of 1936, he was still considerably short of the $33.50 a week goal for which he strove. While Maddox had greatly improved his earnings, he was still far from the income Virginia said they needed as man and wife. But, they were young and in love. So, on 9 May 1936, Lester and his beloved Virginia were married at a minister's house in Marietta.

Due to finances, the newly-married lived with her parents on McMillan Street during the first six months of the marriage. Then, once they had put together a nest egg, they moved into a small duplex on Home Park Avenue where their first child Linda was born. Maddox was a proud father and Virginia looked forward to being a wife as well as a help-mate to her hard-working husband. However, soon after Linda's birth, Virginia suffered from a severe kidney infection and was confined to bed for several months. As a result, Maddox was called upon to help at home and, when he finished his shift as night foreman at the galvanizing plant, he faced another day's work cleaning house, cooking meals, changing diapers and caring for his wife and new baby.

Married life was good for Maddox. He worked hard at Atlantic Steel and made good money, but, now with all the bills of a married man, his financial life was more precarious. One Friday afternoon, Lester lost his week's pay while walking home from the mill. After the loss, he took what few dollars the couple had left and, in desperation, tried to win a cash prize at a street carnival by knocking over stacked milk bottles with a ball. After he lost that too, he and his wife had to borrow from relatives to survive over the next few months.

At the steel mill, Edgar Schukraft had been a long-time mainstay in Maddox's life. When the young and aggressive Maddox showed promise, Schukraft did not hesitate to promote his young subordinate. The two were close, personal friends, but Maddox was not afraid to stand up for what he believed. In one instance, after he pleaded with his boss to give a deserving employee a raise from thirty-seven to forty-two cents an hour, Schukraft balked. After Maddox pushed his point, the boss turned on the underling. "This is no gold mine down here, Maddox," Schukraft said, glaring at him.

An angry Maddox, red-faced and visibly upset, got into his boss's face.

"That's for sure!" he shot back, jutting his chin out. "If it had been, I would have got mine and been long gone by now!"

Getting a pay raise at the mill, as in other industries at the time, was very difficult. Not only were raises rare and salaries low, but most employees seldom took time off from work, even if they were sick, because they were afraid of losing their precious job. Many were reluctant to pause in their duties to get a drink of water or use the rest room for fear of being fired. As a result, these conditions made the plant's employees prime targets for the big unions which, from time to time, courted plant workers where such conditions existed.

It was no secret that plant management took a dim view of unions. Union organizers were not allowed on company property and employees who even talked about seen consorting with them were summarily fired.

One day in the fall of 1941, his supervisor called Maddox into his office and ordered to fire two black men were seen riding in a car with union organizers. Maddox flatly refused.

"I can't do that," he said, "Those are two of my best employees."

"Put it in your report that you're cutting down on your force," the superior countered.

"How can I do that?" Maddox shot back. "We need every man we have. You know we started a third shift only yesterday."

"Then say they are no good," the supervisor replied. "Say they're not doing their work."

"I can't lie about that," Maddox replied. "Both of those men are good workers."

The supervisor was running out of patience.

"How you do it is up to you," he said finally. "Just get rid of those two."

Maddox did not flinch.

"Do as I tell you, Maddox," the supervisor ordered. "Or you won't be working here yourself. Is that clear?"

"If I'm forced to lie to carry out my orders, then I have no choice but to leave," Maddox said. "If those two men are fired, somebody else will have to do it."

Maddox stood his ground and he suffered for that decision. Although he desperately needed the job, he left the employ of Atlantic Steel. His timing could have not been worse for Virginia had presented him with their second daughter, Ginny, shortly before he became unemployed.

A week after leaving Atlantic steel, Maddox went to Birmingham, Alabama, the steel capital of the South, to find employment. He applied for a job at the Bessemer Galvanizing Works. The bosses were delighted to see that Maddox had research experience with Sandelin. That asset, plus his managerial experience at Atlantic Steel, gave Maddox the inside track on an existing vacancy at the plant. He was hired on the spot for 84 cents an hour, an enormous amount at this point in Lester's life.

Although he was making good money, Maddox's time spent away from the galvanizing plant were lonely ones. He was away from Virginia and his daughters. Lester had had to leave Virginia, Linda and Ginny in Atlanta for financial reasons. He simply could not afford to move them to Birmingham. In addition to money problems, while Maddox was away, Virginia was in poor health and simply did not have the energy to pack up and move to Alabama. As a result, he took a room at a boarding house and commuted back and forth to Atlanta on weekends to be with his family.

In December of 1941, only months after Maddox had taken the new job, the Japanese bombed Pearl Harbor and plunged America into world war. Suddenly, there was a tremendous demand for steel. As the nation busied itself building ships, tanks and other military equipment, Maddox and his talents were more important than ever at Bessemer Galvanizing. Suddenly, he found himself working sixty and seventy hours a week.

Only a week after the bombing, however, Maddox almost lost his life in an accident at the plant. "I was standing in a railroad gondola car checking off a list of huge steel ship plates that were being lifted out of the car by an overhead crane," he recalled later. Suddenly, he said he looked up from his clipboard and saw that, just as the crane operator was about to lift one of the five ton loads, one of the heavy chains was slipping from one side. As the load slipped off and the heavy chain snapped back, it struck Maddox in the back with such force that he was lifted up and thrown out of the car on to a concrete floor several feet away.

Instantly, fellow workers rushed to his aid and took him to a Birmingham hospital, where doctors labored to ease his pain and make him comfortable. Maddox's multiple injuries were a challenge to the doctors. "I had hit the concrete floor with such force that some of the bones in my hand had been driven into the end of my arm bones like wooden drift pins. This made it impossible for the doctors to pull the hand bones out of the ends of my arm bones. As a result, they had to break both of my arms near the elbow to extract the hand bones."

Following the accident, Maddox spent two weeks in a Birmingham hospital recovering from the injuries. Later he would say it was two of the hardest weeks of his life. "Not only was I stuck in a hospital, but I was in a strange city without Virginia and my two daughters."

While recuperating, Maddox vowed he was going to move his family to Birmingham as soon as possible.

Following the accident, Maddox returned to work in Bessemer. He decided to take a night job with the US Department of the Navy as an inspector of engineering materials to earn extra money. He found the two jobs demanding on his time and energy. During an average week, Maddox worked between seventy and eighty hours.

Spending so much time on his two jobs took valuable time that Maddox could have used to resolve personal matters. For example, his claim for damages suffered in the accident was not settled. He finally was offered a settlement and, while he felt it was not sufficient, Maddox took the company's offer so he could get on with his busy life.

With the settlement, Maddox had a comfortable financial cushion and enough money to rent a duplex and bring Virginia and his family to Birmingham. "I'll always remember how happy I was to have my family back again under one roof," he said. "I missed them more than words can tell."

After a few months however, the grueling routine of working fifty hours a week in Bessemer then another thirty in Birmingham took its toll on Maddox. He began to feel the effects of long hours on the job. He also realized that Virginia was unhappy in Birmingham. She finally told Maddox that she sorely missed Atlanta. Although Virginia was a native of Birmingham, most of her adult ties were in Atlanta and she began urging her husband to move back.

Maddox knew he could not return to his Atlanta job at Atlantic Steel, so he began asking the Department of the Navy about a possible transfer back to his native city. Finally, his superiors advised him of an opening in Atlanta. They offered Maddox the job and he took it, although the job involved some traveling. While he did not look forward to life on the road, Maddox was eager to return. Two months after he agreed to the transfer, he and his family were back in Georgia.

Home at last, Maddox found himself much in demand as a materials inspector. The war effort had become the primary focus of the nation and steel, needed to build ships, tanks, jeeps, artillery and other implements of war, was vital to the war.

For a while, Maddox enjoyed the inspector's job and was proud to make a contribution to the war effort. The only problem lay in the amount of travel. After he was reunited with his family in Alabama, Maddox promised that he would never again be absent for them for extended periods of time. Now, with his new Department of the Navy job, he found himself away from his family up to two weeks at a time.

Meanwhile at home, Virginia had her hands full with two daughters, Linda who was now four and Ginny, aged two. With the impending birth of a third child, Lester Jr., Maddox became increasingly concerned about Virginia's frailness and feared that the birthing process might be too much for her. He knew his wife family sorely needed him at home.

Maddox made it clear to his superiors that his situation at home was such that his travel must be drastically reduced. He reminded them that, although they said there would be some travel, they promised that his assignments would be in the Atlanta vicinity. That had not been the case, he complained. But each time Maddox brought his situation to his boss's attention, he was told to be patient, and promised that his excessive travel would not last much longer. Finally, disgusted and depressed, Maddox resigned his position with the Department of the Navy and took a job as a salesman on a laundry route.

At the time, Bell Aircraft—later to become Lockheed—had built a huge plant in Marietta north of Atlanta to start manufacturing the B-29 bomber. The moment Maddox learned of the project, he applied for work and was accepted. Following a trip to Buffalo, New York for training, he was placed in production control at the Marietta plant.

Again, Maddox was in his element. He found enormous satisfaction in making a contribution to the nation's war effort. Also, earlier correspondence courses he had taken in accounting and engineering began to pay off. The courses not only enabled him to teach other employees to read blueprints, but when certain key components were in short supply, he could oversee their manufacture. Again, his self-training and his years at Atlantic Steel proved invaluable.

One day, Maddox got a call at the Bell Aircraft plant that there was a fire at his home. Instantly, Maddox left work and rushed straight home where he found that fireman had extinguished a blaze in one of the children's bedrooms. Although there was considerable loss of furniture and clothing, only one room had been damaged. Maddox found his wife and children at a neighbor's house, and Virginia explained that, while she was taking a bath, four-year-old Linda had poked a toy broom into the fireplace. Once it started to burn, the child thrust it back into her toy box hoping her mother would not discover the misdeed. Luckily, his wife had smelled smoke and discovered the potential disaster before it got out of control. Fortunately, the Maddoxes had adequate insurance coverage on the clothing and personal effects so the financial loss caused by the fire was minimal.

At Bell Aircraft, Maddox continued to do well. At a salary of $80.00 a week, it was the most money he had ever made and his impromptu engineering expertise won wide respect among his superiors. When the first fifteen B-29s started rolling off the assembly line, however, the situation changed. A lack of long-range planning caused severe parts shortages and assembly line workers often stood idle for hours at a time. Although there was little or no work, managers asked employees to spend longer and longer hours working overtime. Many times, Maddox worked on Sundays, which paid time and a half.

Maddox was a hard worker who was accustomed to efficiency and productivity. It is not easy to understand, then, why he became disgusted with the waste and mismanagement that surrounded him. "The company had a cost-plus contract with the government and we had employees turning half-hour lunches into an hour or more," Maddox recalled. "Employees would spend hours singing gospel and country songs at a piano in the basement."

Time after time, when Maddox pointed instances of parts shortages to management, his superiors blamed him for the problem, which disgusted him even further. As time passed the situation became intolerable to him. "One Friday afternoon in the fall of 1944, I left Bell Aircraft never to return again. I mailed them my identification badge rather than go back to the plant... I had to get away from the most inefficiency and the most alarming waste of tax dollars I had ever seen."

When he left the aircraft firm, Maddox did not have the slightest idea what he would do to earn a living. He could not go back to steel-making. While there were other defense jobs he could probably get, he did not want any further exposure to the waste and mismanagement he had witnessed at Bell. After a few weeks of soul-searching, Maddox decided it was time for him to try his hand at owning his own business again.

After some investigating, he learned that the frame building he used to house his 1933 soft drink and candy business had been bought by new owners and relocated on the corner of State and Fourteenth Streets. He went to view the new location, and decided to purchase the structure and open another business. After some negotiating with the new owners, Maddox leased the building and, using his $400.00 life savings, he opened a restaurant that sold hamburgers, hot dogs and candy. Maddox did the cooking himself and dubbed the establishment Lester's Grill. "The new location was within walking distance of Georgia Tech and Atlantic Steel, so I got lots of hungry students as well as mill workers."

But Maddox's past was close behind. Six weeks after opening the restaurant, he was called before the draft board and accused of deserting his defense plant job.

"I didn't quit," Maddox replied angrily. "I was drawing a check, but I didn't have a job."

"You left your job at the defense plant and the company will have to replace you," the draft board chairman shot back.

"The company will not have to replace me unless they just have to have another name to put on the payroll," Maddox said. "I didn't have any work and I pleaded for months with my bosses to give me something to do."

Finally, after more than an hour of arguments, Maddox was granted an exemption from military service for reasons of his wife Virginia's poor health and the hand injury he had received at Bessemer Galvanizing Works.

Back at Lester's Grill, business was increasing. Only a few months after opening, Maddox expanded his wares to include a variety of notions. There were heavy gloves and men's socks and caps for the workers at Atlantic Steel. Students at Georgia Tech needed sewing thread, first aid kits and school supplies so Maddox began to stock them. Less than a year after opening his grill, Maddox bought a used 1937 Dodge. He opened a savings account. His wife and three children were well-clothed and fed. He was doing well.

In the fall of 1945, after only a year's operation, Maddox sold the restaurant for $4,500 and bought an operating grocery store at Hampton and Eighth Streets near Georgia Tech. After making the grocery store purchase on a Saturday, he agreed with the sellers he would return on Monday morning to close the deal and take over the business. When Maddox and his wife returned on Monday, however, they were met by a neighborhood woman who informed them that the store had closed for good. "The men who were running the store came over [on Sunday] and carried off several vans of groceries and merchandise," she explained.

Instantly, Maddox and Virginia checked the store's inventory and discovered that much of merchandise they had seen on Saturday had been removed from the shelves. To make the theft less noticeable, the culprits had taken only a small portion of several different items rather than taking a given item's total stock. Maddox became concerned about other items that came with the store. When he bought the business, the seller told him that the grocery's federal sugar, meat and tobacco rationing stamps were on deposit with the various wholesalers. Maddox quickly checked with the wholesalers and learned they held no such stamps. Maddox was infuriated.

Later that day, he met with the seller and their real estate agent at the offices of the seller's attorney. At the meeting, Maddox wasted no time in telling the group about the store's missing inventory and the lies about the federal rationing stamps. He emphasized that the closing would not take place unless the price was reduced to cover the theft and the absence of the federal stamps.

He was shocked at the attorney's reply.

"What they have done in taking out some of the merchandise after the contract for purchase [was signed] is no more than you, I or others would do if they had some items they wanted to take with them," the attorney said.

Maddox's anger reached its peak. He rose from his seat and slammed his chair against the attorney's desk. "I'm not going to try and deal with you crooks," he shouted. "I'm going to get a lawyer, if I can find one, just as crooked as you and let him handle this for me." Maddox stormed out of the lawyer's office and slammed the door behind him.

An hour later, back at home, Maddox received a phone call from the real estate agent saying that, if he still wanted to buy the grocery, the price would be reduced by $1,000. Later that afternoon, he went to the real estate agent's office and closed the deal.

Three weeks later, however, Lester's Grill would come into his life a second time. "The couple that bought the restaurant was having some serious domestic problems," Maddox said, "and a month after the purchase, the man called me."

The next morning, Maddox bought the restaurant back for $3,000, $1500 less than the amount the couple had paid Lester for the grill, but he would not own it long. That afternoon, while he and Virginia were making plans to run two businesses, a man came in and offered Lester $4,000 for the grocery. Elated, Maddox sold the restaurant. He had made a $1,000 profit in only six hours.

Though he had made a considerable profit from his properties, Maddox soon discovered that it was a huge challenge to run a small, independent grocery while competing with major supermarkets. After a few months, Maddox sold the struggling grocery for a small profit and decided to go into real estate. In a short time, he got a real estate sales license and in December 1945, joined the Atlanta Realty Company.

In this new job, Maddox turned again to his natural talents as a salesman and trader. He quickly learned how to price a piece of property so that he could buy it low and resell it later at a profit. Before long, Maddox was turning five and six sales per week at huge profits. "I realized that the real estate business was probably my proper place in the world of commerce."

One evening in November 1946, Maddox and his wife and children were driving down State Street in the family's 1937 Dodge. When the car ahead of him slowed down and pulled toward the right as if to park, Maddox gunned the Dodge's engine to pass. Suddenly, the other car swerved toward Maddox's vehicle. Instantly, Maddox turned the wheel sharply and slammed on the brakes.

At impact, Lester Jr., who was standing in the front seat between his father and mother, was thrown through the car's windshield onto the hood. For a moment, the elder Maddox and his wife were stunned. Then, realizing their son was in grave danger, they jumped out of the car and rushed to his aid. After Virginia pulled Lester Jr.'s bloody body off the car hood, Maddox took his son in his arms. Instantly, he could see that the child had an open wound and needed immediate medical attention.

Luckily, a young man from a nearby home spotted the accident and rushed Maddox, Virginia and the bleeding child to Crawford Long Hospital. Upon arrival, Maddox was directed him through the entranceway to the emergency room. As Maddox rushed inside and pleaded for a doctor's immediate attention, he did not know if his son was dead or alive.

The child was unconscious and had lost a lot of blood. The attending doctors ordered that he be taken into surgery. An hour later, Dr. Kells Boland Jr. came out of the operating room. "The child is in deep shock and has suffered a serious concussion," he said. "He has numerous deep cuts on his hands and face and his lower lip has almost been severed. We will do all we can but I can't promise that he will pull through."

After the child was wheeled out of surgery, Lester and Virginia remained at his bedside throughout the night. Boland had said that, if the child lived through the night, there was a good chance he would survive. The next morning, when the sun arose, Lester's and Virginia's prayers were answered. Their son was alive.

As Maddox and his wife stared down at the small body in the hospital bed, he said, "Hi son, this is daddy. You're going to be just fine!"

The child's face was covered with gauze dressing and only one eye was visible, but as it looked up, tiny creases formed around the edges and Maddox knew his son was trying to smile at his parents.

At the time of the accident, Virginia was five months pregnant with the couple's fourth child. Afterward, her doctor said, as a result of the accident, she might not carry the child for the full term. This news, together with the worry about Lester Jr.'s injuries, threw Mrs. Maddox into a severe depression. As a result, she was unable to care for the children and the household and Maddox was once again called upon to help in the home. For almost three months, he stayed at home and cared for his family. During that time, he paid bills by selling off several pieces of property he had accumulated in the real estate business. Despite the bout with depression, Virginia delivered the couple's fourth child, a son whom they named Larry, on schedule. Once the new baby and mother were back safely at home, Maddox returned to his real estate job.

Over the previous year, Maddox had brokered numerous successful real estate deals. In several, he had sold properties for others and earned a commission. In still others, Maddox bought properties for himself, then found buyers and sold them for a quick profit. Meanwhile, he had accumulated some properties which he was unable to sell. One such parcel was a half-acre lot on Hemphill Avenue. "It was a very depressed area of Hemphill," Maddox later recalled. "The property had never had a structure of any kind and most of the lot was some fifteen feet below street level. The street level portion had been used as a dump for waste, garbage, scrap metal and other junk."

Finally, Maddox decided the only way to unload the property was to clean up the lot, have it filled in and build a structure that could be used for a restaurant, a grocery or some other sort of business. With that idea in mind, Maddox applied to the Small Business Administration, several banks and insurance companies for a loan to improve the property. To his surprise, a $12,500 construction loan was approved by an insurance company. With the loan, Maddox undertook the task of building a 1500 square foot structure on the lot. In the process, he found himself doing much of the work himself. He poured concrete, hammered and nailed and did other jobs in order keep the project under budget.

Throughout the construction, Maddox continued trying to find a buyer, but once it was completed, there were still no takers. He could see his back was against the wall. He had gone into debt to improve the lot and now that the improvements were complete, he was no closer to selling the property than he was before he started. "I knew I would have to do something quick or lose everything. So I immediately applied to the insurance company for another $20,000. With that, I paid off the construction loan and bought used restaurant equipment to open another restaurant."

After having made the decision, Maddox spent hours trying to come up with a unique name for the cafeteria-style restaurant. Finally, he decided on the name Pickrick, a combination of the two words "pick" and "rick" which meant that customers could choose whatever they wished and the restaurant would serve large helpings.

Thus, on 7 December 1947, the doors of the Pickrick Restaurant opened for the first time at 891 Hemphill Avenue. Each of the menus, in bold letters, proclaimed to its customers "You pick it and we'll rick it."

During the years ahead, the eating establishment would become a city landmark. In the process, it would also launch Maddox's political career and bring him to the attention of the state of Georgia, the South and the entire nation.

Chapter 3
The Pickrick Papers

"When I first started putting the Pickrick ads in the paper, I was not a political person; I was a restaurant man trying to sell the best food in town."
—Maddox on the "Pickrick Says" ads

With the establishment of the Pickrick, Maddox was gambling his entire future on a single endeavor for the first time in his life. Deeply in debt with five mouths to feed, Maddox knew he had invested his heart, soul and net worth into the restaurant and had to make it successful. His previous adventures of wandering from one job to another were behind him. He knew it was time to focus his life and stop running endlessly from one undertaking to another. He could no longer afford to waste precious time on low-paying, unchallenging jobs. If he were to fulfill his life-long dream and make his mark as a businessman, his gamble at the Pickrick must pay off.

During the first year, Maddox worked seven days a week for fifty-two weeks and put in more than 11,000 hours trying to get the business off the ground. During that time, with Virginia's help, he made a total profit of just over $1,700. Later, when he sat down to figure his hourly rate, he realized he was making about the same amount he received for delivering newspapers.

Although the Pickrick's neighborhood was economically-depressed, Hemphill Avenue ran through the area. Hemphill, at the time, was part of US Highway 41 running north and south through the city. As a result, a major portion of the Pickrick's business during its early years was hungry motorists passing through Atlanta.

In early 1949, just as the Pickrick was beginning to show a small profit, the Georgia State Highway Department suddenly rerouted the traffic off US Highway 41 on to Spring Street—a few blocks to the east— rather than the normal Hemphill Avenue. This meant that south-bound motorists by-passed Hemphill and the Pickrick and exited onto Spring Street.

Instantly, the Pickrick, as well as the other businesses along that stretch of Hemphill, started losing business. During the first week, business at the Pickrick fell of by almost 40 percent. At the beginning of the second week, the merchants who had been cut out of the US 41 traffic held a meeting to see what could be done. During a meeting of concerned owners, Maddox was designated as their spokesman and he immediately contacted the state highway department and began demanding that the routing change be reversed. "The Spring Street route was not only longer, but there were now nine traffic lights for motorists to contend with rather than two," Maddox said

Finally, Maddox and his friends decided to go directly to Jim Gillis, the state's long-time highway commissioner. After Lester's friend, County Commissioner Archie Lindsey, set up an appointment, Maddox went to Gillis and pleaded his case. Gillis listened to Maddox but did nothing. Gillis' silence did not stop a determined Maddox. He made call after call after call to the Highway Department demanding action.

"You might as well stop bothering me," Gillis finally told Maddox. "The decision has been made to keep US 41 the way it is, and that's all there is to it."

Several days later, a friend suggested that Maddox contact Senator Herman Talmadge, who was not only a friend of Gillis' but who also had influence with federal highway officials. Two days later, Maddox sat down and wrote a long letter to Senator Talmadge. In the letter, Maddox described in detail how the highway department's unwarranted action was causing Hemphill Avenue merchants to lose their businesses. A few days later, Maddox received a telegram from the Georgia Highway

Department stating that US 41 would be rerouted back onto Hemphill as soon as the street signs could be changed. Hemphill Street merchants were delighted with the decision and looked forward toward a return of the business they lost during the fiasco. They knew how and why they prevailed and Lester Maddox became a local hero.

Suddenly, with the return of through traffic, the Pickrick became a gathering place for traveling salesmen and began attracting local diners. While the food was not exotic, it was tasty and had a home-cooked look. The specialty of the house was skillet-fried chicken with a medley of vegetables, home-made cornbread and free refills on the iced tea. During the second year, Maddox discovered that there was an incredible demand for good, cheap food. By then, the working class families in the neighborhood began to eat at the Pickrick. Students at Georgia Tech stopped in between classes for a fast, home-cooked meal. Meanwhile, motorists in increasing numbers learned of the Pickrick and made the restaurant a stopover for lunch or dinner while traveling south down Highway 41. Many of them made a return visit on their return north. Business was booming at the Pickrick and Lester Maddox, the host and entertainer, was becoming a celebrity.

As an entrepreneur, Maddox mastered the art of playing the table-hopping promoter. With coffee pot in hand, he spent hours moving from one table to another, refilling coffee cups, exchanging greetings, chatting, telling jokes and making fatherly comments about children. Whether he knew it or not, Lester Maddox was performing the most essential role in politics—personal contact.

By the fall of 1950, the Pickrick was doing fabulously well as a business enterprise, but Maddox felt it should be doing even better. As a result, he decided to advertise the Pickrick in the *Atlanta Journal*. Since he had only a small advertising budget, Maddox decided he could afford to advertise only in the Saturday paper. Since Saturday was the publication's worst day for sales, advertising rates were much cheaper. Maddox thought it to be a perfect day to advertise. He reasoned that, since there were so few ads on Saturday—mostly church advertisements—readers would be more likely to see his restaurant ads.

On 28 October 1950, the first "Pickrick Says" ad appeared in the *Atlanta Journal*. Maddox wrote the copy himself and hand-delivered it to the *Journal*'s advertising department. Almost immediately, Maddox saw a

positive response from the ad. Business started to pick up. Customers—
both old and new—said they had seen the ad. Even passing motorists told
Maddox they were aware of the ad and offered their comments. He realized the Saturday ads were not only a perfect promotional vehicle, but
they gave him a direct avenue of communication with the public. Thus he
began putting major time and effort into the advertisements.

As his efforts grew, so did the sophistication of the ads. In late 1953,
one ad read:

Dear Pickrick:

I'm a little boy nine years old and I'd rather visit your restaurant and eat Pickrick skillet-fried chicken than eat anything else in
the world. Pickrick chicken is so good I dream about it each
night. Mommie and daddy love your skillet-fried chicken and
other wonderful food too—and we like your cafeteria best of all
because we get to pick out different things from the many meats,
vegetables, salads and spreads.

My problem, Mr. Pickrick, is that mom and dad bring me to
the Pickrick only two or three times each week and I want some
Pickrick skillet-fried chicken each night. What must I do? Should
I leave home?

A skillet-fried chicken lover
Bobby

Dear Bobby:

I appreciate all those nice things you say about the food at the
Pickrick, but please don't leave home. Where there are children in
the home, the family shouldn't eat out all the time. Eating at
home some of the time helps to keep the family together and
happy and you should eat out not more than half your meals.

Be patient—get to the Pickrick as often as possible and, as
soon as you are old enough to work, I'll give you a job at the
Pickrick and you can have skillet-fried chicken every day.

Sincerely,
Pickrick

Maddox never missed an opportunity to capitalize on an idea, someone else's or his own. His ability to make friends by complimenting them
or their children or by replying to their questions with witty responses was
legend. He was skilled in reaching adults through his attention to, and
conversations with, children.

From the first, Maddox discovered a natural talent for making domestic themes attractive in the ads. In one 1953 ad, he explained that Virginia
had stopped working at the Pickrick and the only way he could get her
back was to "let her have some Pickrick skillet-fried chicken." At the end
of the ad, he said that skillet-fried chicken had got Virginia back, but he
was still in trouble with her. Within the Pickrick ads, Lester discovered
that he had a special talent for communicating with the world in a folksy,
often comic manner. The longer Lester wrote the column, the better he
became at developing his talent.

By September of 1954, Maddox's folksy tone and chatty, homespun
wisdom began to win him a faithful following. Not only were the ads
causing the Pickrick to grow by leaps and bounds, but Lester was becoming something of a local celebrity. During the spring of 1955, a
photograph of a balding, bespectacled Maddox with an impish grin was
added alongside the "Pickrick Says" banner. With the addition, the advertisements took on the look of an op-ed piece on the editorial page. It was
a political column posing as a restaurant ad. Along with the new look,
political themes—comments about city taxes, possible candidates for the
next county commission seats as well questions as to why a highway had
not been completed—started seeping into the copy.

Maddox, by his own admission, said his first contact with politics
occurred in the early thirties when he worked at Atlantic Steel. His old
benefactor Edgar Schukraft had been the catalyst. One day, Schukraft—
who was very active in local politics—asked him how he felt about a
heated county commissioner's race. Maddox admitted his ignorance of
the issues and candidates.

"That's wrong, Lester!" Schukraft replied. "You've got a responsibility
as a citizen to concern yourself with politics. If you don't, you certainly
can't complain when a politician takes advantage of you."

That night, Maddox and Schukraft went to a building on Tenth street
in Atlanta to hear the candidates for county commissioner speak. Maddox
listened to what each of the candidates had to say. "I knew then that I

loved the fiery speeches and the competitiveness involved in politics. But somehow I never found the need to get personally involved."

Now, in early 1956, Maddox started to get "involved" and, with each passing week, the political commentary in the "Pickrick Says" ads grew stronger and stronger. In one ad in March 1957, Maddox noted that a candidate would run on a platform to rid the county of illegal gambling and whiskey, yet once he was in office, the vices would continue just as openly as before and illegal liquor would flow just as freely as ever.

In the Atlanta mayor's race that year, Maddox supported and actively campaigned for Fulton County Commissioner Archie Lindsey during the primary. Lindsey was not only one of Maddox's closest personal friends, but he was also a Sunday school teacher at Maddox's North Atlanta Baptist Church and a regular customer at the Pickrick. Maddox had the utmost faith in Lindsey's integrity.

In the race, Lindsey opposed a political legend: long-time Mayor William Hartsfield. By 1957, Hartsfield was a virtual institution in the Atlanta City Hall. After serving as a state legislator and an alderman in the third ward, Hartsfield was first elected mayor in 1936. Over the next twenty-five years, he was re-elected to the post for a record five successive terms. A large part of Hartsfield's early political clout grew out of his long-standing friendship with Atlanta's business community, especially Coca-Cola scion Robert W. Woodruff. City hall rumors had it that Woodruff contributed handsomely to Hartsfield's personal wealth by cutting him in on several Coca-Cola deals.

Once the race was underway, Lindsey capitalized on a police department scandal that was breaking in the Atlanta newspapers. In the investigation, an *Atlanta Constitution* reporter staked out a garage lottery operation for eleven days and observed local policemen not only entering and leaving the premises but also taking money from its occupants.

On the day of the election, both Lindsey and Maddox felt that voters would rush to the polls and, since the scandal was fresh on their minds, oust Hartsfield. But it was not to be. Once the votes were counted, Hartsfield managed to squeaked out a narrow win with a 3,804 vote majority.

Lester was heart-broken. For years, he felt the public was being duped by Hartsfield and what he called the "Atlanta political machine". As a teenager working as a dental lab technician, he had seen the city's illegal lottery operating openly. In the "Pickrick Says" ads, he had called attention to the fact that both illegal gambling and bootlegging were widespread and occurring "right under the noses" of city officials. Maddox knew it existed, and felt the reelection of Hartsfield would change nothing.

For several weeks, Lester tried to explain to friends why Lindsey lost the race. Maybe the power of the Hartsfield "political machine" had been underestimated, he said, or maybe Lindsey's campaign was too weak. Maddox was particularly disappointed that Lindsey was not more vociferous about the law and order issue. Finally, unable to explain why his friend was so thoroughly defeated, Maddox's own political ambitions started to surface. "AND SPEAKING of the Mayor's race." one ad noted, "I've done about all the building there is room for out here, and being one who likes to build and grow, I've been thinking maybe I could build some highways, some park areas, finance an airport or two, and do a lot of other progressive things.... There is only one job in Atlanta that offers me what I'm interested in and I would very much like to have your comments...."

While Maddox did not reveal his reader's responses, they were apparently encouraging because he decided to become a candidate against Hartsfield in the general election.

In 1957, the Democratic party in Atlanta was so strong that the Republican Party was virtually non-existent. As a result, the winner of the Democratic primary was invariably the winner of the election since the general election in November was usually little more than a legal formality.

Since he was neither a Democrat nor a Republican, Maddox decided to take the route of an independent candidate. Georgia law permitted a candidate to petition local registered voters for a place on the ballot. If Maddox could amass the signatures of 2 percent of Atlanta's voters, he could become a candidate against Hartsfield.

Maddox was not an unpolished political candidate. At 42, he was a successful businessman and, as a result of the Pickrick ads, he was well known in Atlanta. Although he had an understanding of the issues, his ability to communicate was not as refined. In the past, his oratorical experience was limited to lodge meetings and small groups at the Pickrick.

Seeking self-improvement, Maddox enrolled in the Dale Carnegie course "How to Win Friends and Influence People." Before he was half-finished, Maddox announced that he was running against Hartsfield in the 4 December general election.

"The best way to clean a house is to start on the roof," Maddox said, when he announced his candidacy on 18 July. "And we need a new cleaner [candidate] who is not tarnished by a political machine."

From the outset, the Hartsfield forces looked at the Maddox candidacy as little more than a nuisance. Hartsfield himself scoffed at the suggestion that Maddox would get more than 2,500 votes and noted that, since Maddox's threat was so minuscule, he would not have to campaign. How could a newcomer—an uneducated restaurateur from a blue-collar background pose a threat to a long-time incumbent like himself? As a result, Hartsfield winked at his supporters about the possibility of Maddox unseating him.

For his first political campaign, Maddox used the Pickrick as his principal base of operations. Virginia had agreed to run the restaurant while he made public appearances and canvassed for signatures. Once he took to the streets, Maddox had little trouble collecting more than 9,000 signatures, more than twice the amount he needed to get his name on the November ballot. Once the signed petitions were in hand, however, Maddox suspected that he might have a problem getting city officials to accept them.

Maddox took no chances. Fearing that someone might try to destroy the petitions, he locked them in the Pickrick safe until it was time to present them to the mayor, as required by law.

On the day of the presentation, Maddox and his supporters gathered outside city hall. Moments later, a Brinks truck arrived and two armed guards bearing the signed petitions handed them to Maddox. With that, he and a crowd of supporters swarmed into city hall and into the mayor's office. A secretary summoned Hartsfield from his inner office.

"Mr. Mayor," Maddox said, "I'm here to present petition signatures as required by law to enter my name as a candidate for the office of mayor in the general election. I would appreciate a receipt for these signatures, sir."

From the start, the race was David versus Goliath. Hartsfield had considerable financial resources and could afford to run a professional campaign. His campaign possessed lavish headquarters on Peachtree

Street, and a large staff of paid employees. Maddox, meanwhile, had virtually no money and a small headquarters which was manned by this family, his friends and some volunteers. He paid for his campaign literature and other expenses himself. The budget was so tight that virtually every expenditure required a major decision.

But what Maddox lacked in money, he had in enthusiasm and took to the campaign trail with a revolutionary fervor. In late October, six weeks before the election, the Hartsfield campaign paid a local polling house, Rawson and Associates, to canvass voters to determine the possible outcome. Once the results were in, the Hartsfield camp could not believe them. Incredibly, the poll had found that Maddox was leading in six of the city's eight wards. Two days later, Hartfield's supporters held a fundraiser and collected $50,000 for their candidate to use in the final days preceding the election. Suddenly, Hartsfield started campaigning.

On election day, the sheer power of the Hartsfield forces managed to crush Maddox. Once the votes were counted, Hartsfield had transformed his narrow 3,800 vote majority in the primary into a resounding 2-1 victory in the general election. The final tally showed Hartsfield with 41,300 votes while Maddox received 23,987.

On 7 December 1957, three days after he had been defeated by Hartsfield, Maddox used almost all the ad space to explain why he got in the race, the forces that resulted in his defeat and a subtle hint that he would not seek public office again:

> "LESTER ASKED me to tell you that he would rather be Lester Maddox than Mayor Maddox, but he wouldn't mind being Mayor Maddox for a few years in order to help provide Atlanta with better government... I agree with many of Lester's friends, he is a better restaurant man and businessman than he is a politician and I believe he is going to take my advice and stay out of politics in the future."

Although Maddox had run and lost, he had learned the basic ground rules of practical politics. He had polished his public speaking skills; he knew what it felt like to walk up to people on the street and ask for their vote; he learned the rhythm of a campaign; he learned that a political race was a merciless affair in which a candidate could neither give nor expect leniency from his opponent. These experiences would prove to be valuable lessons in the future.

Despite Pickrick's suggestion that Maddox remain out of politics, Maddox yearned for a political career. In early 1958, he made his intentions perfectly clear: "PICKRICK SAYS: Up until last year, most of my politicking was what you might call 'Undercover.' I couldn't hold back any longer so I climbed out from beneath the cover and lo and behold if a fellow from over on Mitchell St. didn't come along and cover me up again (but good).

"AT THE PRESENT time, I'm pushing the cover back and it looks as though my politicking will be completely out in the open in the not-too-distant future."

In the same ad, Lester continued his attacks on politicians about the way they had been spending taxpayers' money:

> AND OFTEN a man caught gambling with a dollar or two of his own will be arrested and sent to prison—yet occasionally some public officeholders are found to be gambling and misusing millions of dollars belonging to other people and are never punished. Often such a scoundrel will leave office and you'll hear the remark: "He was the greatest this or that our city, county, state or nation has ever known..."

By the summer of 1959, Maddox had turned the ad into a forum for his personal political views and he had an enormous following. In fact, the most widely-read item in the Saturday *Atlanta Journal* was Lester's column, especially among the local political pundits.

"Most readers—especially people with a political interest—would read "Pickrick Says" first," remembered one long-time political observer. "Most people would get the Saturday paper, then go straight to the 'Pickrick Says' ad to see who Lester was lambasting in his column."

In October of 1959, when the new census revealed that the population of Atlanta had reached one million, Maddox jumped on his soapbox in a huge three-column "Pickrick Says" ad and attacked the US Supreme court:

"It is a great day for Atlanta and the South and the nation," he wrote, but it may not continue unless the citizens "impeach the present members of the US Supreme Court and thwart the efforts of others who would destroy our state and national constitutions, thereby destroying our individual freedoms and rights which in turn would destroy private enterprise.... Each of us have plenty to fight for and fight we must. We cannot afford to let the other fellow do our fighting. The best way to lose all that we cherish and hold dear is to do nothing."

In November 1959, Maddox took some potshots at both Georgia public officials and the national integrationists. In the ad, he wrote:

"The public officials responsible for construction of the Atlanta Expressway should never come before the taxpayers and boast of any progress...when the lousy job they have permitted on the expressway overshadows any and all good they have accomplished in government...

"WHAT SHOULD have been completed and in use within five years will probably not be accomplished within fifteen years. Who is responsible for this delay of ten years and millions of tax-payers dollars being wasted? Had this expressway been completed in 1953, tens of millions of dollars would have been saved in real estate, labor and construction cost....

"AND WHY SHOULD interracial societies and newspapers give so much publicity to lawlessness in the South since the Supreme Court desegregation ruling of 1954? Why is there no comparison with lawlessness in the South previous to the 1954 ruling? How could they fail to mention the greater lawlessness in other regions of the country since the 1954 ruling....? If all this has happened since the 1954 ruling, could it be that said ruling had indirectly brought about the breakdown of law and order? Is the "law of the land" determined by the US Constitution and the "will of the people" or by members of the US Supreme Court?"

With each and every ad, Maddox star rose higher and higher. Many blue collar whites—people who had no access to government and felt they were the victims of government—found that Maddox spoke for them. These same people—whom the media later referred to as "the little people"—would form the core of his political power base. In spite of Maddox's popularity, there was an intellectual elitist population in Atlanta which saw Maddox as little more than a trouble-maker, a misguided, small-time player who posed a threat to the orderly transition from a racially segregated to an integrated Atlanta.

Meanwhile, the "Pickrick Says" ads were doing more to boost the *Journal*'s Saturday sales than any other single factor. As Saturday sales increased, so did advertising and some local merchants began to tell the *Journal's* advertising department to use a similar lay out as Lester's ad. Finally, the ads caused Cox newspaper officials to add a new Amusement and Entertainment section to the Saturday editions in which restaurant and movies would be featured. At one point, the *Journal's* advertising director told Maddox that his ads were the topic of discussion at various local and regional trade meetings.

As the "Pickrick Says" ads grew more and more toward the political extreme, however, so did the controversy surrounding them. They became so controversial that, before the ads were sent to the composing room, they were scanned by the *Journal's* attorneys for potential libel suits. Finally, by late 1959, Maddox's commentary in the ads became so politically flagrant that the advertising department notified him they would no longer print them.

Maddox was not intimidated. After taking a few days to think the situation over, he decided to go to the competition. Shortly, he began publishing "Pickrick Says" ads in the small independent papers in metro Atlanta with the heading "The Atlanta Newspapers Refused to Run This Ad!" Three weeks later, the *Journal's* advertising department called and politely told Maddox they had reconsidered and now would be happy to start running his ads again. In fact, they agreed to print three ads they had previously rejected.

But his problems with the Atlanta papers were only beginning. Shortly afterward, Maddox was told that, since his ads contained so much commentary about the national political scene, he was going to have to start paying the national advertising rate. After Maddox threatened to take the ads elsewhere a second time, he was notified that the newspaper's executives had held a "special meeting" and he could continue at the old rate. Despite giving in a second time, the newspaper no longer allowed Maddox to pick the location of his ad in the paper. Although the Pickrick ad started to appear all over the paper—in the sports pages, with the comics or even with the obituaries—Maddox's popularity only continued to grow.

In September of 1960, Maddox poked fun at the *Atlanta Journal* reporter who described him in the "Atlanta After Dark" column as "an uninhibited ad writer." Chiding the reporter, Maddox wrote, "Big words like that [uninhibited] usually bother me. I couldn't find a dictionary so I started asking my customers what 'uninhibited' means... One of my educated customers told me that uninhibited means 'with the brakes off and the throttle wide open.' In other words, say and do as you think."

"I sure was relieved to get the real meaning," Maddox wrote, "Because I thought he was calling me the same thing a drunk called me last week..."

By late 1961, with the growing specter of the civil rights movement, the ads began to read like pamphlets for the John Birch Society. In September, when Maddox was embroiled in the mayor's race against Ivan Allen and civil rights activists were urging a boycott of Albany city merchants, the "Pickrick Says" ad called for Albany citizens to buy rather than boycott. It read, "BE A PART OF ALBANY week in Georgia.... Buy from those grocers, druggists, clothiers, department stores, service stations.... WHITE ALBANY stand up for Georgia—for America... Even if you must miss the Pickrick, go ALBANY!"

In another ad, in response to a letter from an integrationist, Maddox turned almost vitriolic when Pickrick noted, "I do hope you will get your integration wishes—a stomach full of race-mixing, and a lap full of little mulatto grandchildren, so you can run your fingers through their hair."

By then, the ads were becoming increasingly crude and prejudicial. Interestingly enough, Maddox's critics charged that the newspapers were the culprit. They claimed that, by running the ads, the Cox newspapers were inflaming racial feelings to the flashpoint and, as a result, any local civil unrest lay at the doorstep of the newspapers.

Meanwhile, at the same time he was one of the most popular columnists at the *Journal*, he was the bane of the editorial department at the *Journal*'s sister publication, the *Constitution*. There Maddox was lambasted day after day by publisher Ralph McGill and editor Eugene Patterson.

"To them, I was a racist, a bigot and just about anything else they could think of to make me out as some kind of devil," Maddox remembered. "One day I went down to the newspaper offices on Forsyth street and, starting at the front door, I made my way through the offices looking for black faces. If I was a racist while employing forty-five blacks among my sixty-five employees, many in supervisory jobs, surely this liberal paper must be staffed by African Americans. Yet everywhere I looked there were white faces with only an occasional black pushing a broom."

Later, after Maddox brought this to the attention of the public, an employee invited him back to the *Constitution* offices. There Maddox said he found a white secretary with her face blacked Amos and Andy style. "Now you can't say that we don't have a black in a prominent position at this newspaper," the employee allegedly said.

By the summer of 1962, no one seemed to be beyond the pale of Maddox's wrath. In the column, he criticized such notables as President Kennedy, his brother Robert, Dr. Martin Luther King Jr., Nikita Khruschev, Atlanta Mayor Ivan Allen as well as Ralph McGill and his associate Eugene Patterson. By then, Maddox's political ideas had become both cohesive and national in scope. He could face anybody and argue a political issue with intelligence, fire and a certain folksy, down-home sincerity. His experience writing the "Pickrick Says" ads had matured him politically.

When Christmas of 1962 rolled around, the Pickrick had been open for 15 years. During that time, it had become one of the most famous restaurants in Atlanta and was serving more than half a million people a year. Maddox's dream of owning his own successful business—sparked at age twelve when he was delivering the *Georgian-American*—had been realized a thousand times over. During those years, his most powerful personal political contribution had been the "Pickrick Says" ads. They had not only made him a political figure in the minds of many Atlantans, but, more than any other single factor, they laid the groundwork for Maddox's later political successes.

Chapter 4
First Tastes of Politics

"Professional politicians really don't know how to handle a political out-sider who 'lets it all hang out.'"
—Maddox on his early political attempts

As Maddox's political popularity grew and the Pickrick thrived, Hartsfield's popularity was at an all-time low and rumors were that he would not be a candidate for reelection as his term neared. Aware of Hartsfield's political troubles, Maddox began plotting a strategy: He would look for a strong "conservative" candidate for mayor. If he failed to find one, he would enter the race himself.

Finding no candidate and convinced that Hartsfield could not win if he sought another term, Maddox decided to seek the office. As the primary heated up, four more candidates also entered the fray for the mayor's post: State Representative M. M. "Muggsy" Smith, State Senator Charlie Brown, Fulton County Commissioner Jim Aldredge and businessman Howell Smith. Meanwhile, "Atlanta's political machine" had not chosen a candidate and, while rumors flew that Hartsfield would not run, Maddox and the others looked to Ivan Allen Jr., heir to an office supply company fortune, as Hartsfield's likely successor. Maddox knew, as did the other candidates, that the powers-that-be told Hartsfield in 1957 that they would support him for only one more term. If he chose to run again, he was on his own. They could not oppose him, they knew, but they could refuse to support him. Hartsfield was well aware of the fact that, without their backing, his chances for reelection were slim.

Once campaigning was underway, pressure began to mount for Allen's candidacy. Editorials appeared in the Atlanta Constitution singing his praises. At his own expense, Atlanta banker and prominent democrat Mills Lane conducted a poll of some 90,000 customers at the Citizens and Southern Bank which resulted in a resounding call for Allen's candidacy.

Still Hartsfield had not made his position known. In later years, Ivan Allen said that, at the time, he went to Hartsfield and urged him to run. Allen said he told Hartsfield, if he would run, he would contribute $10,000 and take a leave of absence from his job to manage the campaign. If that were not satisfactory, Allen said, he urged Hartsfield to let him know so he could launch his own campaign. Finally, Hartsfield, who was seventy-two years old, announced that he would not seek re-election.

While the first race against Hartsfield had been David versus Goliath, Maddox's second race for mayor was classy, rich boy versus blue-collar, poor boy. Ivan Allen Jr. was the son of Ivan Allen, Sr., the wealthy founder of a chain of office supply stores. Allen was well-educated, well-connected and had the finances to run a well-organized campaign. Maddox, meanwhile, was a high school drop-out from an economically-poor background whose only claim to fame was a successful restaurant and the "Pickrick Says" ads.

Of the race, Allen later recalled, "I was quite aware that my most serious opposition would come from Lester Maddox, a 10th grade drop-out who ran a blue-collar fried-chicken restaurant called the Pickrick (and who) had sprung out of the lower and middle-class white neighborhood suddenly when the Supreme Court handed down its decision on school desegregation. As polarization set in, his star rose higher. Undoubtedly, he would scream 'nigger-nigger-nigger' throughout the campaign."

Despite the social differences between the two principal candidates, the battle lines were drawn early in the campaign and, as predicted, the principal issue turned out to be race. Throughout the campaign, Allen referred to Maddox again and again as a racist and bigot and charged: "You represent a group that would bring another Little Rock to Atlanta!"

Maddox countercharged that Allen was using race to cloud the real issue which was corruption in government. Maddox charged that Allen was confusing the issue because he represented the group that reaped the benefits of the corrupt government, the cleaning up of which was the principal plank in his platform.

During one rally at which both Maddox and Allen were present, Maddox told this story of how he caused Allen huge embarrassment. After a speech in which Maddox charged that Allen was the ordained candidate of the finance czars, he pulled a pair of his wife's silk stocking out of his coat pocket and held them up for the crowd, announcing, "A pair of silk stockings for the silk stocking candidate."

The animosity between the two men escalated even further as the race progressed. Eventually, the race would become a personal vendetta for Allen.

As the campaign drew to a close, Maddox took issue again and again with the *Atlanta Journal* and *Constitution* which characterized him as a racist and demagogue. In one campaign appearance after another, Maddox charged that the newspapers themselves were prejudiced because they failed to make a distinction between a segregationist—which he claimed he was—and a racist—which he says he was not and never would be.

On 13 September 1961, voters went to the polls to cast their ballots in the primary. Of the 101,000 votes cast, 39,000 went to Allen and 21,000 to Maddox with the remaining 41,000 scattered among other candidates. Since neither Allen nor Maddox received a majority, a run-off was scheduled for 22 September.

In the run-off, Allen polled 64,313 to Maddox's 36,091. Allen's margin of victory surprised the experts. It was a bitter defeat for Maddox. It was further proof, if further proof were needed, that city-wide elections in Atlanta were controlled by a strong political force composed of bankers and other businessmen, the Atlanta newspapers, and the in-crowd at city hall.

At a news conference after the run-off, an *Atlanta Constitution* reporter asked Maddox what he planned to do now that the race was over. "I don't know,' Maddox said with a sly laugh. "I might run for governor."

For Maddox, the possibility of a statewide race was very real. With two races under his belt, he was now a seasoned professional politician.

Within the scheme of Atlanta city politics, he knew he was a force with which to be reckoned. Twice he had gone up against the mighty Atlanta political machine and, although he had lost both times, he had ably presented himself and his platform.

As Governor Ernest Vandiver's term was reaching a close in 1962, Maddox was still convinced that he had something to offer. He saw his two earlier losses for Atlanta mayor as do-or-die attempts against a political behemoth where all the cards were stacked again him. Not only was he bucking a powerful political machine, but he also found himself vilified by both papers as a segregationist and demagogue. Maddox reasoned that, in a statewide campaign, he could take his conservative views to the hinterlands where he would not have to face either a firmly-entrenched political machine nor the Atlanta newspapers.

Fearing that many supporters of former Governor Marvin Griffin would believe Maddox to be a plant to split the conservative vote in the governors race, Maddox decided to run for the state's second-highest post, the lieutenant governor's office. Despite his willingness to run, Maddox was faced with two problems. As before, he did not have the means to finance a state-wide campaign. Also, he was virtually unknown outside of Atlanta, especially in the rural areas of south Georgia. For the second problem, Maddox had several thousand posters printed—at two cents each—which simply read:

MADDOX
MADDOX
MADDOX

Despite lack of money, which would discourage most candidates, Maddox loaded the posters and several boxes of campaign literature into his Mercury station wagon, bought a road map and hit the highway. Once he arrived in the small rural towns of south Georgia, he parked the station wagon, got out and started walking the streets, shaking hands and handing out literature. He would go anywhere he thought he could get a vote. There were drug stores, barber shops, service stations, hardware stores, cotton gin companies, farm implement supply houses, mom-and-pop groceries and even beauty parlors. He left no stones unturned. At town squares, a confident Maddox would walk up to people and introduce himself.

In the mountain country of north Georgia, Maddox plied the politician's trade in the same fashion. If he drove through a town and saw a crowd—whether it was a football game or a cattle auction—he pulled over and started politicking. Throughout the state, Maddox left a trail of the "MADDOX MADDOX MADDOX" posters. If he spotted a billboard bearing the likeness of one of his opponents, he stopped and nailed up one of his posters on the stanchions supporting the billboard. He was fast becoming a master of running a campaign on a shoestring.

Early on, it became clear that the two men to beat in the race were Maddox and Peter Zack Geer, the executive secretary to Governor Ernest Vandiver. Geer, despite his youth, was a seasoned politician, a segregationist and an attorney who was well-connected with Democratic party officials throughout the state.

During one rally in Atlanta, Maddox lashed out at Geer as "Governor Vandiver's office boy." He accused the young redhead of running his campaign "from the governor's office" and charged that he was not only using "postage stamps, but state employees, cars and airplanes" as well. To drive the point home further, Maddox charged that Geer's boss had "surrendered" on school segregation and even demanded by telegram that Governor Vandiver resign. Upon receiving the telegram, Vandiver dismissed Maddox as a "pip-squeak."

At one joint rally, Geer, calling Maddox "a tenth grade drop-out", emphasized that his own legal training and experience under Vandiver would be invaluable assets as lieutenant governor. Again, he pointed out that Maddox had no law school training.

When it was Maddox's turn to speak, he turned directly to his opponent. "What you say, sir, is true," he said. "Being a legal scholar can be a fine asset, but such training is not always used in the right direction. In fact, some of the best legal minds in the country are out there at the end of Boulevard in the federal penitentiary and I do not doubt that there are countless others not quite so brilliant on the outside who should be in there."

. From the start, Maddox tried to steal Geer's segregation thunder. In that effort, he launched a telegram campaign. In one instance, he wired President John F. Kennedy a telegram urging him to appoint Martin Luther King Jr. "ambassador to Africa, Russia or elsewhere." Later he sent a telegram to Albany, Georgia officials who were firmly resisting a civil rights campaign endorsed by King: "Georgians and Americans everywhere are grateful for your courageous stands against Communist-inspired lawless agitators who would destroy law and order, and destroy freedom, liberty and constitutional government." In another instance, he wired his old enemy, Atlanta Mayor Ivan Allen, a telegram which called upon him to stop urging hotels and restaurants to serve NAACP delegates at a forthcoming convention.

Despite his boundless energy and will to win, Maddox learned quickly that running a statewide campaign was a grueling task. Many nights, Maddox would find himself campaigning until midnight. Many days, his longtime friend J. L. Allen would drive the station wagon so he could concentrate solely on shaking hands, making speeches and telling people about himself. Due to a dire shortage of funds, Maddox found that his campaign was mostly a one-man show. He wrote his own speeches, nailed up most of the posters, oversaw the printing of his pamphlets and then personally passed them out to voters.

Late one night, Lester and Allen, weary and tired from a long day of campaigning, pulled into a small hotel in south Georgia. While Allen slept for the next day's drive, Maddox spent two hours writing a speech for a rally the following day on one of his posters.

The next morning, he and Allen were up at 7:00 A.M. and on the road. En route to the rally, they made several stops along the roadside to nail up posters. When they finally arrived for the big event, Maddox started searching frantically through the station wagon for the poster on which he had scribbled his speech. But it was nowhere to be found. Then he realized that, in his haste, he had nailed the speech—along with the poster—to a pine tree forty miles away. Despite this, Maddox, who never found himself at a loss for words, delivered an extemporaneous speech to a rousing ovation.

In the 12 September primary, more than 750,000 Georgians went to the polls. Although the votes were scattered among the nine candidates, Geer and Maddox were the front-runners. In the final tally, Geer polled 187,770 while Maddox got 138,065 votes and the two were scheduled for a run-off on 21 September.

In the run-off, however, two major forces arose against Maddox. The first was Carl Sanders, who had won the Democratic nomination for governor in the primary, immediately threw his support behind Geer. This move was enormously helpful to Geer since Sanders was extremely popular.

The second major obstacle to Maddox was his old nemesis Atlanta Mayor Ivan Allen Jr. who had not forgotten the bitter race Maddox ran against him the previous year. In particular, he had not forgotten the embarrassment over the "silk stocking" incident.

As a result, Allen launched an all-out "Stop Maddox!" campaign. Not only did he throw his support behind Geer, but wherever he could, Allen actively used his influence with blacks in Atlanta and Democrats throughout the state against his old foe.

The night before the election, Maddox charged that several public officials and state employees were politicking for Geer: "Certain public officials have lately abandoned their duties to work for my opponent," he said. "They are lavishly entertaining in state offices in order to blandish certain politicians to support my opponent. State employees are being ordered to neglect their jobs and work in my opponent's favor."

In the election, the two major Atlanta newspapers, the thorn in Maddox's side in previous elections, played only a minimum role. A *Journal* editorial before the election, noting that both Geer and Maddox were segregationists, stated: "Inasmuch as the job requires so little, either is capable of filling it."

Due to a huge rainstorm sweeping through the state, however, voter turnout was extremely light and slightly more than 400,000 people bothered to go to the polls. Late that evening, when all the precincts were counted, Geer defeated Maddox 224,897 to 181,695.

For the third time, Maddox had placed second. Handicapped by minimal finances and a lack of name recognition in crucial South Georgia, he proved himself a major contender for the state's second highest office. More than anything else, he learned the ropes of running a statewide campaign. His political savvy had matured. Now he felt perfectly at ease in front of a crowd and he could stand face to face with an opponent and hold his own. Finally, Lester Maddox was ready to seek the governor's office, but first he had to deal with the civil rights movement.

Chapter 5
The Pick Handle Incident

"We're not ever going to integrate. The Pickrick belongs to me and not to President Johnson or the agitators or the news media or Khruschev or anybody!"

—A defiant Maddox takes a stand, 11 August 1964

Nineteen hundred and sixty-one was a banner year in Atlanta for the civil rights movement. In the spring, the city's Chamber of Commerce and black leaders announced an agreement to end segregation of downtown lunch counters (and protests thereof) within thirty days of the desegregation of Atlanta's public schools. Shortly afterward, four white high schools were integrated with the admission of nine black students and later Georgia Tech integrated its student body by admitting three blacks.

During the following year, upon the urging of the police chief, hiring restrictions were lifted against black officers in the Atlanta Police Department. The US Supreme Court declared the state's "County Unit System"—a measure designed to keep political power in the state's rural areas—unconstitutional. During the election immediately following the ruling, a black man, Leroy Johnson, was elected to the state senate. The social integration of African Americans into Atlanta's white community was rapidly expanding.

From the very first, Lester Maddox and his Pickrick restaurant were natural targets for the civil rights demonstrators. Martin Luther King Jr.'s headquarters—located near Auburn Avenue in central Atlanta—was only four miles from the Pickrick. King and other civil rights leaders, as a result of the Pickrick ads, were well aware that Maddox was a staunch segregationist and a vociferous spokesman for the cause. It was only logical to expect that sooner or later the civil rights activists would "test" the Pickrick.

Civil rights activists first came to demonstrate at the Pickrick on 3 July 1962. During the NAACP's national convention in Atlanta that summer, the organization sent pickets to several local restaurants and hotels that had resisted integration. When the group of some fifty picketers appeared outside the Pickrick on Hemphill Avenue, diners glowered through the restaurant's windows at the demonstrators and their signs.

After some three hours, the pickets had dwindled to only a handful and Maddox was glad that the matter was being settled without incident. The following day, Maddox sent a telegram to the convention and thanked them for the picketers, noting that the action had not only increased his business, but had earned him 50,000 votes in the lieutenant governor's race.

The first actual sit-in attempts at the Pickrick occurred on 18 May 1963. On that day, four African Americans and three white demonstrators—representatives of the Committee on Appeal for Human Rights—walked into the restaurant and took seats. Immediately, Maddox stepped in and escorted one demonstrator to the front door, then ordered his African American employees to remove the other six. Finally, after an African American employee managed to remove another demonstrator, the others left "rather than see these Negro men lose their jobs."

In early January 1964, civil rights demonstrators launched their most vicious assault to date on Atlanta businesses. A primary focus of the attack was on hotels and restaurants. In mid-January, Leb's, a popular restaurant in downtown Atlanta, was the target of a massive sit-in effort and some 20-30 agitators—both black and white—stormed into the restaurant, seated themselves on the floor and refused to leave. When owner Charley Leb asked police to remove them, they refused. Instead, police officers blocked the entrance and prohibited customers from entering the restaurant. Inside, demonstrators were destroying restaurant equipment, urinating in food containers, and generally wreaking havoc on the place. When Maddox, a long-time Leb friend, arrived at the scene, he saw that police officers were refusing to allow anyone to cross the street and enter the restaurant.

"When I saw what was happening," Maddox said. "I couldn't believe it. Leb could neither open nor close his restaurant. In effect, his livelihood was being effectively shut down."

Although Maddox was told to remain outside, he waited until a policeman standing guard turned his back, then he darted into the restaurant. Inside, he found Charley Leb in a state of shock.

"This is America, Lester," he said. I've got my whole life tied up in this restaurant and now it's being destroyed. How can this be happening?"

Lester shook his head in amazement.

"If I can help you in any way," Maddox said. "Just let me know."

Finally, having assessed the situation, Maddox turned and left. Back outside, Maddox was faced with several hundred demonstrators who, carrying signs and chanting slogans, continued to block the restaurant entrance. Finally, he managed to elbow his way through the crowd. Once he was in the street again, several demonstrators recognized him as owner of the Pickrick and began to chant: "Maddox is next! Maddox is next! Maddox is next!"

A stunned Maddox turned to face the group.

"We're not going to just shut you down, Maddox," one shouted, "we're gonna make you lose everything you've got."

A nearby policeman, sensing that trouble was imminent, approached Lester.

"You have to move on, Mr. Maddox," he said. "We've got to clear this area."

Maddox angrily turned to the policeman.

"Officer," Maddox said, "These people have been here since yesterday and they aren't being cleared out of the area. When you tell them to move, that's when I'll move on."

The policeman glared at him.

"That's a police order, Mr. Maddox!" the officer barked. "You have to move on! Now!"

By then his youngest son Larry had joined Maddox. Seeing that defiance was futile, Lester turned to his son.

"We'll move, but we're going to go down that sidewalk," he said, indicating the sidewalk in front of the restaurant which was packed seven or eight deep with demonstrators. As Maddox and his son started to move, the demonstrators slowly backed up and let them pass. As they did, the threats started again.

"We're going to get you Maddox!" one young demonstrator shouted. "We're going to get you good!"

Some twenty minutes later, Maddox and Larry were back on Hemphill Avenue at the Pickrick. That night, a concerned Maddox considered what he had witnessed at Leb's and weighed the threats demonstrators had leveled against him. From all indications, the Atlanta police had no intention of stopping the demonstrators from destroying property at Leb's. If the promised threats were carried out against him, he would in all likelihood get the same treatment. Although he had never fired a gun in his entire life, he went to a gun shop the following day and bought a pistol. He vowed he was going to protect himself and his property.

In late April 1964, a new group of demonstrators—both black and white—appeared at the entrance to the Pickrick. Maddox, having learned from the May 1963 experience, once again called upon his African American employees.

"I blocked the doorway," Maddox recalled, "and refused to let them enter. Then I called for my employees."

Finally, after threats from Maddox and arguments from black employees that their jobs were being jeopardized, the group left. Even then, Maddox had set the stage for the pick handle incident four months later.

"We just happened to have a 100-foot-long, high-pressure water hose and some pick handles around in case we ran out of firewood," Maddox commented later.

Despite Maddox's bravado, the civil rights movement was not about to allow him or the Pickrick off the hook.

The death of the Pickrick was sealed on 2 July 1964 when President Lyndon Johnson signed the Civil Rights Act into law. Now, the activists had the power of federal law behind their demonstration efforts and anyone who refused them service in a public place would be defying federal law. Thus, less than twenty-four hours after the legislation was signed into law, demonstrators were back to test the Pickrick.

Around 2:45 P.M. on 3 July, three African American students from Atlanta's Interdenominational Theological Seminary pulled into the Pickrick parking lot. Once they arrived at the entrance, they discovered the doors had been locked for the normal three-hour afternoon closing period. When they learned the Pickrick would re-open at 5:30 P.M., they promised to return.

Three hours later, when the civil rights activists pulled into the parking lot a second time, an elaborate stage had been set to meet their challenge. An angry throng of Pickrick customers and Maddox supporters—several of which were armed with wooden pick handles—milled around the parking lot and near the restaurant entrance (The original wooden handles that Maddox handed out to his son and other supporters were inaccurately reported to the public as ax handles.). Maddox himself, dressed in a somber dark suit with a pistol bulging in a holster under the coat, was prepared to repel the African Americans. His oldest son, nineteen-year-old Lester Maddox Jr., was armed with a pick handle and stood dutifully at his father's side. Meanwhile, a flock of television, newspaper and wire service reporters had been alerted and were standing by to witness the confrontation.

Maddox, upon seeing the car park, strode from the entranceway toward it. His son was close behind. As the car's driver, the Reverend George Willis Jr. of Youngstown Ohio, opened the door to get out, Maddox stepped up and kicked it shut. Moments later, the Reverend Albert Dunn of Hillsboro, Texas emerged from the passenger side of the car, put on his jacket, and started toward the Pickrick. Instantly, Maddox, angry beyond words, drew the pistol and started shouting orders for the African American man to leave. The third occupant of the car, the Reverend Woodrow T. Lewis of Sumter, South Carolina, never got out.

What happened next has been widely argued by both witnesses and attorneys in court. However, according to an Atlanta Journal report published the following day, as Maddox, pistol in hand, approached the car, he shouted to the African Americans: "Get out of here and don't ever come back!"

The Reverend Dunn quickly returned to the car, alarmed by Maddox and the converging crowd of pick handle-wielding Pickrick customers. After the Reverend Dunn retreated to the car, one member of the crowd struck the car hood with a pick handle. As the car continued moving away, other whites poked at the African Americans through the open car windows. Meanwhile, several reporters and photographers ran alongside the car and questioned the three African Americans.

"We're still hungry," the Reverend Willis told one of the reporters. "We'll be back."

The promise to return never materialized. Instead, three days later, the three African Americans filed two separate lawsuits against Maddox. In the first, filed in Fulton County Civil Court, Willis and Dunn swore out warrants against Maddox claiming that he had pointed a pistol at them. The second suit, filed three days later in US District Court, sought a restraining order against Maddox for refusing them service at the Pickrick. The federal suit charged that Maddox violated the public accommodation section of the new civil rights law when he refused to allow them to enter his restaurant.

Overnight, Maddox became a celebrity. The photo of him carrying the pistol, accompanied by his pick handle-armed son, was published in newspapers and broadcast on television stations all over the nation. He was hailed by segregationists as a man who would stand up against forced integration. Thousands of Georgians, who had earlier only heard of Maddox through his political races and the restaurant ads, showed their support by patronizing the Pickrick. During the days after the incident, the restaurant's parking lot was full and, for hours at a time, long lines waited outside the entrance for service. In several instances, Maddox finally turned people away simply because he could not serve them all.

From the first, local authorities did not have the stomach for pressing Maddox too harshly on the pistol-pointing charge. During a preliminary hearing on 8 July, in which bailiffs had to turn spectators away from the packed courtroom, Judge Osgood Williams listened to testimony from both Maddox and the African Americans. Based on conflicting evidence, Judge Williams found probable cause for the charges and ruled that Maddox be bound over to criminal court. Meanwhile, Maddox was allowed to sign his own $1,000 bond and go free. Over the succeeding months, criminal court prosecutor John I. Kelley, who was not up for re-election, showed no desire to prosecute Maddox. Finally, when new prosecutor William Spence took office in January, the Maddox trial was set for 12 April 1965.

Meanwhile, federal authorities were not as kind to Maddox. In fact, they wasted no time sending out the message that they had zero tolerance for those who refused to obey the new civil rights law. On 13 July, the US Department of Justice, in an action personally orchestrated by Attorney General Robert Kennedy, intervened in the suit on behalf of the African Americans. Days later, the Attorney General assigned a battery of constitutional lawyers to the case and named Burke Marshall, chief of the Justice Department's civil rights division, to oversee the government's case.

Maddox, on the other hand, had only two attorneys, William G. McRae and Sidney Schell. Although both were considered capable attorneys, neither was noted for his expertise on constitutional law. Before deciding on the two, Maddox conferred with several other attorneys in an attempt to find the best counsel possible. Finally, discouraged by the vast amounts of money required to retain big-name constitutional lawyers and to appeal such cases to the US Supreme Court, Maddox chose McRae and Schell. Ultimately, Maddox correctly surmised that most attorneys, due to the social ramifications involved, simply did not want to take the case.

While the Pickrick incident was the first court case which openly defied the new civil rights law, it was not the first to challenge the law. That came when Atlanta attorney Moreton Rolleston, owner of the Heart of Dixie Motel, filed a suit against the new law the same night President Johnson signed it. In the suit, Rolleston claimed that, if integrated, his motel would lose millions in business. He placed that loss at $11 million and asked for that amount in his suit.

Noting that both cases were challenges to the same law, US District Judge Frank Hooper decided to convene a three-judge panel and hear the cases back-to-back. This would allow any decisions to be appealed directly to the US Supreme Court. The judges Hooper selected for the panel were himself, District Court Judge Lewis Morgan and Elbert Tuttle, chief judge of the Fifth Circuit Court of Appeals. The Heart of Dixie Motel case was heard first.

On the morning of 17 July, promptly at 9:30 A.M., the proceedings got underway. Federal attorneys and Rolleston, representing himself, needed slightly more than two hours to argue their cases. Once they had heard both sides, the judges called a recess and announced that the second case would begin at 1:30 P.M. From the moment the Pickrick case got underway, there were three basic questions to be decided. First, was the public accommodations section of the civil rights law constitutional? Secondly, if the law was constitutionally valid, was the Pickrick covered by it? Thirdly, did the Pickrick serve interstate customers and did the bulk of the food served at the restaurant move in interstate commerce?

For more than three hours, federal attorneys called numerous witnesses before the panel to prove that the restaurant did serve interstate customers and its food moved in interstate commerce. Once government testimony was concluded, Maddox's attorneys argued that, although food may have moved through other states to arrive at the Pickrick, its preparation and resale for public consumption within the state of Georgia did not constitute interstate commerce.

Three days later, the judges announced they were ready to deliver an opinion. As Maddox and his attorneys waited outside the federal court clerk's office, he was jovial about the forthcoming decision.

"I'm not going to integrate," he told reporters as he waited. "I've made a pledge.

Musing on the consequences of the decision, he said, "Even if they take everything, I'm not going to worry. Didn't Lyndon Johnson say he was going to eradicate poverty?"

Moments later, Maddox, his lawyers and the federal attorneys were ushered into the court clerk's inner office to learn of the judges' decision.

Thirty minutes later, the door reopened and the ruling was etched on the faces of the participants. Rolleston, as well as Maddox and his lawyers, was crest-fallen. In the ruling, both the Pickrick and the Heart of Dixie Motel were enjoined from refusing service to African Americans and were given twenty-one days—until 11 August—before the injunction took effect. This delay would allow attorneys for Maddox and Rolleston to prepare appeals and seek a possible stay from the Supreme Court.

That night, as Maddox worked with his attorneys to prepare an application for a stay, he was already trying to come up with a fallback position in case the nation's highest court ruled against him.

"I'll close the Pickrick," Maddox vowed, "if the Supreme Court rules against the rights of free enterprise."

On 10 August, the day before the injunction was effective, Justice Hugo Black handed down a decision, which denied stays in either case. Both Maddox and Rolleston refused "to abide by the provisions of the public accommodations law," Justice Black wrote, "and therefore deserved to be enjoined."

On the morning of 11 August, the day the injunction took effect, civil rights activists were back at the Pickrick. At 10:30 A.M., two young African Americans appeared at the entrance and asked to be served. Moments later, Ozell Rogers, head of the restaurant's bakery department, appeared and asked the two to leave with the claim that "you're putting 75 people out of work." The two African Americans left.

When Maddox arrived at 11 A.M. and heard about the new integration attempt, he grew angry and defiant.

"We're not going to integrate," he told a crowd of assembled supporters. "The Pickrick belongs to me and not to President Johnson or the agitators or the news media or Krushchev or anybody."

Despite Maddox's defiant stand, the Pickrick would shortly be put to a new test. Twenty minutes after making the statement, a car with five African Americans—a woman and four men—pulled into the parking lot. After four of the occupants got out and walked to the entrance, they were blocked by Lester Maddox Jr. Immediately, the elder Maddox appeared and pleaded with the African Americans to leave, claiming that, if they remained, he would have to close and put his employees out of work.

After they refused, Maddox grew angry and said, "You're not about to come in here. If you live a hundred years, you'll never get a piece of fried chicken here."

With that, the determined African Americans waited outside until the Pickrick's normal afternoon closing time at 2:30 P.M. While they waited, Maddox escorted his white customers past the African Americans around to a side door.

During those three and one-half hours, the assembled crowd of whites argued with the demonstrators over the civil rights issue. At one point, a white man lunged at the blacks, but he was instantly pulled away by a policeman. Finally, Ozell Rogers appeared again and pleaded with the African Americans to leave, but again they refused.

After a summer shower sent the demonstrators, the police, the newsmen and Maddox's supporters dashing for cover under the Pickrick's canvas canopy, several whites tried to crowd out the African Americans, but they clung tenaciously to the support columns. Finally, when the restaurant closed at 2:30 P.M., the crowd dispersed. The demonstrators announced they would be back when the Pickrick reopened. When the Pickrick reopened, however, the African Americans were nowhere to be seen.

Meanwhile, the events of the day had spoken for themselves. Maddox had refused service to the five African Americans in spite of the federal injunction. He was going to be in hot water with the Department of Justice and the courts.

Two days later, on 13 August, Judge Hooper issued an order demanding that Maddox show reason why he should not be held in contempt and set a hearing for 20 August. That same day, integrationists decided to further hammer home their point and two more African Americans appeared at the Pickrick and demanded to be served. In the incident, Calvin Jones and Gary Robinson, along with two FBI agents, made their way through the restaurant's first two entrance doors before Maddox appeared and blocked them.

"You sorry, no-good devils," he said. "You just put 66 people out of work. You sorry communists. You've stolen my business, now get out of my door."

An hour later, Maddox set up a podium near the restaurant entrance and, in an emotional announcement to some eighty supporters and friends, stated that he was closing the Pickrick "for good."

"My president, my congress and the Communists have closed my business and ended a childhood dream," Maddox said, tears streaming down his face. "They have killed my business and helped kill the American free enterprise system."

The following day, a story in the Atlanta Journal stated that Maddox had closed the Pickrick on the advice of his attorney.

"I told him [Lester] not to violate the court order," said attorney William G. McRae. "If anybody came there and requested service and he didn't want to serve them, to shut the thing down."

Although Maddox closed down food service at the restaurant, he was still faced with the earlier show-cause order issued by Judge Hooper.

In the 20 August hearing, Maddox and his attorney McRae came before the three-judge panel again. This time Judges Hooper and Morgan were still seated, but Court of Appeals Judge Griffin Bell had replaced Elbert Tuttle on the panel. In the ensuing proceeding, Bell took an active role against McRae.

"We're not going to have this thing rammed down the throat of the South," McRae said.

Bell warned McRae that the court had no time for political speeches and reminded him that he was speaking for Maddox and not the South.

McRae argued that, as a result of closing, Maddox was losing an estimated $200 a day. With that, Judge Bell countercharged that Maddox should not have closed. Then Judge Bell posed the most damaging question.

"What irreparable harm would he suffer if he ran it and went by the law?" Bell asked.

"We're not going to integrate it to find out," McRae said.

Finally, after hearing arguments, the judges ruled that the earlier court order would remain in effect. Two weeks later, the panel made the temporary order a permanent injunction.

During the few weeks after the Pickrick closed, Maddox set up a souvenir stand near the front entrance which featured red-painted pick handles stamped with the words "Pickrick drumsticks." Also offered for sale were bumper stickers, political pamphlets, American flags and cans of a carbonated drink Maddox called "Gold Water." As customers flocked in, Maddox said proceeds of the sales were going for "bread and meat and fighting back the attack of my government and the Communists."

For almost a month, Maddox cornered the market on pick handles. E. R. Bates, owner of Bates Hardware Company who sold the pick handles to Maddox at cost, said he not only bought out the entire stock of two local jobbers, but he had exhausted the stocks of five factories. Bates said that, while Maddox had obtained a few pick handles on his own, he had supplied more than 10,000 handles from his sources.

During this gimmick period, Maddox announced that he would erect a three-story, white frame tower on the Pickrick grounds, which he would call "the monument to the death of free enterprise." Once built, Maddox dedicated the bizarre-looking structure on a cold Sunday afternoon in late September. The 500 people who attended the ceremony were charged thirty-five cents for adults and twenty-five cents for children to view the "historical exhibits" inside. These exhibits included framed quotations of Thomas Jefferson, Daniel Webster, Nathan Hale and Lester Maddox—along with a copy of the US Constitution—resting in an open coffin.

By early October, the novelty of Maddox's publicity gimmicks began to wear thin and he admitted he was in "horrible" financial trouble. During the month and a half since the Pickrick was closed, Maddox kept his employees on the payroll. Although he had done well selling souvenirs, he was deeply in debt and creditors were demanding payment. Finally, he announced publicly that he was going to have to "do something to survive."

After conferring with his attorneys, it was decided that the restaurant would reopen under the name the Lester Maddox Cafeteria. Since the Pickrick was a corporation and Lester Maddox was its agent, the attorneys decided that the corporation could lease the restaurant to Lester Maddox the individual. With that, the restaurant doors opened again and the Pickrick was back in business.

Aware of the legal arguments surrounding the reopening, Maddox posted a sign at the front entrance, which qualified the terms for eating at the restaurant. The sign stated that the Pickrick could not serve interstate travelers and the act of seeking service was the same as giving one's word that they were not from out-of-state. The sign explained that the restaurant did not discriminate against persons because of "race, color, creed or national origin." However, the sign noted, "no integrationists" would be served.

During the first two days the restaurant was open, business boomed. Friends and supporters flocked in again to congratulate Maddox on his courageous stand. On the morning of the third day, however, a group of four African Americans appeared for service. Three members of the group were the Reverends Willis, Dunn and Lewis, who tried to integrate the Pickrick on 3 July. After Maddox blocked their entrance, the four left and went to Judge Hooper who issued another show-cause order on civil contempt. According to the order, the Lester Maddox Cafeteria was under the same restrictions of the earlier injunction issued against the Pickrick.

Back in court again, the opening of the Lester Maddox Cafeteria was called a "subterfuge" and Maddox was ordered to accept every customer regardless of his or her race, creed or national origin. With the order, Maddox was warned that he would be fined $200 a day for each day he did not comply. This was the final death knell for the Pickrick.

After three hours of discussion with his attorneys, Maddox decided he had no alternative other than to close the restaurant forever.

"Together we [he and his attorneys] drew up a statement of surrender," Maddox recalled later. "I would bow down to the police state."

Several days later, Maddox was finishing "clean-up operations" at the restaurant when an African American appeared at the entrance. Once Maddox peeked through the window, he saw the man and knew he wanted to be served. Without saying a word, Maddox took a small sign and hung it on the door. The sign said CLOSED.

Meanwhile, Maddox still faced the pistol-pointing charge in criminal court. The trial got underway on 12 April 1965 in the courtroom of Judge Dan Duke.

Once testimony began, civil rights worker George Willis testified that Maddox had pointed the pistol directly at him. He said Maddox was "pointing it directly in my face... I was looking down the hole in the barrel."

Albert Dunn, another civil rights worker, testified that Maddox "had the pistol on me.... It was the pistol that determined my moves from there on."

After several newsmen testified about the sequence of events, there were strongly conflicting versions as to exactly what Maddox had done with the pistol. Although all agreed that Maddox had a pistol, there was no agreement as to whether he waved it, pointed it or simply kept it at his side.

Maddox attorney Sidney Schell paraded a long line of prominent citizens before the court to testify to his client's character. These included two superior court judges, a civil court judge and two ministers, including Maddox's pastor at the North Atlanta Baptist Church.

Finally, Maddox himself took the stand and recalled his childhood dream of having his own business and his poverty-stricken days growing up in Home Park. When asked about the specific incident, Maddox said: "I pulled my gun because I had reason to believe that my life and property were under threat. I did not pull my gun to deny service to anyone.... The action I have taken is what I would expect you (the jurors) to take."

Finally, having heard both sides, Judge Duke charged the jury and sent them off to the jury room to make a decision. After only thirty-five minutes of deliberation, the jury returned a not guilty verdict.

"Thank God we still have juries," Maddox commented later.

During the summer of 1965, the Pickrick building and property was bought by Georgia Tech as part of a campus extension program. Once the new owners gained control of the building, it was extensively remodeled and refurbished and today it serves as the university's job placement center. Although Maddox has visited the site several times, he has refused to re-enter the old building to this day!

After he was elected governor in 1966, Maddox took part in an official tour of the Georgia Tech campus in the spring of 1968. As the rosy-faced female student guided the group across the west side of the campus, she stopped directly in front of the refurbished Pickrick Building and turned to Maddox.

"Governor Maddox," she said. "I'm sure you recognize our new jobs placement center."

Maddox smiled with recognition.

"Let's go inside and look around," the student guide said, then she turned and started toward the building. As the other members of the group followed the tour guide, the governor hung back.

When they reached the door, the guide noticed that Maddox was not among them. She turned and saw him standing in the same spot where they had had the earlier discussion.

"Wouldn't you like to come inside, Governor Maddox?" the tour guide asked.

Maddox smiled sheepishly.

"No, y'all go ahead!" he said. "I'll just wait out here."

To this day, there is no record that Maddox ever entered the old Pickrick building since its closing.

Chapter 6
"This Is Maddox Country"

"There was no way I could sell out and withdraw as a candidate... for no amount of money would I betray the trust of one little Georgia boy or girl..."
—Maddox on efforts to buy him out of the primary

During the height of the civil rights unrest at the Pickrick during the summer of 1964, long-time friend Courtney Wynne paid Maddox a visit. Wynne was well known as an expert on the operating restaurants and, for many years, Maddox had sought out his advice about business matters at the Pickrick.

After the two were seated in a back booth, they talked briefly about the restaurant business. Finally, the conversation turned to politics and Wynne, well aware that Maddox was fighting tooth and nail to protect the restaurant against civil rights demonstrators, planted a seed in Maddox's head.

"You know, Lester," Wynne said, "This thing could get you elected governor."

Maddox looked at his old friend for a moment, then smiled.

"You might be right!" he replied.

At the time, however, Maddox was so preoccupied with keeping his business open and free of demonstrators that he did not have time to think about his political ambitions. Standing up for your beliefs is one thing, a serious Maddox explained, keeping a restaurant business open and running to feed your family was quite another.

Over the next ten months, Maddox would lose his battle and be forced to close the Pickrick and sell the property it stood on. In early September 1965, however, exactly one year after the Pickrick closed, the seed that had been planted by Courtney Wynne germinated into reality.

Maddox had long dreamed of becoming governor of Georgia. He had toyed with the idea and hinted at that dream in his "Pickrick Says" ads, but, in reality, it always seemed to be just beyond his grasp. Now, on the heels of the pick-handle incident and his closing the Pickrick, Maddox sensed that the dream could well become a reality. As a result of the restaurant ads and his two losing mayoral races, Maddox was well known in and around Atlanta as a "political person." During his campaign against Peter Zack Geer, Maddox—traveling all over Georgia in the white station wagon to nail up signs and make speeches—had become quite famous throughout the state. Now, after his widely publicized fight with Washington and the civil rights activists, he was famous not only in Georgia, but throughout the South and most of the nation. Maddox knew he was building a strong base of support among voters who faithfully voted for candidates who espoused a strong segregationist platform.

On 25 September 1965, one year after the Pickrick closed, Maddox announced his candidacy for the state's Democratic nomination for governor. With the announcement, he promised to promote a platform of "constitutional government, free enterprise, God, liberty and Americanism."

"I knew I had a good chance of winning," Maddox recalled. "In every previous campaign, I had continued to gain political strength. In the lieutenant governor's race, I beat everyone but Peter Zack Geer. I knew I had lots of people out there that liked me and my views."

The following month, Maddox took money from the sale of the restaurant and opened the Pickrick Furniture Store. Although he had this wild political dream, he still faced with the task of providing daily bread for his family. As usual, when Maddox announced he was running for office, Virginia knew that she would be expected to run the family business. During the eighteen years they had owned the Pickrick, Virginia ran the restaurant while her husband was "off politicking", as she called it. Now, Virginia knew that she must manage the furniture store.

In the Democratic primary, the three early candidates were Maddox, former governor Ellis Arnall and Hoke O'Kelley. Arnall was an Atlanta attorney and a staunch Roosevelt liberal who served as governor from 1943-1947. Hoke O'Kelley, an elderly, Gwinnett County landowner who had entered several previous gubernatorial races and always lost, was not considered a serious threat. Thus, among the three, Arnall was considered the odds-on favorite.

Once the race started to heat up, however, former Governor Ernest Vandiver, a favorite of the Talmadge political machine, decided to join the fray. Instantly, the balance of power was upset and, with Vandiver's announcement, the race became a two-horse affair between Arnall and Vandiver.

In the late spring of 1966, the situation underwent another dramatic change when Vandiver dropped out. While serving in the state house from 1959-1963, Vandiver suffered a near-fatal heart attack. In the press release that announced his withdrawal, Vandiver stated that, although he seriously wanted to run for governor again, his doctors warned that a hotly contested political campaign might cost him his life.

With Vandiver's departure, the powerful Talmadge faction was left without a candidate. Immediately, Senator Herman Talmadge himself recognized the political vacuum and announced that he was interested in returning to Georgia to seek the governorship. That interest, however, met a quick end when the state's "big mules"—bankers, lawyers, businessmen and others who controlled the state's political money—informed Talmadge that he should remain in Washington and allow wiser heads to choose someone for the race. A week later, that "someone" was James Gray, a wealthy Albany television station and newspaper owner. Then, just as everyone thought the race had taken its final form, two more candidates—former Lieutenant Governor Garland Byrd and State Senator Jimmy Carter—quickly joined the fray. With their entry, a total of six candidates formed the field.

With that, the final balance of power in the race began to take shape. With Vandiver out, most observers now viewed the race as a three-way affair between Arnall, Gray and Carter. Arnall would get the new south liberals, Gray would get most of the Talmadge Democrats and Jimmy

Carter would prove especially strong in rural and middle Georgia as a result of his alliance with farmers. Carter, a Navy man and former officer on a nuclear submarine, was so confident of his chances that he had dropped out of the race for congress in his home district to enter the governor's race. Meanwhile, Maddox—mostly as a result of the pick-handle incident—was expected to get the bulk of his votes from the state's hard-line segregationists. Byrd and O'Kelley were considered very dark horses.

Once the campaign was underway, each of the Democratic candidates attempted to tailor his platform on the vagaries of how the Republican nominee, West Georgia Congressman Howard "Bo" Callaway, would shape his. All the candidates knew that the winner must face Callaway in the 8 November general election. Callaway was chosen as the Republican nominee at a party caucus months before and he was considered a formidable opponent for the Democrats.

Maddox, as always, was faced with a shortage of money to finance his campaign. While the other serious candidates had some financial backing, Maddox had very little and was forced to rely on small contributions and his own personal resources. Maddox recalled later that it took him a year (September 1965-April 1966) to raise $1,000. This was almost totally small contributions of up to $10. In late May, however, when Maddox's political strength started to show, some hefty donations started coming in and he raised another $17,000. Maddox contributed $18,000 from his own pocket. This total of $36,000 was Maddox's campaign budget for the primary. Even with that amount, he said there were many days he "didn't know whether I'd be able to pay my lodging and make it back to Atlanta."

One day, while Maddox was planning out his campaign, a salesman for an outdoor advertising firm paid him a visit.

"Mr. Maddox," the salesman said, "I'd like to help you get elected."

"Well, sir," Maddox replied, "I can sure use all the help I can get."

"Billboards," the man replied. "That's what you need! Big billboards with your picture on them, from the Tennessee line to Florida and from the Alabama line to the Atlantic Ocean. We can do the job for you for only $96,000."

Maddox laughed.

"Sir, I appreciate your offer," he said, "but to tell you the truth, if you had said $960, I still couldn't afford it."

Maddox learned during the 1962 lieutenant governor's race that proper placement of his owns posters near his opponents' highway billboards often served to neutralize the larger sign's effect. With this in mind, Maddox ordered 50,000 posters with the words: "This is Maddox Country" printed on them. Then, he and J. L. Allen Jr. loaded up his station wagon and started criss-crossing the state nailing up the posters and making speeches. Before long, Maddox learned that his opponents' workers were coming along behind him and removing many of his posters. As a result, he bought a 12-foot ladder, secured it atop the station wagon and started nailing the signs so high his enemies could not reach them.

During the campaign, Maddox and his helpers covered more than 100,000 miles from Valdosta in the south, Blue Ridge in the north, Savannah to the east and the Alabama line to the west. Day after day, with the old white station wagon loaded with posters, campaign literature, bubble gum for kids and boxes of small American flags, he plied the campaign trail.

The Maddox campaign was not only faced with a lack of campaign funds, but also the general belief among Democratic party bigwigs that Maddox lacked both money and organization and, thus, without either, was just another also-ran in the contest. One of those bigwigs was state highway commissioner Jim Gillis a man with huge political power in the state. Early in the race, Maddox decided to contact Gillis and explain to him that he was a serious candidate and could become governor.

After Maddox's call was put through to Gillis, Maddox explained, "Mr. Jim, I'd like to talk to you about putting your support behind the winning candidate. I'm going to be the next governor of Georgia and if you're not with me now, you will be when it's over."

Gillis did not answer at first. "We're not against you, Mr. Maddox," he said finally. "We like you and appreciate the position you stand for. But some of the fellas say you're just too hard-headed."

"Well, Mr. Jim," Maddox replied, "the fellas may be right about my being hard-headed if they mean I'll stick by what I believe, but they're going to have to decide whether they want a hard-headed Democrat or a Republican."

Finally, Maddox realized he had made little progress with Gillis. The established political structure, he surmised, was too unyielding to allow an under-financed outsider with no ties to the party hierarchy to become governor.

Not only did Maddox have to fight the Democratic Party in the 1966 race, as always, he also had to fight the Atlanta newspapers. From the start, Maddox charged that their political cartoons, news stories and editorials lashed out at him as "some sort of throwback to the dark ages, a racist, bigot and hate monger."

As late August rolled around and the campaign started heating up, it became obvious that Arnall was the candidate to beat. The former Governor, who was credited with a progressive term in the governor's office, made it clear that he was a Democrat through and through.

"I'm a local Democrat, a state Democrat, and a national Democrat," Arnall repeated, "and anyone that doesn't like it can go to hell."

Although he had a respectable voter following, Arnall also had some stern critics. After his term as governor, he had conducted a national speaking tour, which was critical of Georgia and its people. In the speeches, he had referred to Georgians as being backward, poverty-stricken and poorly educated. Many Georgians had not forgotten that, in his book, *The Shore Dimly Seen*, Arnall had described most Georgians as throwbacks to another age and beckoned Georgians and the south to rejoin the union. His public comments, coupled with the book, did little to improve his image among proud, if short-sighted, Georgians. In fact, he had made some bitter enemies among the state's Democratic die-hards.

Arnall was also criticized for his old-fashioned, 1940s campaign style. On television, critics whispered that Arnall came across as a simple, country bumpkin with tired, outdated ideas. The polished oratorical style and the Roosevelt idealism that had wowed voters when he won the governor's race against Eugene Talmadge in 1942 was little more than a weak parody on 1966 television.

Meanwhile, in his own campaign, Maddox made sure that voters understood Arnall's ultra-liberal message and he told one group of prospective voters that Arnall was "Earl Warren, Jacob Javits, Nelson Rockefeller, Hubert Humphrey, Lyndon Johnson and Bobby Kennedy all wrapped into one, plus Martin Luther King."

On the other hand, James Gray portrayed himself as the responsible segregationist. Born in Massachusetts, Gray was Dartmouth-educated and had settled in Albany in the late forties to build a prosperous television and newspaper business. In many ways, his campaign rhetoric against the civil rights movement was similar to Maddox's in that he tossed around words like "socialism," "left-wing," "Communism," and "tyranny". Gray, although he took a firm stand against integration, was much more low-key in his demands than Maddox.

On that subject, the one plank in his platform he emphasized almost daily was the federal school desegregation guidelines. Gray continually said the guidelines were designed to turn schools into "propaganda factories that graduated robots that had been indoctrinated, not educated."

If he were elected, Gray said he would file a suit contesting the "constitutionality of the guidelines: "The vicious school guidelines being implemented in Georgia's public schools at this very moment actually have the hidden purpose of not only destroying local control of schools, but turning teachers into propagandists, instead of educators."

Meanwhile, former lieutenant governor Garland Byrd's platform was similar to Gray's. In speeches, Byrd consistently attacked racial integration and Washington by hammering away at the school desegregation guidelines that accompanied federal school aid. If elected, Byrd said he would encourage every Georgia school system to rescind its agreement to follow the desegregation guidelines. If the systems lost federal funds as a result, Byrd said he would ask the general assembly to pass legislation, which would provide state funds to replace the canceled federal aid. He estimated that the cost of replacement would be about $10 million a year, but explained that no tax increase would be necessary to finance the replacement funds.

Of the five major candidates, Carter's position was the vaguest. Carter tried to place himself somewhere between Arnall on the left and the segregationist Maddox-Byrd-Gray cadre on the right. Time and time again, Carter claimed that he was the only one who could reunite the six-candidate Democratic field and go on to defeat Callaway. "Everybody else [in the race] has too many people against them to reunite the party," Carter proclaimed.

Carter's overall strategy was to woo blacks and white liberals in the cities. His advisors felt that this urban support—coupled with his strong support in central and South Georgia—would assure him a spot in the runoff.

In the end, however, Carter's strategy, as well as Gray's and Byrd's, failed. While Carter, Byrd and Gray were in the back room forming strategy and planning television and newspaper ads; Maddox was traveling across the state, making speeches, shaking hands and nailing up posters.

When Maddox first announced his entry into the race, his political strength was sorely underestimated. Few among the Democratic party faithful accepted him as a serious candidate. He was a three-time loser, they said, and did not stand a chance against the likes of Arnall and others. By early September, however, the laughter had died away and, in the polling, Maddox was closely following front-runner Arnall. One wire service political analyst wrote, "Lester Maddox entered the governor's race and everyone said: Ha! Ha! Now nobody's laughing." Suddenly Maddox was riding a huge wave of popularity and the other candidates knew that the fiery underdog could well prove to be the victor.

In early September, only days before the 15 September election, Maddox got a startling telephone call from a person he will only identify as Bud.

In the phone conversation, Maddox said Bud told him he had been approached by three men on an airline flight who asked him to deliver a message to Maddox.

"What's the message?", Maddox asked.

"They're interested in seeing another candidate elected," Bud replied, "and they feel that you being in the race is interfering with his chances. They said it would be worth a lot to them if you would consider withdrawing on some pretext like ill health."

Lester pondered the statement.

"What did they mean about it being worth a lot to them?" he asked.

Bud hesitated before answering.

"They offered to pay you...," he said finally, "Maybe $250,000 to drop out of the governor's race."

Again, Maddox was silent for several moments. Then he laughed.

"It's just some kind of joke, Bud," he asked.

"Oh, no!" Bud replied. "It's no joke. They said another candidate dropped out of a statewide race several years ago and he was paid $100,000 for saying his health was bad." At first, Maddox did not answer. "I would take the offer seriously," Bud continued. "Anybody that would pay a man $250,000 to get him out a race could probably afford to pay $5,000 and have him taken care of permanently if he refused."

Finally, determined to discover who the perpetrators were, Maddox told Bud he could not meet with the men that day as suggested, but he would make arrangements to meet them the following day. Maddox explained that he was to make a campaign speech in Macon the following day. That would be the most convenient time, he suggested. He said he would meet with the men at the Dempsey Hotel in Macon at 2:00 p.m. Satisfied with the answer, Bud said he would relay the message.

The following day, Maddox arrived in Macon at 10:00 a.m. with his younger brother Wesley and his driver J. L. Allen Jr. They went directly to the local FBI office and asked that they be met by an agent at a downtown intersection. When two agents arrived, Maddox explained that he was due to meet three men at the Dempsey Hotel who wanted to buy him out of the governor's race. After listening to Maddox, the agents said the matter was out of their jurisdiction and suggested that he contact local law enforcement authorities.

Taking their advice, Maddox called the Macon Police Department and asked to speak to the chief of detectives. After being told that the detective was having lunch at the nearby Len Berg's restaurant, they went to meet him. The detective listened to Maddox's story. The officer laughed and told him, "I don't believe it, but if you think there is anything to it, I suggest you get yourself a lawyer."

"I was bothered by his response," Maddox recalled later. "But in one last attempt to get help, I decided to got to the Bibb County Courthouse and seek the assistance of the state solicitor."

Once he had spoken with the county solicitor, however, Maddox was told that the office had no jurisdiction in such matters. Since he was not a public official, the solicitor explained, the offer could not be considered a bribe.

Meanwhile, Maddox was scheduled to make his speech at the S&S Cafeteria at noon and, with no time to waste, he and the others hurried to the lunch meeting. Once the speech was over, Maddox and his crew left the cafeteria, drove to the Dempsey Hotel and checked in. As Maddox and J. L. Allen started to their room after check-in, he spotted *Atlanta Constitution* reporter Sam Hopkins standing in the lobby with Macon newspaper reporter Billy Watson. Although the *Constitution* had been Maddox's mortal enemy in the past, he decided that he should inform Hopkins and Watson of the upcoming buy-off attempt. After explaining the situation, Maddox finished by saying: "All I ask is that you try to listen outside my room when they come there with the money." The two reporters agreed to the request and, after ordering driver J. L. Allen to remain in the lobby, Maddox proceeded to his room.

Moments later, there was a knock on the door. When Maddox opened it, Bud was standing outside.

"They're ready, Lester," he said. "They want you to come down the hall to their room."

Then Bud reached inside his jacket and withdrew a piece of paper.

"All you have to do," he said, handing the paper to Maddox, "is sign this and the money is yours."

Maddox said he cautiously took the folded piece of paper from Bud, then immediately explained that he had to go to the rest room. Once the bathroom door was closed, Maddox unfolded the letter. It was addressed to George Stewart, Secretary of the Georgia Democratic Party, and it read:

"Due to my physical condition, it would be both impossible and unwise for me to complete my campaign for Governor of Georgia and therefore, this is my formal notification to you that I am withdrawing from the Democratic primary election for the Governorship. I would appreciate your returning my $2500 qualification fee at your convenience."

Amused, but still cautious, Maddox placed the letter in his sock, then returned to the door. Bud led him down the hallway to a nearby room to meet the awaiting party.

At the meeting, in addition to Maddox and Bud, were three attorneys who Maddox later identified as Bobby Lee Cook, Jake Cullens and "another attorney from Atlanta." Once Maddox was introduced to the men, Cook said he and the others had brought the cash to get Maddox out of the governor's race. One of the men immediately pulled a suitcase from under the hotel bed and opened it. Then he took out several bundles of bills and handed them to Maddox.

"The tens were in ten thousand dollar bundles and the twenties were in twenty thousand dollar bundles," Maddox recalled later. "Man, that was a lot of money, the most cash I had ever been in the presence of in my life, but I knew I couldn't accept one dime of it."

For a moment, Maddox looked at the huge bundles of money he held in his hands, then threw them on the hotel bed.

"What's the matter?" Maddox said the first attorney asked him. "All you have to do is sign the letter to Mr. Stewart asking that your name be withdrawn as a candidate because of your health, and you can take this money and along with your wife and children have anything you want..."

Maddox slowly shook his head.

After Maddox refused to take the cash, Cook turned to his cohorts and instructed them to take the money and leave because he wanted to speak to Maddox in private. The other two balked at the suggestion that they leave the room with the money, claiming it was too dangerous. Finally, it was decided that the money would be placed under the hotel bed, then they would leave.

Once the other two had left, Maddox said attorney Cook tried vigorously to persuade him to get him to sign the letter and accept the money. Finally, however, after Maddox made it clear that he had no intention of dropping out, the attorney gave up and Maddox left the hotel room. Outside in the hallway, he walked past Bud and the other two attorneys back to his own room.

Moments later, Bud appeared at the door again and asked Maddox to return the withdrawal letter. Maddox fumbled on his person, then looked around and finally told Bud he had misplaced it. For a moment, Bud glanced around the room, then hurriedly left.

Moments later, Maddox reappeared outside the hotel room where he met J. L. Allen and the two reporters. They said they were unable to hear everything that was said in the other room, but they had heard him exclaiming about the money. Maddox quickly provided Hopkins and Watson with details of the incident, after which the two eager reporters hurried off to file their stories.

While he was eager to identify the culprits who sought to buy him out of the race, Maddox refused to reveal the identity of Bud. When asked to do so thirty years after the incident, Maddox simply said, "I'd rather not say. Let's just say he was a distant relative." Likewise, several years after the incident, Maddox lost the withdrawal letter he said was presented to him for his signature.

When the Sept. 15 election day finally arrived, all the polls had Arnall leading the pack. In the minds of political pundits, the question to be decided was whether Arnall's run-off opponent would be Lester Maddox,

James Gray, or Jimmy Carter. Everyone knew that Maddox would make a stronger-than-expected showing, but doubted his ability to win.

When the precincts closed that night and the returns started coming in, Carter ran extremely well and held a solid second place lead throughout most of the night. Once the late rural returns were counted the following morning, however, Maddox started to nudge Carter out of second place and, by early afternoon, had replaced Carter as the runner-up candidate. Finally, when all the votes were tabulated and declared official, the outcome was Arnall, 231,480 votes; Maddox, 185,672; Carter, 164,562; Gray, 152,973; Byrd, 39,994; and O'Kelley, 13,271. Arnall would now face Maddox in a run-off rather than either Carter or Gray.

Only a day after the run-off candidates were decided, many political pundits and most of the media predicted that Arnall would easily defeat Maddox. Sam Hopkins, the *Atlanta Constitution*'s political reporter, wrote, "Arnall was lucky he got the man in the run-off he wanted all along."

Meanwhile, finishing third behind Maddox had been a bitter disappointment for Jimmy Carter. When he first entered the governor's race, all the political observers claimed that Carter, with his impressive credentials, would be a very strong contender. Despite a strong showing in rural Georgia and strong support in Atlanta, he had nevertheless finished 20,000 votes behind Maddox.

When Carter lost the 1966 primary to Maddox, he confessed that it was one of the most embarrassing moments of his life. A hard-scrabble tenth grade dropout who sold fried chicken for a living had soundly beaten the worldly, polished Navy man, an Annapolis graduate and atomic submarine officer. Although Carter tried not to show it at the time, he would make life difficult for Maddox when he was elected the state's 76th governor in 1970.

Following the Democratic Primary in 1966, Maddox neither planned nor attempted any change is his strategy. Both his position, and that of Arnall, were well defined during a long, hard and tiring campaign. Maddox was the outsider, the defender of the people from governmental tyranny. Arnall was a liberal, old-school Democrat who was loyal, not only to his state and national party, but also to the philosophy of Franklin D. Roosevelt.

Arnall's campaign strategists John Greer and Walter Sanders knew that they were in a real political dogfight. The results of the primary sobered them to the fact that Maddox was, indeed, a major force in the state. They quickly advised Arnall not to spend any money on the run-off campaign. They saw the election as a clear-cut contest between an FDR liberal and what they considered a misguided, hard-line segregationist. They felt that everything Arnall stood for had been adequately aired during the primary. As a result, he campaigned lightly. In one television address to voters, he once again branded Maddox as the "axe-handle candidate." After the speech, he called in reporters and had his picture taken at a table with the state and federal constitutions on one side and a collection of pistols and axe handles on the other.

Meanwhile, some observers were saying that Arnall did not have a chance against Maddox. In the primary, the four top candidates behind Arnall had all been varying degrees of segregationists. It was only logical, these observers said, that the majority of these votes would go to Maddox—the biggest segregationist of all—in the run-off. Further, they claimed that most Georgia voters were not ready for Arnall's brand of freewheeling Roosevelt liberalism.

Maddox, meanwhile, wasted no time in attempting to enlist the support of the other losing candidates, especially James Gray. Even though Maddox had suspected that Gray was the person behind the buy-off offer, he was also very impressed with Gray's organizational and speaking abilities. Maddox believed that, if he won the primary run-off, Gray could unify Democratic office-holders behind his general election campaign against Callaway.

Several days after the primary, Maddox flew to Miami Beach to meet with Gray, who was relaxing with his family after the long, grueling primary. The meeting, which lasted less than hour, did not result in an open Gray endorsement of Maddox. However, Gray did agree to offer some token help in the runoff. Gray helped raise money for Maddox's run-off campaign and contributing some himself. Also, Maddox taped some campaign-related TV commercials at Gray's station in Albany.

Once Arnall and Maddox were back on the campaign trail for the run-off, Arnall continued to attack Maddox as "the axe-handle candidate" and told prospective voters that, if Maddox were elected, it would not only be "an embarrassment to the state, but a severe obstacle to continued state growth."

The following day, Maddox came back with the charge that Arnall was "a wild socialist who is the granddaddy of forced racial integration."

During the days leading up to the run-off, Arnall expressed supreme confidence in victory and, in several speeches, pointed out that he had never lost a political race while Maddox had never won one.

After the polls closed at 7:00 P.M. on 28 September, the political forecasters who claimed that a runoff between Arnall and Maddox was pointless proved to be right. Once the voting booth results started pouring in, the end came swiftly for Arnall. By 9:30 P.M., Maddox had a commanding lead of some 90,000 votes. While Arnall's strength showed up well in the urban precincts, Maddox scored huge totals in the state's rural areas. In Houston County, where voters gave Carter an overwhelming margin in the primary, Maddox easily defeated Arnall by almost 1,000 votes, clear evidence that Carter voters cast their ballots for Maddox. After only three hours of vote counting, it became clear that Maddox was bound for a resounding victory.

When Arnall told his supporters at the American Motor Hotel that he was going to the lobby to congratulate his victorious opponent, his supporters yelled, "No!"

Despite this, Arnall, his wife and daughter Alice graciously went downstairs into the overflowing hotel lobby and met with Maddox and his family.

Atlanta Mayor Ivan Allen, who had defeated Maddox in the 1961 race for mayor, apparently still remembered the silk stocking incident. On the day following Maddox's stunning victory over his candidate Arnall, Allen unleashed a fiery verbal barrage against Maddox.

"It is deplorable," Mayor Allen said, "that the combined forces of ignorance, prejudice, reactionism and the duplicity of many Republican voters have thrust upon the state of Georgia Lester Maddox, a totally unqualified individual, as the Democratic nominee for governor. The wisdom, justice, and moderation espoused by our founding fathers must not be surrendered to the rabble of prejudice, extremism, buffoonery and incompetency."

During the run-off campaign, Allen spoke out vehemently against Maddox. While his "Stop Maddox!" campaign had worked during the 1962 lieutenant governor's race, it had had the reverse effect this time and only served to turn the swing voters away from Arnall and toward Maddox. Two days before the run-off, one South Georgia voter told Maddox, "You know, I hadn't made up my mind until I heard what Ivan Allen was saying about you. Now I'm voting for you!"

Once the official results were in, Maddox immediately named James Gray chairman of the state's Democratic Party. Whether this was a payback for Gray's slight support during the run-off is uncertain. Maddox has never said why he chose Gray for job. If it were a political payback, it was well disguised. Maddox's close friends and advisers at the time believe that he was genuinely awe-struck by Gray's Ivy League education, his sophistication and his ability to communicate.

Meanwhile, it was a sweet victory for Maddox. Now he stood on the very edge of achieving the dream he first revealed in a Pickrick ad twelve years earlier. He had jumped the first hurdle and was on the way to becoming governor of Georgia.

Chapter 7

Maddox vs. Callaway

"It was best for the Democratic party that I won the primary run-off rather than Ellis Arnall. If Callaway...had faced the liberal Arnall in the general election, he would have clobbered him."
— Maddox remembers the general election

Even before campaigning for the 8 November general election got underway, stalwarts in the Georgia Democratic Party were already trying to forget that Lester Maddox was their party's nominee. Only one day after the primary run-off, former governor Ernest Vandiver declared, "Maddox can't beat Bo."

When asked whether he would support Maddox, Vandiver replied curtly, "I don't have any comment on that at this time."

On the same note, Senator Herman Talmadge said he did not want to have anything to do with the general election. "Why should I become involved in something that I haven't gotten into so far?" he asked inquiring news reporters.

Atlanta Congressman Charles Weltner, the epitome of Southern racial liberalism who had voted for the Civil Rights Bills of 1964 and 1965, was appalled at the Maddox nomination. Despite his dislike of Maddox, Weltner was now required by the Democratic Party oath to support Maddox in the gubernatorial race. Weltner, who was up for re-election, was not prepared for that. Thus, his reaction to the Maddox win was far more drastic than either Vandiver's or Talmadge's. At a press conference in his small office in Atlanta's old post office building, he read a short statement: "Today, the one man in our state who exists as the very symbol of violence and oppression is the Democratic nominee for the highest office in Georgia. His entire public career is directly contrary to my deepest convictions and beliefs. And while I cannot violate my oath, neither can I violate my principles. I cannot compromise with hate. I cannot vote for Lester Maddox..."

With that, Weltner resigned not only from his congressional seat, but the Democratic Party as well. (Maddox said later that the real reason Weltner resigned was because it was "a way out of certain defeat" in his re-election effort.)

Meanwhile Callaway was eager to launch his campaign against Maddox. When asked about his opponent, Callaway commented: "Time after time, Lester Maddox has shown you can't underestimate Lester Maddox. Now the race begins. My opponent has been chosen... This is the beginning and I can't wait to get started."

From the very outset, the 1966 general election was billed as one for the history books. In recent years, a powerful new Republican faction had raised its head among Georgia voters. Over the past five years, most white Georgians had become so angry about forced integration that they were ready to vote for anyone—even the long-hated Republicans—who could provide some relief. Also, newly affluent Georgians increasingly believed their taxes were being given away by Democrats through various social programs. These voters had made their voices heard in 1964 when Republican Barry Goldwater easily won Georgia's electoral votes in the presidential election. Now, two years later, their ranks had swelled to record levels and, for the first time in almost 100 years, the Democratic Party's gubernatorial nominee faced a strong Republican in the general election. This Republican was Howard 'Bo' Callaway.

From the start, most political observers realized that the 39-year-old Callaway had everything a candidate could ask for. Heir to a South Georgia textile fortune, Callaway was a graduate of West Point, a combat veteran of the Korean War and a sitting congressman for Georgia's third district. During his congressional term, he had spoken out for states' rights and had voted against the 1964 Civil Rights bill. While he represented old Southern Democrat segregationist ideals, he presented these views in a vocabulary of couched euphemisms and respectable synonyms.

His family's political connections had originally resulted in his entry into politics. For many years, Callaway's father Cason had served with distinction on the state's University System Board of Regents. In the early fifties, however, the elder Callaway had to step down due to a severe eye problem. Anxious to secure an appointment for young Bo, he went to Gov. Herman Talmadge and asked him to name his son to the post. Talmadge immediately granted the elder Callaway's request. Young Bo served as a member of the board of regents under Democratic Governors Talmadge and Marvin Griffin. Callaway remained active in Democratic Party politics. In fact, he endorsed Griffin in the 1962 Governor's race against the ultimate winner, Carl Sanders. In 1964, Callaway decided to become a Republican and rode Barry Goldwater's coattails into the third district congressional seat. It was the first time a Georgia Republican had been elected to the US House of Representatives since Reconstruction.

Everybody knew early in the 1966 election year that the Democratic Party's standard bearer, whoever it might be, would face a formidable Republican candidate. Callaway, with his polished oratorical style and shrewd understanding of both state and national issues, was a challenging opponent as a person. In addition to his personal appeal, he had generous campaign financial backing from both the national Republican Party and the Callaway family, as evidenced by Callaway's sixth-floor campaign headquarters at exclusive 1430 West Peachtree building in downtown Atlanta, a technological showplace like few Georgians had ever seen.

The space-age look of the headquarters might have been designed by a Hollywood set director and its electronic equipment—including computers that could make instant calculations on voting trends—could have come from the drawing-board of an IBM electrical engineer. Hot-line telephones had been set up between the headquarters and Callaway's district office. Election Day emergency procedures had been implemented. A closed circuit television camera instantly videotaped everyone that stepped off the elevator into the headquarters. 31-year-old Bill Amos, a construction engineer and political strategist who headed Callaway's congressional campaign in 1964, headed up Callaway's "Command Post", as he liked to call it.

Callaway and Bill Amos staged a colorful noontime parade down Peachtree Street to kick off the Republican's campaign. It was an extravagant affair. Pretty "Go Bo" girls—decked out in glittery white and blue costumes—passed out campaign stickers and buttons to the assembled crowds. A bevy of proud, enthusiastic young Republicans—businessmen, college students, housewives and professional women—swelled the ranks. Several republican congressional hopefuls—confident of victory in the upcoming election—waved from an open convertible. Callaway himself smiled and waved proudly as the procession moved slowly through the Five Points business section in a downpour of confetti from overhead skyscrapers.

Maddox, on the other hand, although he was the Democratic nominee, had no party money to finance a campaign. At the time of the primary run-off, the Democratic Party's coffers were not only empty, but severely overdrawn by an amazing $200,000. Maddox himself, who was already deeply in debt from the primary and run-off, could only draw on his personal resources. As a result, he increased the loan amounts against his home and his insurance policies to launch the campaign.

Despite the lack of money, Maddox did not complain too loudly. As a politician, he had always taken a dim view of contributions because he felt that, once he accepted them, he would have to repay the favor if elected. Thus, time and time again during his general election campaign, he proudly proclaimed that the people, not the kingmakers, had put him where he was.

When Maddox launched his general election effort, he used the same formula that had proven successful in the past. First, he ordered 50,000 "Maddox Country" posters. Once printed, he loaded the posters in his old white Pontiac station wagon, then enlisted his faithful campaign driver, J. L. Allen Jr., into service. With road maps in hand, Maddox and Allen set out across the state nailing up posters, handing out flyers, making speeches, kissing babies and shaking hands.

Maddox's campaign headquarters at the Henry Grady Hotel on Peachtree Street, although respectable, was a far cry from his opponent's sophisticated setup. Maddox's personal office was a cramped, enclosed glass cubicle off the hotel's first floor lobby. Nearby, he had several regular hotel rooms filled with campaign literature and office desks for his staff that consisted of two sisters, his brother Wesley, and several volunteer workers.

The most striking similarity between Callaway and Maddox as candidates was that both were segregationists, although Callaway was not nearly as vociferous as Maddox. In Congress, he had voted against President Johnson's Great Society, the Civil Rights Act and federal integration guidelines. Maddox, on the other hand, had made his stand against forced integration during the well-publicized incidents at the Pickrick. Whereas Callaway fought segregation as a legislator, Maddox carried a pistol and armed his family and supporters with pick handles to fight integrationists.

Other than the segregation issue, however, the two candidates were dramatically different. As a result, each candidate developed a campaign that pointed out their differences.

Time and again, Callaway pointed to the appearance of campaign workers. "Look at the people that surround us," he said, indicating his campaign workers. "Mine are young, aggressive, hard-working and dedicated. The people hanging around my opponent's headquarters are the same old cronies that have been hanging around for years."

Callaway's observations were, in fact, true. Most of the old-line political hacks that were ever present during the days of Eugene and Herman Talmadge sided with Maddox and often hung around his campaign headquarters. Setting aside the literal truth of the accusation, however, Maddox countered these accusations against his campaign workers: "We have some people with dirt under their nails, thank God, but none with dirt in their hearts."

In many ways, Callaway's attacks on Maddox mirrored those of Ellis Arnall. He argued that Maddox was irresponsible and had flouted the law at the Pickrick. Also, he hammered away at Maddox's lack of government experience, all the while emphasizing his own tenure as a congressman.

Throughout the campaign, Maddox was closely associated with the pick-handle incident. While it had won him enormous popularity among hard-line segregationists, it was an albatross around his neck among liberals and racial moderates.

With this in mind, Callaway preached over and over that Maddox's election would result in four years of lawlessness and the likely closing of Georgia schools. He contended that many teachers feared that schools would be closed under Maddox and, in one speech in Columbus, he told the crowd that if Maddox were elected, he "would enforce only the laws he believes in. And that's not liberty, that's anarchy… How do you have a society of liberty with a man whose only claim to fame is violating the law?"

Even Maddox could see that, while the pick-handle incident helped him, it also hurt him. In several instances, Maddox threatened to cancel press conferences or leave rostrums when explicit questions about race were raised. During one speech he said a majority of the black people would vote for him "if they knew my platform and not just one incident in my life…"

Meanwhile, Maddox portrayed Callaway as the "silver-spoon candidate," reminiscent of his campaign against Ivan Allen Jr. in the 1961 mayor's race. During one campaign appearance, rather than waving a silk stocking, Maddox waved a bloody shirt and reminded the assembled voters that Republicans (referring to General Sherman under President Lincoln) "had burned the state once."

Maddox, drawing on his own blue-collar background, loved to exploit the "rich boy" image he had created for Callaway. In one campaign rally in Jonesboro, Maddox said facetiously that voters should not hold it against Callaway that he was a millionaire textile heir: "It's not his fault that he doesn't understand people," Maddox told the crowd. During another rally in Rome, with its heavy concentration of blue-collar workers, Maddox reminded voters that, during one Depression-era strike, the Callaway family had put its employees "behind barbed-wire fences in concentration camps."

Maddox also drew upon his own background to distance his image from that of Callaway's. In one speech, he said, "I didn't get a college education. I wish I had. I wish every boy and girl could get one. Sometimes a person who has missed this has a greater desire to help others get one…I know what it is to go weeks and months without a paycheck, to do without food or clothing, to sacrifice for a child's education. I know how to earn an income—I have not been given one free."

While it was never stated publicly, the tacit, overriding question in the campaign was the issue of racial integration. With many white voters alarmed by racial incidents in Atlanta as well as rapidly-expanding desegregation throughout the South, Maddox symbolized a welcomed wall of resistance against integration. During many speeches, he would receive his loudest ovations with the line: "A man's home is his castle. Unless we can preserve our right to private property, there can be no liberty in America."

While Maddox and Callaway battled it out as a Democrat and a Republican, a third political force in the election slowly emerged. After Maddox won the Democratic nomination for governor, the state's blacks and white liberals were devastated. They feared that "this rabble-rousing segregationist" might actually be elected to the state's highest office. With Callaway, these same voters—especially blacks—felt equally alienated and called the Republican "a silk-stocking segregationist who is no better than Maddox." This group failed to find a voice in either candidate.

Bumper stickers and placards reading "Go Bo and take Lester with you" began to appear throughout the state, making it obvious that neither candidate was acceptable to many of the state's informed voters.

In early October, a group of disgruntled blacks and white liberals gathered in Atlanta and decided to band together and launch the WIG (Write-In Georgia) movement. Founded by Norman Shavin, an *Atlanta Constitution* columnist, and Betty Platt, a Savannah public relations consultant, the WIGS were basically a collection of blacks, white liberals, Jews and others who could not stomach the choice between Maddox and Callaway. The attendees decided to form a union and put their collective efforts behind a third candidate for a write-in campaign, an option Georgia voters could exercise at the time. Once they had agreed to unite, those in attendance spent considerable time discussing who their candidate would be. Finally, after several names were mentioned for the write-in effort, the group decided their man would be Ellis Arnall. When Arnall learned of WIG's decision, he refused to take part in the organization's effort. Neither did he repudiate it, so the write-in campaign moved forward.

At one point, Maddox attempted to determine exactly where Arnall stood on the issue. He telephoned the former governor at his Newnan home. Reportedly, Arnall told Maddox, "I will neither be a party to encouraging a write-in campaign…nor will I be a party to preventing one. It is a completely free decision for every Georgia voter to make." "Arnall's Army"—as the WIG faction came to be known—was a loosely organized, hodgepodge of under-financed, but dedicated amateurs, who wanted to make a difference in the election. The only prominent white official associated with the WIG cause was Atlanta Vice Mayor Sam Massell who used his influence to get office space for a WIG campaign headquarters in the 5 Forsyth Building in downtown Atlanta.

Meanwhile, WIG Workers, with money from their own pockets as well as personal resources, provided desks, filing cabinets, typing paper, postage stamps, typewriters and paper clips. Although the political fervor for change was present, their campaign was basically little more than a paper effort consisting of press releases, handbills, pamphlets and letters pleading for votes and contributions.

Since the WIG faction was so poorly financed, it had little or no paid advertising. Betty Platt said later that the WIGS could only afford 215 inches of advertising during the entire campaign. Shavin said WIG collected about $25,000 for the effort, most of which came in $1.00 contributions.

A three-man executive council made up of Shavin, civil rights activist Hosea Williams and Savannah businessman David Rabhan made high level decisions for WIG faction. For years, Williams was an assistant to Martin Luther King Jr. in the Southern Christian Leadership Conference and a proven organizer within the Negro community. Rabhan, a native of Savannah living in New York, returned to Atlanta to work in the WIG campaign.

Along with the WIGS, Maddox had to fight still another weak, but nevertheless present, force in the campaign: Democrats for Callaway. In virtually every race he had ever run, Maddox had faced a "hate-Maddox" faction that claimed his election would create chaos and do irreparable harm to the Democratic party. These forces, supported by the Atlanta newspapers, decided they would temporarily support a Republican in the general election.

City Judge Robert Heard of Elberton, the leader and organizer of Democrats for Callaway, made his way across Georgia telling voters that a vote for Lester Maddox would be "a vote for extremism in all its violent forms, for intemperateness, for provocative acts, for those types of things which if allowed to fester and influence over four years would absolutely destroy the state as a haven for responsible citizens seeking security and opportunity."

While Democrats for Callaway had little or no real influence on the election's outcome, the group served as a welcomed opportunity for

Maddox to lambaste the Atlanta newspapers. "When prominent individuals announced that they were Democrats for Callaway," Maddox said, "it made headlines. When prominent individuals announced that they were endorsing Maddox, there were no headlines."

As usual, Maddox, since he had little money, pursued the campaign style he knew best: moving from Georgia town to Georgia town in his Pontiac station wagon. Along the routes and byways, he continued to nail up "Maddox Country" signs on trees and telephone poles and especially on the support columns for billboards featuring Callaway. In the tiny hamlets, he loitered in public squares to shake hands with prospective voters, give bubble gum to kids and pass out American flags to adults. He would stop in at a country barber shop and ask every man present to cast his vote for him. The routine was grueling and demanding, but the energetic Maddox kept going.

Meanwhile, Callaway, flush with cash from his wealthy family and the National Republican Party, conducted an impressive television, newspaper and billboard advertising campaign. Also, there were radio spots as well as ads in the regional issues of national magazines.

Maddox, a veteran of running shoestring campaigns, had learned years before that there were many ways to get publicity without paying for it. During the 1962 race for lieutenant governor, his telegram campaigns had won him invaluable press coverage. Also, he had an unerring sense for being at the right place at the right time.

Midway through the campaign, both Callaway and Maddox sought votes at the annual Peanut Festival in Sylvester, Georgia. The event called for a huge parade complete with marching bands and majorettes down the city's main street. Included in the spectacle were both candidates, waving to the crowd in widely separated, open cars. When the Maddox car stopped at a corner where newsmen were assembled, he got out, waded into the crowd and started shaking hands. Several minutes later, when Callaway appeared, Maddox ran up alongside his car and poked out his hand.

"Good to see you, Mr. Callaway!" Maddox said. "I was beginning to wonder if you were still in this race!"

Callaway smiled sheepishly, shook the hand of a smiling Maddox, then got out of the car. For several minutes, as the two chatted amiably, reporters scribbled notes, flashbulbs went off and the TV cameras rolled.

Footage of the two candidates together aired on the nightly news. The next morning their photos were in every newspaper in the state.

But Maddox carried his talent for free publicity even further. Shortly after the Peanut Festival, Maddox challenged Callaway to face off with him in a television debate. Maddox said publicly that this forum was the best way to let all the voters know where each candidate stood on the issues. Immediately, three statewide television stations offered free airtime for such a debate, provided that both candidates would appear and agree to a set of rules to govern the confrontation.

After Callaway initially ignored the challenge, Maddox turned up the heat. In one speech after another, he urged voters "to get my opponent to accept the free television debates we've been offered, so I can come before the people of the state with my program...I was going to use Mr. Callaway in my administration, but if he's not going to settle down, I won't be able to work with him. I will need somebody more stable.

"When I started this race," Maddox continued, "I had five opponents. One week and two days ago, I had one opponent. Now I'm down to half an opponent and I can't even find him...Little Bo Peep has lost her sheep and doesn't know where to find them."

Meanwhile, as reporters pressured Callaway again and again about the proposed debate, he knew, sooner or later, he was would be forced to take the challenge seriously. On one hand, the Republican knew that such a debate would most likely benefit Maddox more than him. Not only would the free publicity be immensely beneficial for Maddox, but also Callaway was well aware that his cagey opponent could be cunning in such a situation. On the other hand, he also knew that the debates would allow him to drive home his points about the differences between the two of them. Finally, two weeks after the initial challenge, Callaway agreed to the debate.

After some negotiations, the two candidates promised to appear together on two programs, one on WSB-TV in Atlanta on Sunday, 16 October, and another on WAGA-TV in the same city four days later.

In the first debate, both candidates spent most of the time arguing non-issues. Also, both men, especially Maddox, tended to run over their allotted time and again and again had to be called down by the moderator. As the face-off progressed, however, little new information about either man's qualifications to be governor was revealed.

Early in the debate, Maddox charged that Callaway had hired off-duty policemen from the Columbus Public Safety Department to prevent Negroes from entering Callaway Gardens, a recreation park controlled by one of the Callaway family foundations. Callaway countered that the Gardens had remained open and all laws had been obeyed while Maddox, in a similar situation, had closed down his restaurant.

Finally, near the end of the face-off, Maddox turned to Callaway and asked him point-blank if he was a segregationist. Instantly, Callaway avoided the question by saying there was no easy answer.

In the WAGA-TV debate four days later, the candidates and the air were more heated, but mostly the two retraced earlier ground. In this foray, Maddox produced an affidavit from a Columbus policeman to confirm his earlier charge that Callaway had hired off-duty cops to prevent blacks from entering Callaway Gardens. Callaway countered that selling the Pickrick did not make Maddox a martyr. Actually, he said, the sale was in Maddox's best interest because he knew that the land was part of an urban renewal program for Georgia Tech. Maddox replied that, in the sale, he had received only half of the restaurant's true value.

Though during most of the second debate, nothing new was revealed about either man, it was not without developments. While delivering his summation, Maddox abruptly got up from his chair, walked over to Callaway and offered his hand. The startled Callaway did not accept Maddox's hand until Maddox's offer of a handshake was captured by a camera. Once Callaway finally grasped his hand, Maddox held it and launched into a harangue demanding Callaway "campaign on the issues." For the cameras, Callaway remarked that Maddox's action was "a very dramatic departure" from the debate rules the two had agreed upon.

Moments after the cameras stopped rolling, however Callaway and Maddox turned on one another and launched into an angry, shouting match. The Republican, his face red with rage, shouted that he was glad Maddox "had stopped slinging mud at me and my family." Maddox, angry at Callaway's earlier charge that he had attended KKK rallies, snapped, "You don't know the truth when you see it!"

Fearing that the angry confrontation might escalate into violence, Callaway's aides rushed in, grabbed their candidate and headed for the door. Meanwhile, Maddox continued to vent his emotion toward Callaway. As incredulous newsmen and cameramen watched, he continued shouting at his opponent as his aides whisked him out a studio side door.

Up until the very last day of the campaign, both candidates campaigned vigorously in rural Georgia. After a record 2,500 people turned up for a Callaway rally in tiny Gray, Georgia, the Republican proclaimed: "I've been going all over this state looking for Maddox Country, and I still can't find it."

Maddox was equally confident of victory. On election day, after he and Virginia had cast their votes, he drove out to the West Pace's Ferry Road site where the new governor's mansion was under construction.

As they peered at the soon-to-be-finished Greek Revival structure, a pensive Maddox turned to his wife.

"Do you like the color of the bricks, Babe?" he asked.

On 8 November 1966, Georgia voters went to the polls to cast their ballots to choose the state's seventy-fifth governor in the general election. The flamboyant nature of the issues as well as the heated debate between the candidates had launched a huge turnout and both Callaway and Maddox were calling for a resounding victory.

By the time the polls closed at 7:00 P.M., Maddox's headquarters in the Dixie Ballroom of the Henry Grady Hotel in downtown Atlanta was jammed with enthusiastic supporters. When Maddox and his wife arrived at 8:00 P.M., they were greeted with a tumultuous round of applause. The walls of the huge room were decorated with red, white and blue bunting and a lavish center-table bore several punch bowls and a huge layer cake that prominently featured the Georgia State seal and a photo of Maddox. Everyone, including Maddox himself, expected a huge victory celebration before the end of the evening.

As results began to trickle in from the less densely populated rural areas, Maddox held a slim margin and his supporters' enthusiasm began to grow. At 8:45 P.M., with slightly less than 5 percent of the votes counted, all three major television networks, using their computerized projection techniques, declared Maddox the winner.

The television pronouncement only made the crowd more bubbly with anticipation and several supporters started getting ready to celebrate. A five-piece rock and roll band played "Dixie" and supporters were shouting and laughing joyously. Meanwhile, Maddox himself was uncharacteristically subdued. "It feels great," he said, sipping a glass of water and trying to share his supporters' enthusiasm.

As the long evening wore on, however, Maddox's slim lead began to vanish and, by midnight, Callaway was less than 2,000 votes behind. The margin was so thin that a single large precinct could throw the election results either way. At midnight, the two candidates were in a dead heat with more than 85 percent of the precincts counted. Finally, at 1:00 A.M., Maddox, tired and emotionally drained, could see that the election was becoming a virtual toss-up. He told his supporters to go home, get some sleep and save their celebrations for later. Soon after the crowd began to disperse, Maddox and Virginia left for the evening.

The following morning, while Virginia made coffee, Maddox telephoned his campaign headquarters. When he asked a worker the latest results, he was startled by what he heard.

"The big DeKalb County vote is in," the worker said. "As expected, it went big for Callaway. He's 32,000 ahead."

"We'll be up there after breakfast," Maddox said. "We'll make it up."

Throughout the morning, the results teeter-tottered back and forth and, by 1:00 P.M. that afternoon, Maddox regained another slight lead. By 4:00 P.M., however, Maddox and Callaway were closely matched at 450,000 each. Both candidates knew that the very last vote would have to be counted before the outcome could be determined. They would have to wait.

By the end of the week, the laborious task of counting the Fulton County absentee ballots, as well as the various returns that trickled in from remote areas of the state, was complete. Once all the results had been tabulated, the unofficial total had established Callaway as the winner of a narrow 2,500-vote plurality. This was far from the clear majority Callaway needed to be declared the winner. The WIG write-in, which accounted for almost 53,000 votes, had prevented either Maddox or Callaway from receiving a legal majority of votes. A majority would have been one-half of all votes cast plus one. Callaway had fallen far short of that requirement.

Back at Maddox campaign headquarters, the candidate and his aides were shaking their heads at the dilemma presented by the lack of a clear majority.

"What happens now?" one aide asked.

"It goes to the general assembly," said aide Tommy Irvin. "The legislature will have to decide the winner."

Most Georgians—politicians and voters alike—assumed that, in a state-wide election in which there was no clear majority, the general assembly in joint session would decide the outcome between the two candidates with the highest number of votes. This was what the state constitution called for, they claimed. As a result, since Democrats held a huge majority in both houses of the assembly, Maddox would surely be named the winner. Fearing this, Callaway supporters began to file lawsuits, which challenged the section of the state constitution that empowered the general assembly to elect the governor in such circumstances.

The first, filed by the American Civil Liberties Union in federal court, claimed that the US Constitution, as well as several one-man, one-vote US Supreme Court decisions, would be violated if the state's general assembly were allowed to elect the governor. A second suit, filed on behalf of John Barton and Nancy Jones of Sandy Springs also challenged the legislature's right to elect the governor and called for a popular vote runoff between Callaway and Maddox.

Both lawsuits were considered simultaneously by District Judge Lewis Morgan and US Circuit Judges Elbert Tuttle and Griffin Bell. Their ruling stated that a legislative election of the governor would overturn the overall will of the people. Thus, the section of the Georgia Constitution, which allowed election of the legislature, was invalidated. Instead of calling for a new election or a run-off, however, the three judges allowed time for an appeal to the US Supreme Court.

Once the ruling was made, it set off a firestorm of speculation about the various ways the general election could be resolved. One possibility was to hold a re-run of the general election between Callaway and Maddox with no write-ins. Some speculated that, if the matter went to the general assembly, enough legislators might abstain from voting that no clear majority would be gained. This would have the same result as the general election, the pundits claimed, and still leave sitting Governor Carl Sanders in the chair. This theory, when carried even further, suggested that Sanders could then swear in Lieutenant Governor George T. Smith, step down and allow Smith to become the new governor. Of these options, many agreed the most likely decision was that Maddox and Callaway would have a run-off with no write-ins.

Despite all the possibilities, everyone agreed that Carl Sanders should remain in the governor's chair until the matter was resolved. Sanders announced that, during the interim, he would begin to draw up the annual state budget and allow both Callaway and Maddox to participate only as observers. Traditionally, the incoming governor drew up the budget for the first year of his administration.

Early on, Maddox stated publicly that he would remain silent on the litigation. But he soon changed his mind. On 18 November, his frustration got the better of him and he said he expected the court to order a runoff "not for Georgia or for Lester Maddox, but my opponent." Maddox's distrust of the nation's highest court ran so deep that he refused to believe that the judges would possibly vote in his favor.

Meanwhile, both candidates, anticipating a two-man runoff, campaigned lightly. Callaway made appearances around the state thanking voters for their support. During one speech, he committed a grave error when he spoke out against the Democratic Party. "We have killed the dragon," he stated. "We have shown that the Democratic Party can be beaten in Georgia."

Meanwhile, Maddox conducted what he described as his "fourth campaign" of the year and made several brief appearances around the state thanking his supporters. During one such appearance in central Georgia, Maddox's old white station wagon finally broke down and he had to finish his tour in a friend's car.

On 12 December 1966, the US Supreme Court handed down a surprising ruling. In a 5-4 decision, the high court reversed the lower court's ruling and decreed that the state assembly could, in fact, decide the outcome of the governor's race.

In the decision, Justice Hugo Black's majority opinion stated that nothing in the US Constitution "either expressly or impliedly dictates the method a state must use to elect its governor." Further, he wrote, it would have been constitutional for the state legislature to elect the governor in the first place.

Meanwhile, Justice William O. Douglas vigorously dissented by arguing that the election was started by the people and should be completed by the people. To allow the legislature to complete the process would dilute or reverse the vote of the people, Douglas opined, and that was a clear violation of the constitution's one-man, one-vote rule. Despite the dissent, the court had made its ruling.

On the afternoon the decision was announced, both Maddox and Callaway were in attendance at a briefing session for new legislators at the University of Georgia and commented on the high court's ruling. "It's a real victory for states' rights and individual freedom," Maddox said, speaking positively about the nation's highest court for probably the first time in his entire life. Callaway, when questioned by reporters about the ruling, stated grimly that he felt confident the state representatives would choose the candidate who had received the most votes. Although he was trying to remain positive, Callaway knew that he was now playing a losing game.

Despite the Supreme Court ruling, there were still efforts by Callaway supporters to change it. One suit, filed in state court by Atlanta attorney Henry Henderson, called for a special election. Still another suit demanded a runoff. In a 5-2 decision, the state's Supreme Court, while not specifically denying the legislature's power to authorize a run-off, reaffirmed the assembly's "power and right" to choose a governor in such a situation.

Meanwhile, Callaway publicly called for a run-off and tried to discuss it in a personal meeting with Maddox. Meanwhile, Maddox knew the US Supreme Court decision had given him a lock and he decided to play a cat and mouse game with Callaway.

After Callaway's staff alerted the press, a crowd of reporters was waiting when the Republican walked into Maddox's campaign headquarters at the Henry Grady Hotel. When Callaway asked to meet with Maddox, a staff member informed him that his boss was too busy to speak with him. As reporters began to question Callaway, one of Maddox's aides bluntly asked Callaway, "Would you mind getting your press conference out of our headquarters?" Several minutes after Callaway's departure, Maddox emerged from his office and announced that Callaway had failed to make an appointment.

On the morning of 10 January at precisely 9:30 A.M., Lieutenant Governor Peter Zack Geer rapped the gavel and called the joint session of the Georgia General Assembly to order. In the normally somber house chamber, an elaborate stage was set for the making of history. Television lights from the three major networks blared and the spectator's gallery—which included Maddox's four children—was packed with interested citizens, curiosity-seekers, and a host of supporters representing both candidates. Many had waited in the wings for hours to get a seat.

The first order of business was the canvassing of the votes in the general election. In the past, this procedure was little more than a formality but this time the participants wanted to be sure they complied with the letter of the law because of the unusual circumstances. The legislators' task was to elect a new governor so the state could get on with business.

During the morning hours, Maddox remained in his private room at the Henry Grady hotel and watched on television as the sealed returns of Georgia's 159 counties were opened, tabulated and then announced. Counting the write-in votes was especially time-consuming because voters had spelled Ellis Arnall's name so many different ways.

Around 3:30 P.M. that afternoon, when the canvassing started drawing to a close, Maddox and his wife had lunch in the hotel coffee shop. Then, accompanied by plain-clothed law enforcement officers, they rode in an unmarked patrol car to the capitol where they were led discreetly to the ground floor office of State Auditor Ernest Davis. There Maddox seated himself in front of a portable television and continued to witness the general assembly proceedings.

Two hours later, in the house chamber upstairs, Geer announced the official results of the general election: Callaway 453,665; Maddox 450,626; write-ins 52,831. Noting that the vote did not give a clear majority to either candidate, Geer announced that the joint assembly in a roll call vote must make the choice. He then ordered the voting to begin.

Although Geer had stated there could be no abstentions in the voting, eleven legislators—ten Negro and one white—did just that. One Negro legislator—Democrat Richard A. Dent of Augusta—cast his vote for Maddox. Several legislators—knowing their constituents were watching—explained their votes as they cast them. Representative George Busby, later to be Georgia's governor, voted for Callaway. Democrat Elliott Levitas, a partner in Arnall's law firm, also voted for Callaway. As the voting droned on, one Democratic legislator after another called "Maddox." Suddenly, victory began to look certain for the beleaguered Maddox.

The 130th vote—the one Maddox needed for victory—was cast by Representative Tom Murphy of Bremen, the man Maddox had recently named his House Floor leader. Maddox was jubilant when he heard Murphy's vote.

"I told you so!" Lester said, jumping up out of his chair and kissing Virginia. "I told you so! I told you so!"

By 7:18 P.M., the roll call vote was complete and the joint session of the assembly had confirmed Lester Garfield Maddox as the state's 75th governor by a 182-66 margin. Instantly, a cordon of Georgia state troopers whisked their new boss from his hideaway in the state auditor's office up to the house chamber where the general assembly was patiently waiting. As Maddox entered and strode toward the podium, a round of applause erupted from the collected gallery and the lawmakers.

Once Maddox had reached the rostrum, his wife Virginia, his children and several aides gathered around him as the loud ovation continued. After a few moments, the applause stopped and the assembled crowd grew quiet.

Maddox, his face pink with joy, turned to the microphone.

"My heart is full," he said. "I am grateful to you, the members of the general assembly and the people of Georgia for honoring me with his high office. I accept it with no friends to favor and no enemies to punish. God bless you!"

As Maddox moved away from the microphone, members of the general assembly and those in the gallery rose to their feet and burst into another round of thunderous applause. Earlier, Maddox had told his state trooper escort that, once the speech was finished, he wanted to be taken directly to the governor's office. Instantly, the troopers, as instructed, formed a flying wedge and cleared a wide path through the crowd so that Maddox and his family could get down the stairs to his new office, where Governor Carl Sanders waited to greet him.

Meanwhile, outside the governor's office on the second floor, the crowd of spectators which had witnessed this historic event filled the narrow hallway. As they did, one of the portraits of the former Georgia governors, which lined the west wall, fell to the floor. Eye-witnesses said no one was standing within 15 feet of the painting when it suddenly fell. Quickly, a concerned bystander carefully picked up the errant portrait and restored to its proper place. As it was replaced, spectators gasped at the incredible irony of the incident: It was a portrait of Ellis Arnall.

Chapter 8
Governor Lester Maddox

"I could not be a great surgeon, or a fine artist, or a talented musician, but I could be an honest man. I wanted to see what one free and honest man could do as governor of Georgia, a man free of pressure groups and all the influences of special interests and political machines."
—Maddox previews his administration

Lester Garfield Maddox was the man of the hour at the Georgia state capitol on the morning of 11 January 1967. As he stood on the inaugural platform on the capitol steps and prepared to take the oath of office, he was about to be honored before a large crowd of congressmen, current and former public officials, family members, supporters and curiosity-seekers. Among the dignitaries in attendance were Mississippi Governor Ross Barnett, Mitt Talmadge (matriarch of the Talmadge political dynasty), former governor Marvin Griffin, and Congressmen Bill Stuckey, Jack Flynt and Elliott Hagan.

It has been a long and hard year for Maddox. The strain of an unsettled general election, the court cases, the long wait between the election and the final resolution had taken their toll. He felt the essence of the day and realized, perhaps for the first time, that governing is quite different from campaigning. Now, he must run the state government and he must do it well. Average would not be good enough for Lester Maddox. He must do an excellent job in order to prove his critics wrong. He knew he must make the best of his opportunity to calm the political waters and prove himself to the people of Georgia.

In his inaugural address, Maddox called for improvements in education, prisons, treatment of the mentally ill, state highways and assistance to local governments. For metropolitan Atlanta, he stressed that "the completion of I-285 is our most important task at this time."

Regarding the fears of violence, Maddox addressed them clearly: "There will be no place in Georgia during the next four years for those who advocate extremism or violence in any form.

"When the record of this administration is written four years hence, let it be said that in the conduct of daily affairs of the office of governor and the people's interests were protected first, last and always."

The following day, Maddox's inaugural address was hailed throughout the nation for its conciliatory, even-handed tone. Following his address, many of Maddox's critics were beginning to have second thoughts. Most of the members of the Assembly who voted for him felt justified after hearing his first official remarks. Some of the fears raised by the newspapers and Maddox opponents seemed to evaporate with the calm expression of his official intentions. Maddox always believed that the public would support him once it ignored the media attacks against him and realized that he was not the ogre he was made out to be.

Several days later, Maddox and his wife and family moved into the old governor's mansion in Ansley Park. The new mansion was still under construction and was not scheduled for completion until the following fall. When Maddox and his family arrived with their belongings, Maddox roamed the premises, making a full tour of the mansion for the first time. He had visited the building on three previous occasions, but all he had seen were the kitchen and reception room. During the Marvin Griffin administration, the Pickrick catered three official affairs at the mansion.

After his tour Maddox said, "I wanted to be governor of Georgia, but somehow, not in my wildest imagination, did I ever think that me and my wife would be occupants of this house."

After the inaugural festivities, Maddox was not immediately prepared to name his new team. He needed, and took, a few days to study his appointments. However, he did name three appointees to his immediate staff, Bob Short as executive aide and press secretary, Morgan Redwine as executive secretary and Jack Gunter as executive counsel. Early on, he made his intentions clear about his appointments: "I will always try to find a person for any position, executive or otherwise, who I feel would be better qualified to fill the position than I would. In doing so, I am free to do what I must do, without having to supervise and watch over those I select."

Maddox was knowledgeable enough to know that his three most important appointments were state revenue commissioner, highway department director and state purchasing agent. Recognizing the importance of collecting taxes on time and in the full amount, he named State Senator Peyton Hawes of Elberton, an opponent in his 1962 race for lieutenant governor, to the revenue post. Also, aware of the need to have a highway director that could work with local officials in planning, building and maintaining roads and highways, he reappointed long-time director Jim Gillis to the highway job. Although Gillis had not supported Maddox, he was an experienced and well-respected highway man who had served satisfactorily under several governors. Clayton Turner, an Atlanta credit manager, became supervisor of state purchases.

Another important post to be filled was that of budget director. Maddox faced the serious task of formulating a multi-million dollar biennial budget in less than a week. Because Georgia had no governor-elect until the day before Maddox took office, Governor Carl Sanders put together a budget based on rather inflated requests of the various state departments.

Maddox's task was clear: he must cut the spending plan, but only in those areas that were not vital to the future of the state. To that end, Maddox turned to Sander's budget director, Wilson Wilkes. With many years of accounting experience and former Chair of the House Appropriations Committee, Wilkes was very familiar with the budgets of previous years, but he was well aware of all the nooks and crannies of Sanders' generous but unaffordable budget. Maddox knew that Wilkes could quickly help him amend Sanders' budget.

Since Maddox had little experience in state budgeting, he relied heavily on the advice of Wilkes and a capitol old-timer, Walter O. Brooks, in forming a state budget. Wilkes and Brooks quickly showed Maddox all the shortcuts he needed to put his own fingerprints on his first budget. For days, Maddox, Wilkes and Brooks labored over the proposed budget to reduce the bottom line to an affordable figure, while redirecting spending toward Maddox's programs. Maddox knew he had to be careful with his first budget, since his priorities and programs would be carefully scrutinized. He knew full well that his first budget would require careful tailoring since it would not only set the tone, but also serve as a blueprint for his entire administration. As a result, his first budget address to the General Assembly called for record increases in budgets for education, law enforcement, welfare and corrections—the heart of his "Society of Liberty" campaign platform.

A week after the inauguration, Maddox's administration team began to take shape. Long-time friend J. O. (Jack) Partain was named to replace Sanders' appointee John Harper on the Pardons and Paroles Board; Gen. George J. Hearn was renamed the state's adjutant general; Orville Schaefer was reappointed director of the Department of Family and Children's Services and Asa Kelley, a respected Albany attorney, was named director of the Department of Corrections. For his spokesmen in the state legislature, Maddox chose State Senator Frank Coggins of Hapeville as senate leader and State Representative Tom Murphy of Bremen—later to become a legend in state politics—as floor leader in the house. Next, Maddox asked the state senate to return Governor Sander's last minute appointments to state boards and commissions. Maddox believed, and the Senate agreed, that he should make the appointments rather than Sanders.

In his first press conference, Maddox announced that "all visitors to the governor's mansion will get a cool sip of cow's milk or a soft drink, if they're thirsty, but no alcohol." Also, he explained that prayer services would be held "in the executive offices at 9:30 A.M. on the mornings I'm here."

As Maddox launched into the administration, he felt the best way to root out corruption within state government was through state employees and local leaders. As a result, he appointed his Committee of 1000, a watchdog group whose purpose was to report state government wrongdoings directly to his office.

People making up the Committee of 1000 were local businessmen, low and middle rank state employees, courthouse employees, and private citizens from every voting precinct in the state. All allegations of wrongdoing were to be reported to his long-time friend J. L. Allen, who served as chief of staff for the committee.

"For years, I have said that people should be more involved in their government," Maddox said, in defense of the group. "I promised to have a people's administration and the Committee of 1000 is one more example of that."

Although Maddox would be severely criticized for his "super snoopers," its members would prove invaluable over the next four years by identifying wrong-doing and reporting it to Maddox for needed reform.

Most previous Georgia governors promised open government when they were elected, but Maddox truly tried to bring "little people"—people who had no access to government or who were victims of government—into the governmental fold. Thus, three days after his inauguration, Maddox designated the first and third Wednesday of each month had been "People's Day" and any Georgia citizen could appear at the governor's office and have his or her say on any subject. Although it angered Maddox, the media referred to the event as "Little People's Day," a name that stuck throughout the administration.

The very first People's Day was held on 19 January 1967. When Maddox walked into his office that morning, fourteen-year-old Sammy Ousley, an eighth grader at Grady High School, was waiting first in line.

"I appreciate your being the first person to come in," Maddox said, shaking the youngster's hand. "Come on over and have a seat."

With that, the youngster took a seat in a chair beside the governor.

"What can I do for you?" Maddox asked.

"I just wanted to see if I could really come in and meet you," the teenager said.

Maddox smiled.

"Well, you're here," he said, eyeing the youngster. "Why aren't you in school?"

"I told the teacher I was sick so I could be out and come up here."

Maddox eyed the youngster seriously.

"For a young man like you," he said, "There is nothing more important than a good education."

"That's what my mother says," young Ousley replied.

For a moment he paused, then looked up at Maddox.

"You won't tell her, will ya?"

"No," Maddox said, remembering his own depression-era youth when he skipped school to help earn money for his poverty-stricken family.

"But next time, attend your classes and make an appointment to see me after school. Okay?"

"Okay," the youngster said happily.

For the next few hours, Maddox listened to more than fifty citizens get various problems off their chests. An elderly couple wanted welfare; a new divorcee wanted a bill passed that would split a man's salary between him and his ex-wife; another man wanted a job; a Paulding county man wanted a road paved; an African American woman wanted Maddox's help to get an early prison release for her son; another woman said she wanted to tell Maddox she was praying for him. Toward the end of the day, a schoolteacher, accompanied by ninety-four fifth graders, made an appearance and asked to have their pictures made with the new governor.

Over the following months, Georgians from every walk of life appeared at the governor's office to see their governor. Of all the thousands who came to see Maddox to air their grievances, probably the most famous was school teacher-turned-stripper Patti White.

White stood in line for some time before she could get in to see Maddox. When Maddox looked up and saw her 36-22-36 frame standing in his office doorway, he turned to an aide.

"Who's that?" he asked.

Before the aide could answer, Patti strode forward.

"How do you do, Honorable Lester Maddox," she said, offering her hand.

"I'm so happy you could come," Maddox said shaking her hand nervously and inviting her to be seated.

"I have a question," she said. "Why is it so difficult for the state legislature to pass a bill raising teacher's salaries?"

"Are you a teacher?" he asked.

"I used to be," she explained. "I had to get out because the pay was so low."

"Then you weren't in it for love of teaching," Maddox commented.

White explained that she loved the teaching profession, but she also had to pay her bills so she turned to stripping for a living.

"I'm doing all I can for education," Maddox said, "and I promise before my term is over, I'm going to get teachers the biggest raises they've ever had."

Satisfied, the woman finally got up and left the office. Several photographers snapped her photo as she swayed her shapely hips on the way out. Observers said Maddox was "visibly shaken" by the woman's visit.

Throughout Maddox's term, People's Day was a roaring success. For the first time, anyone—black or white, rich or poor—could bring his or her particular problem to the attention of the state's highest executive. More than anything else, People's Day humanized Georgia state government. For years, state government had been a vague, distant institution to which many Georgians had no access because they did not know the right person, had not made a large enough political contribution or simply had no political clout. Now, for the first time ever, they could visit and talk directly with the highest state officer.

Although People's Day was the principal means by which Maddox opened state government to Georgians, there were also frequent events in which Lester and Virginia opened the doors of the governor's mansion to anyone and everyone who wanted to come.

During one such event on 16 April 1967, Virginia was graciously welcoming guests to the mansion when she was pulled aside by an African American woman, Mrs. Albert Hill of Macon. Hill explained that four young black men with her had escaped from the prison work camp in Wilkinson County the night before and wanted to talk to Governor Maddox.

Immediately, Virginia motioned to a state trooper on duty who took custody of the four. Thirty minutes later, the trooper returned to Maddox's side.

"Governor," the trooper explained. "something unusual has happened. Four young black men have broken out of a South Georgia prison and they want to talk to you. We have them under guard in the summer house."

Thirty minutes later, Maddox met with the convicts and listened to a sordid tale of brutality and mistreatment in the Wilkinson County work camp. One of the men complained that guards constantly threatened to "shoot his legs off." Another charged that he had gone six to eight days with only one meal and was then placed in solitary confinement after he complained. Another said the men had to use commodes that would not flush, had no visiting privileges, received mail only once a week and were crowded into small barracks with up to thirty other prisoners at a time.

Maddox was shaken by what the men told him. Later that afternoon he convened a press conference. "I want the most thorough investigation of the Department of Corrections ever conducted," Maddox declared. "If the stories are true, we are not going to tolerate these conditions in our state prisons."

When the prison's warden was notified of Maddox's orders, he was defiant, dismissing the accusations as lies. Maddox, on the other hand, believed there was truth to the charges. "Those convicts could have been in Chicago by now. They came up here knowing for sure they would be sent back to jail and possibly back to the same work camp."

For years, Georgia had one of the cruelest prison systems in the South. The stories told about South Georgia chain gangs and their supervision by sadistic guards were nothing short of horrific. Some prisoners cut their Achilles tendons so they would not have to work on prison farms or roadside gangs. Prisons were rampant with stories about unruly inmates being tied over barrels and beaten with rubber hoses. In one case, an inmate had drowned after stripping naked and swimming out into a partially frozen lake to retrieve dead ducks for a guard. Maddox himself had heard the stories and now he was prepared to do something about it.

Over the next two years, the Georgia's state prison system underwent the most radical reform in its history. The probe Maddox ordered included all seventy-three of county work camps as well as its sixteen prison branches. The state health department and the fire commissioner's office were instructed to inspect for sanitary and fire hazard conditions. The results were shocking. Health inspectors discovered widespread examples of bug infestation, inadequate water supplies, poor sewage disposal and generally unhealthy conditions. The state fire commissioner's report designated most of the county camps as firetraps. Meanwhile, Maddox made several surprise visits to prisons and work camps to see the problems for himself.

After learning that the Wayne County work camp was one of the worst, Maddox made several surprise trips there to talk to prisoners. Earlier, he had learned that talks with prison officials only resulted in cover-ups and misinformation. The truth of prison conditions could only come from prisoners and Maddox questioned them extensively about food, working conditions and treatment. After seeing the conditions at the prison for himself, Maddox declared that the overcrowded wooden buildings that housed prisoners—they had been declared fire traps— would be replaced. Also, he promised better sewage disposal, improved food and more humane working conditions.

During the visits, one of Maddox's favorite pastimes was to sing gospel hymns with prisoners. After a round of hymns at the Wayne County facility, including "The Old Rugged Cross" and "I'll Fly Away," Maddox counseled the inmates to "serve your time, then never come back to prison."

As the investigation progressed, Maddox's personal visits turned up other problems in the state's prison system. Several times, he had heard stories about corruption in the warden's office at the Ware Prison Camp at Waycross. Thus, armed with complaints, he decided to make a surprise personal visit there.

In anticipation of exposing wrongdoing, a Maddox aide requested a list of the camp's purchase orders for the weeks preceding the governor's visit. The aide also obtained from the Department of Corrections a copy of the camp's menu on the day the governor was to arrive.

After Maddox and the aide flew to Waycross, they caught a ride with a state trooper to the prison on a Saturday morning. After arriving and finding the warden absent on a visit to his daughter, Maddox spoke briefly with the deputy warden and began visiting with inmates. He asked about their families and what it meant to be away from home for long periods of time. He asked about their children and their wives and whether or not they were adequately supported. As he walked down the corridors, the prisoners, knowing he sympathized with their plight, chanted "Maddox! Maddox! Maddox!" Finally, he asked that the inmates be gathered together in the dining hall to sing gospel hymns.

Meanwhile, the aide asked for entry into the camp's kitchen pantry to examine its inventory. Once inside, he discovered none of the items that had been listed on the camp's purchase orders. There were no sides of beef, no bacon and no sausage in the prison cooler.

Later Maddox and the aide asked an explanation for the several sides of beef, some fifty pounds of sausage and a similar store of bacon which were missing from the prison's food pantry. Nervously, the guard explained that the warden oversaw the prison larder and that no one else was allowed. Immediately, Maddox ordered that the warden be suspended.

During another prison investigation, the state fire commissioner's report revealed that the worst fire hazard was at the youthful offenders facility at Alto. As a result, while safety improvements were underway, Maddox wanted to see for himself and made a personal visit to the prison.

While talking to the young prisoners, he discovered that a seventeen-year-old California youth named Melvin Murdock was eligible for probation but he was financially unable to afford the trip back to his home state.

"We're going to send that boy back to California," Maddox said, when he finished the prison tour. Eagerly, he took his executive secretary's hat and started passing it around. In ten minutes, $65.00 was raised for the cause and Maddox personally pitched in the rest.

As he rode back to Atlanta that night, Maddox decided to conduct an experiment with the young offenders he had talked with earlier. He decided to implement an early release program in which reprieves would be granted to all inmates under the age of 19 who had less than six months to serve and had good behavior records. The following day, Maddox informed the Department of Corrections of his idea and ordered them to put it into force.

A month later, the first group that qualified for early release under the new program was transported from the prison to Atlanta for official cere-monies. For the event, a total of 153 boys gathered into the house chamber at the capitol. Also in attendance were numerous prison officials, members of the Pardons and Paroles Board and the boys' parents.

During his address, Maddox pleaded with the young men to disavow crime. "I'm sticking my neck out," he reminded them. "I'm putting my head on the chopblock for you… Don't chop it off!"

With their release, each of the boys signed a pledge promising to obey the law and abstain from alcohol. Six months later only eight of the 153 reprieved youths had been arrested again.

After the early release program with youthful offenders proved so suc-cessful, Maddox decided to extend it to the adult prison population. and on 1 December 1967, a total of 547 prisoners—an astounding 7 percent of the prison population—were given early releases. Before making the announcement, Maddox drew up a set of guidelines for qualifying. All of those released must have three months or less remaining and at least one year's good conduct record. None of the men to be released could be sex offenders and each had to sign a pledge promising not to associate with people of questionable reputation or to drink alcohol.

During the ceremony which marked their release, each of the men was given a letter from Maddox suggesting ways they could begin their new life. "If this program is successful," the letter stated, "We shall probably do it again. Don't penalize those who are to follow.... Try turning to Him whose birthday you are about to celebrate...who said, 'I am the way, the truth and the light...' Try it. It worked for me. I wouldn't 'con' you. Good luck."

There was nothing Maddox hated more than leaving a job partially-done and, since he had gone the extra mile to reform the corrections department at the bottom—the prisons themselves—he saw no reason to not make changes at the top in the Pardons and Paroles board. For more than forty years, the board had been a sacred cow to Georgia governors and, as a result, no significant effort had been made to correct widespread reports of corruption. For years, it had been whispered in correction department corridors that, if prisoners could raise enough money to hire a certain lawyer, they stood a much better chance of being paroled than their poorer fellow inmates. Maddox himself had heard the stories and decided to look into the matter.

Soon after he took office, Maddox called his old friend Jack Partain, a former military man and Atlanta insurance executive, and appointed him to the Pardon and Paroles Board to combat the corruption. Partain would later become one of Maddox's most trusted colleagues during his administration.

Partain and Maddox had first met him when he ran for mayor against William Hartsfield in 1957. During the campaign, Partain was a member of a major Atlanta civic organization and, after candidate Hartfield was invited to speak to the group, Partain questioned the group's president as to why Maddox, the other candidate, was not invited. Finally, after some friendly coaxing, Partain convinced the president to allow Maddox to appear before the group. Maddox was so impressed with Partain's sense of fairness that the two became fast friends.

Shortly after Partain's appointment, Maddox ordered State Attorney General Arthur Bolton to launch a full investigation into the activities of the board. The rumored corruption Maddox hoped to uncover soon became evident to Partain. "Only a week after I was appointed, I got a taste of what Lester was talking about," Partain said. "Another board member came to me and said: 'Here is the case of a woman in prison for killing her husband. She has a brother who is president of an oil company over in Mississippi and the family is very wealthy. You know, if we wanted to get her released, it would probably be worth $25,000.'"

During the following weeks, the attorney general's investigators reviewed hundreds of cases in which prisoners had been paroled under suspicious circumstances. Finally, they settled on twenty-nine cases in which they suspected special treatment for inmates. In those twenty-nine cases, the same attorney had represented all twenty-nine of the paroled prisoners.

With the announcement of his findings, Bolton recommended sweeping changes in the state's approach to pardons and paroles. Once Bolton's findings were made public, Maddox immediately called for the resignation of board members Jake Claxton and Rebecca Garrett. Both refused Maddox's demand. Shortly thereafter, several members of the House of Representatives drew up articles of impeachment against both Claxton and Garrett.

Garrett's son, Sims, a well-known Atlanta lobbyist, came to her defense. In meeting after meeting with House members, Garrett agreed not to seek reappointment if they would not impeach her. Since Garrett did not have long to serve, an agreement was reached. Shortly afterwards, the assembly began impeachment proceedings against Jake Claxton, but Claxton resigned before passage of the legislation. After Maddox's crack down on the department and its operations, the attorney who handled most of the successful paroles never appeared before the board again.

Partain, who Maddox made Chairman of the Board, then set about the task of appointing two new members to the reformed board. "Before the investigation, board members but did not have to give reasons for recommending parole or reprieve, but afterward, they had to say exactly why they had reached their decisions," Partain said.

"Before the reforms," he continued, "everybody and their brother was representing inmates before the board. Now, only attorneys—Georgia attorneys—could represent prisoners and there was extensive paperwork to be filled out before they could make an appearance."

The new set of regulations not only made the Pardons and Paroles process fairer and more efficient, Partain said, but also rendered it more public. For the first time, records of hearings were made available for public scrutiny. Board decisions, as well as the hearing proceedings, were made part of the public records. Thus, with the naming of the new board members and implementation of new regulations, rumors and stories about buying pardons and paroles simply disappeared.

In April 1967, Maddox approached another serious task: filling vacancies in the state court system. His critics had charged that Maddox's judicial appointments would be mostly ultra-conservatives that conformed to his right-wing political philosophies. Well aware that his critics would not be satisfied with whomever he appointed, Maddox was careful to select not only qualified, but popular, judges to fill vacant slots.

Maddox's first opportunity arose during the spring of 1967 when it was his duty to appoint a new member to the state supreme court. For the post, he chose John E. Frankum of Clarkesville, who had served with distinction on the State Court of Appeals. Next he appointed Judge George P. Whitman Sr. from the Fulton County Superior Court to replace Frankum, setting off a chain of events that gave him four additional appointments. Once the round of appointments was complete, however, both the Atlanta media and his harshest political enemies praised Maddox.

On 31 December 1967, Maddox and his family moved into the new $1.8 million governor's mansion on West Paces Ferry Road. A month later, Maddox flung open its doors for all citizens and declared, "Georgia's state house is the finest in the nation. It doesn't belong to the Democrats or the Republicans or to the Lester Maddoxes. It belongs to the people of Georgia."

The New Greek revival structure featured several large, lavishly appointed staterooms, reception areas and banquet facilities on the first floor. Living quarters for the state's first family as well as a plush presidential suite made up the second level.

Once the Maddox family had moved in, Maddox became personally involved in the completion of the mansion. Noticing that the mansion did not have a fence, he angrily criticized the lack of security. "The new mansion and the mansion grounds were left wide open to any Tom, Dick or Harry that wanted to come in," Maddox said. "Can you show me a governor who would want to live in a state house that did not have a security fence?" After ordering that $160,000 be spent on a fence, Maddox took much criticism for spending the money.

Later, after Maddox learned that a security fence had been omitted from the construction plans to build a swimming pool and a tennis court, he ordered that the swimming pool be closed because it belonged to "all the people of Georgia." "I don't have time to go swimming," he said, "and it would be impossible to have all the people in Georgia swimming in it at once, so I want it closed."

Later he learned that the new mansion did not have a flagpole out front from which to wave the Stars and Stripes. "Now what kind of state house is it that doesn't have a flagpole to display that glorious symbol of truth, justice and the American way?" Immediately, Maddox ordered that a flagpole be installed.

By the spring of 1969, slightly more than two years into his administration, Maddox's original staff of aides had undergone a series of wholesale changes.

First, his original executive secretary, Morgan (Bucky) Redwine, was fired after only three months in the post.

In late March 1967, Maddox called Redwine to account after two underaged dating couples in possession of alcohol were arrested in Redwine's car. According to one of the youths, Redwine had not only arranged the dates, but he had purchased the alcoholic beverages and loaned them his car.

Calling Redwine "careless," Maddox fired his executive secretary and insisted that he would terminate any member of his staff who violated his moral standards. "Bucky is a very able man," Maddox commented, in announcing Redwine's dismissal. "He just got careless and made a mistake."

The Redwine incident was but one of several occasions when Maddox demonstrated that his strict rules of moral conduct applied to his staff, as well as to others. Once Maddox became furious with a young staff member who returned from a trip to the Bahamas clad only in her bikini. "Everyone who works for the people should have the highest standards of conduct," Maddox said. "Running around half-naked is not what I call a high standard."

Maddox also acted quickly and decisively when his Chief of Staff, Lyons attorney T. Malone Shape took a client who owed the state several thousand dollars in back sales taxes to see Maddox's revenue commissioner, Peyton Hawes.

His client, Sharpe told Hawes, owned half interest in a restaurant as a partner to a well-known state official. The two, he said, simply could not afford to pay their tax bill. "Worst of all," Sharpe confessed, "they've already collected the taxes and spent the money. But, since my client's partner is a man with a good reputation and since he and his wife are friends of Governor Maddox, we thought you might forgive them the taxes or at least work out some way for them to pay as they can realizing, of course, that they have no money."

Having mastered the art of politics years earlier, Hawes listened respectfully and took Sharpe's plea under advisement. After Sharpe and his paying customer departed, Hawes called Maddox.

"Governor Maddox," he said, "Malone Sharpe was here with a client asking for relief from a tax bill the man owes the state."

"Who is it," Maddox inquired.

"He's a fellow who says he goes to church with you every Sunday," Hawes replied.

"I go to church with a lot of people," Maddox reportedly responded, whereupon Hawes identified the man by name.

"How much does he owe?" Maddox asked.

"Somewhere around $12,000," Hawes replied.

"And he doesn't want to pay?" Maddox questioned.

"That's right, Governor," Hawes responded. He wants us to either forgive his debt, reduce it or let him pay on the installment plan. I thought I'd let you know, since he claimed to be your close friend and because he was here with your Chief of Staff."

Maddox paused for a moment, then said to Hawes, "Padlock his place and that goes for every other deadbeat who won't pay their taxes!"

Once Redwine was out, Maddox wasted no time in replacing him. Tommy Irvin, a state representative from Mt. Airy, moved almost immediately into the job. Tall, affable and able, Irvin not only knew state government and politics, but he was also a Maddox supporter, having assisted the new governor in his campaign against 'Bo' Callaway. In addition, Irvin was a valuable ally during the Maddox transition. He sat in for Maddox on the early, Sanders-arranged budget meetings and was extremely helpful in making cuts, which rendered the former governor's budget more affordable.

Irvin's stay, however, was short. Following the Democratic Party's convention debacle in Chicago in 1968, several members of the capitol
"clique" deserted their party and became Republicans. The leader of this
group was Agriculture Commissioner Phil Campbell, a Talmadge man,
who was immediately rewarded by the national Republicans with a job in
the US Department of Agriculture. When Campbell resigned his state
agricultural post, Maddox immediately appointed Irvin to replace him.

In May 1969, having reassigned Irvin, Maddox was again without an
executive assistant and he frantically started searching for a qualified person. Maddox was well aware that he needed an experienced hand, a
person who not only knew state government, but also could deal effectively with the day-to-day politics of the governor's office. Finally, he
found the man he was looking for in the Department of Corrections. His
name was Zell Miller.

Miller was not new to politics. In 1964, while a history professor at
Young Harris College in north Georgia, Miller took on powerful and
popular Congressman Phil Landrum in Georgia's ninth district. After losing to Landrum, Miller landed a job with Governor Carl Sanders, who
made him director of the state probation department. That job, however,
did not last long. Miller, still longing to hold high political office, resigned
to again challenge the mighty Landrum in 1966. This time, Miller lost by
a larger margin than before. Broke, jobless and with a wife and two children to support, Miller sought employment again in state government
and became personnel director in the Department of Corrections. In the
post, Miller had proven himself likable and capable and, when Maddox
finally offered him the executive secretary's post, Miller immediately
accepted.

During the last two and one-half years of Maddox's administration,
Miller proved to be an able "assistant governor." During that period, he
learned the inner workings of state politics and the governor's office at
Maddox's feet. It was an excellent training ground for Miller's later political career. In later years, Miller expressed his admiration and thanks to
Maddox for his early political training and explained that Maddox "has
been like a father to me."

Another key appointment in the Maddox administration was Bill
Burson. Early on, Burson had made an impression on Maddox as a
speaker, an organizer and administrator. Born and raised in a mill village

in Thomaston, Burson had first-hand knowledge of poverty and the plight of the common man. Like Maddox, Burson grew up in a household with a strong religious mother who encouraged him to leave the mill town and make something of himself. After graduating Phi Beta Kappa at the University of Georgia, Burson became a decorated war correspondent in Korea with United Press International.

Following the truce there, Burson returned to Atlanta. His UPI boss assigned him to cover the state capitol where he became an acclaimed reporter. Burson was so skilled at finding stories, in fact, that Governor Herman Talmadge asked one of his staff for the reporter's name.

"That's Bill Burson of the UPI," Press Secretary Walter Brooks replied.

"Well, hire him," Talmadge ordered. "He's smarter than we are!"

Although Maddox failed in his effort to make Burson head of the Department of Industry and Trade, he wanted to find him a place on his team. The opportunity arose when Orville Schaeffer resigned as Director of the Department of Family and Children's Services. Maddox felt the job would be perfect for Burson and wasted little time in appointing him to replace Schaeffer.

Aggressive and outspoken, it did not take Burson long to clash with Maddox. He moved quickly to expand the federal food stamp program into Georgia's rural counties, often bypassing county commissions. He also began to add African Americans to county welfare boards. This, of course, angered the governing bodies of the counties and, for relief, they came to the governor. Maddox courteously heard their complaints, but ultimately stood by his director. Burson resigned his post in 1970 when he sought, and won, the elective office of State Treasurer.

By May of 1967, Maddox's Committee of 1000 was paying off. The committee was particularly helpful in providing information about instances in which state property being stolen was being misused. In one press conference, Maddox said, "I'm warning these people now that we know about them and that these serious violations must be halted."

Another glaring form of wrongdoing uncovered by Maddox's Committee of 1000 was the misuse of state vehicles. "We know that various individuals have been misusing state vehicles," he said. Maddox contended that these individuals were using state property for their own personal use.

Never before had Georgia state government had a system of internal monitoring in which employees were asked to report their superiors' wrongdoing to the governor. Already the committee had provided invaluable information toward reform of the prison system, the Pardons and Paroles Board and the Department of Industry and Trade.

During his campaign, Maddox promised to clean up the state's Department of Industry and Trade. Ostensibly, the commission's purpose was to curry favor with companies that were looking at the prospects of expanding or moving to Georgia. This meant that employees were involved in extensive wining and dining which led to widespread overspending and other irregularities. Over the years, the department had became a dumping ground for old girlfriends and political cronies and, as a result, the department was hugely overstaffed with underqualified people.

Only weeks after taking office, Maddox and a State Senate Committee conducted a joint study of the department and found grounds for concern. After the results of the study were announced, Maddox asked Director Jim Nutter to resign. Nutter submitted his resignation, but the department's board of directors refused to accept it. Maddox, determined to have his way, launched into a fight with the board and demanded that its members resign so that he could name his own director. After several weeks of stalemate, Maddox recommended Bill Burson for the director's job, but chairman Peter Knox and the bulk of the board refused to approve Burson, claiming that he was not qualified. Immediately, Maddox began canvassing his allies in state government and the legislature for a man of impeccable qualifications for the job.

Several days later, Maddox got a call from his old friend Courtney Wynne suggesting General Louis Truman. "He is the commandant of the third army at Fort McPherson," Wynne said. "Did you know he is due to retire from the army soon and he plans to make Georgia his home upon retirement? He's a highly qualified man."

Maddox was delighted at the suggestion. He called Fort McPherson immediately and asked for General Truman. Truman, a cousin of former President Harry Truman, had an excellent reputation with influential people in Georgia and he was not a child of politics.

Truman, while he did not accept the post immediately, did agree to take it several months later prior to his retirement. Several days after

Truman's acceptance, Maddox met with members of the Industry and Trade Board and his nomination met with unanimous approval. Shortly afterward, Maddox got the department's advertising budget raised from $200,000 to $500,000 a year.

Over the succeeding years, Truman and Maddox worked together to clean up the department and insure the honesty and efficiency Maddox had promised during his campaign. Over that same period, by traveling throughout the nation as a team, Maddox and Gen. Truman brought more new industry to Georgia than all administrations over the previous twenty years combined.

During one of his trips with Truman to bring new industry to Georgia, Maddox became aware of another problem in his beloved state. Maddox and Truman were in Akron, Ohio to visit with the board of directors of Goodyear Tire and Rubber Company. During the visit, Maddox was pulled aside by Russell DeYoung, chairman of the board. De Young complained about that a South Georgia speed trap had caught on of the company's executives in tiny town of Ludowici.

For years, Maddox had heard rumors about Ludowici and Long County and its infamous reputation for unethical enforcement of traffic laws. At the time, Ludowici, Georgia was a small town of less than 2,500 people located directly on Highway 301, a secondary northwest-southeast route, which paralleled the Georgia coast between South Carolina and Florida. The city's speed limit jurisdiction had been extended several miles along Highway 301 on both ends of town. Motorists traveling along on the open highway would round a curve, then suddenly see the city's 25 mph sign. By the time the motorist could slow down, however, it was too late because a waiting city patrol car—its siren blaring—was already in pursuit.

Once ticketed, the motorist was required to post a cash bond in order to go free. The case would be scheduled for some later date, but by then, the motorists would be hundreds of miles away. Thus, the cash bond would be forfeited to the city's treasury and, for generations, the city of Ludowici had sustained itself with traffic fines from Highway 301.

Another favorite scam by Ludowici city officials concerned car repair. City policemen would stop a car and, after finding some minor mechanical problem, declare the vehicle unsafe for travel and order the driver to take the car to a particular and preselected car repair shop to have it fixed before proceeding. Once the problem was repaired, the owner of the shop would charge the motorist five to ten times the normal rate. Also, Ludowici single traffic light would, by design, suddenly turn red without warning and claim one unsuspecting victim after another.

Once he returned from Ohio, Maddox launched an investigation into the various unscrupulous operations at Ludowici. From the first, the person he suspected of being behind the scams was Ralph Dawson, the "boss of Long County." Maddox knew that, in order to be effective, he would have to bring Dawson to account for his actions.

Before attacking Dawson personally, he called on the "good" citizens of Long County to pressure their officials to bring a halt to the illegal activities. He argued that it was useless to spend millions to try to bring new industry into Georgia while such unsavory local practices were taking place. He explained that an evil few was ruining the reputation of all Georgians.

At first, Maddox's pleas worked and complaints about the speed trap and other schemes leveled off. After a few months, however, complaints began again and Maddox knew he had to take drastic action. With that, he erected huge billboard signs along Highway 301 on both entrances to Ludowici, which warned approaching motorists of the scams waiting in Ludowici. Aware of Dawson's power over local law enforcement, he sent highway patrol officers to guard the signs around the clock to prevent Dawson and his henchmen from destroying them.

Apparently, the signs had the desired effect because, two months after they were erected, a delegation of Long County officials, headed by Dawson, paid the governor a visit. Dawson complained about the negative publicity Maddox had brought against Long County and demanded he stop.

After a brief exchange between the two men, Maddox grew angry. "Don't you understand?" Maddox shouted. "With this sort of activity, you're not just hurting Long County, you're hurting the good people that live there. You're hurting the whole state of Georgia, and still you've got the gall to come in here..." Maddox took a step closer to Dawson, then seeing that his reason was getting no place, he started waving his finger in Dawson's face. "You're the most corrupt, dishonest, nasty and crookedest person I've ever known," he shouted. "The longer you stay here, the longer it's going to take to clean it up after you're gone!"

With that, Maddox grabbed hold of Dawson's arm and, pulling him out of the chair, began to escort him to the door. Maddox opened his office door and shoved Ralph Dawson out into the outer office and slammed the door. Then, he returned to the chair where Dawson was seated, grabbed Dawson's hat and flung it into the outer office.

Maddox spent the next twenty minutes emphasizing to Dawson's group that he was not going to tolerate illegal activities such as the speed trap and automobile scams at Ludowici. Finally, after the lecture, the delegation got up and quietly filed from the governor's office.

Although Maddox had some success in quelling the corruption in Ludowici and Long County, at least temporarily, it was not the only den of local corruption along Georgia's coast. Highway 17—which paralleled Highway 301 just east of Ludowici—was another hotbed for exploiting motorists and, in many ways, more corrupt than Ludowici and Long County.

US 17 is a meandering highway that enters Georgia from South Carolina just above Savannah and winds its way along coastal Georgia through Liberty, Bryan and McIntosh counties into the city of Brunswick, thence to Jacksonville, Florida. Before the completion of Interstate 95, US Highway 17 was a major thoroughfare from New York to Miami and, like Highway 301 at Ludowici, it was heavily traveled by vacationers en route to Florida.

Along Highway 17, the standard roadside attractions—shops which featured fresh pecan rolls, soft ice cream and arts and crafts—beckoned travelers. Also, for those with a taste for vice, there was prostitution in out-back house trailers as well as no-win dice and shell games. The establishments which sponsored these gambling games were known as "clip joints." For years, they were so infamous that many state tourist departments, even the American Automobile Association, warned its members of their existence. The problem was so prevalent in Georgia that at the time Maddox was elected Georgia was known as the "clip joint" state.

"I was determined to clean up the mess," Maddox said. "And spare our state and its law-abiding citizens from the embarrassment we all suffered as a result of it. My examination of the situation revealed that local law enforcement officials not only refused to stop these illegal games, but condoned them."

Maddox did not need long to identify the ring leader of the 'clips joints' as Tom Poppell, the Sheriff of McIntosh County. Poppell was the leader of the "court house" gang in Darien, the county seat of McIntosh County. What Ralph Dawson had been in Long County, Tom Poppell was in McIntosh County.

Maddox paid his first unannounced visit to the clip joints along Highway 17 in May 1967. Stunned employees did not have time to hide their illegal punch boards and dice games from the intruders. Thus, Maddox and the troopers caught them in the act and warned them that neither he nor their fellow Georgians condoned their activities. Once a full investigation was complete, troopers found gambling, prostitution, violations of state and local liquor laws, health code violations, and even illegal immigrants in most of the establishments.

Only days after the Maddox visit, a New Hampshire couple reported to the Better Business Bureau in Savannah that they had been "clipped" for $160 at a pecan stand in Darien. After filing the report, an official of the agency advised the couple to return to Darien and enter a complaint. Back at Darien, however, the couple was arrested as witnesses under a rule by the local district attorney who required the arrest of anyone involved in such cases.

Once the BBB official in Savannah got word of the arrests, he called state law enforcement officials who in turn called Maddox. He wasted no time calling authorities in Darien: "Either release that couple by midnight or I'll fly down there and release them myself."

Immediately, a hearing was held and the couple was released. A few days later, the controversial pecan stand was padlocked on orders from the circuit's new solicitor general.

Poppell obviously got the message for, after the governor's inspection tour, complaints of flimflams along Highway 17 subsided.

There seemed to be no end to Maddox's house-cleaning in Georgia state government. After revolutionary reforms in the prisons, Pardons and Paroles, Department of Industry and Trade and corruption in local government, Maddox still had more work to do.

Here are some of his other accomplishments:

For years, the state's purchasing department was run on "a good old boy system." With each new administration, legislators, politicians and their friends decided who would provide the state's oil, gas, office supplies and other equipment. Although the state required competitive bids, in many cases, recipients of state contracts were the firms whose officials either had political clout or had made substantial contributions to the governor's campaign. Maddox charged that, in many cases, "nobody knew what the items would cost or even if the purchased goods were actually delivered." Maddox ordered Turner to restore competitive bidding and award contracts to the lowest qualified bidder.

Maddox completed I-285, the perimeter road around the city of Atlanta, which he had called "The most important task at hand for Atlanta." For years, having the power of road-building was a powerful tool in Georgia politics. A man who had the power to pave a road or change the route of a major road or highway was extremely powerful. If you were road commissioner you could easily use the post as a spring board to higher public office.

For more than thirty years, Georgia governors promised to make state government more accessible to blacks. Once elected, however, their actual efforts amounted to little more than lip service.

Meanwhile, Maddox was sincere in his belief that amalgamation of the races was not a good thing. In the infamous pick-handle incident, Maddox absolutely refused to allow blacks into his restaurant. He based his position on the rights of private property owners, the same rights advocated by Sanders, Talmadge and others.

Lester Maddox would be the man who truly paved in-roads for African Americans in Georgia state government.

After only ten days in office, a delegation of black leaders, including State Senator Leroy Johnson and the Reverend Martin Luther King Sr., arrived in Maddox's office. The delegation wanted to know precisely what Maddox was going to do for black Georgians.

After a few exchanges between them, Maddox finally replied, "I'm trying to be the best governor this state has ever had and I can't possibly do that by working against any group of citizens or creating any special conditions for any group. So, even though you have fought for some of my predecessors and, by your own admission, fought even harder to keep me out of office, I want to assure you that I'll do more for you than my predecessor did."

Over the next four years, Maddox kept his promise and did more for blacks in Georgia than all other previous governors combined. Maddox installed the first black officer in the Georgia State Patrol. He instituted food assistance programs in 158 counties which aided poor whites and blacks alike. Before the Maddox administration, only thirteen counties had such programs. Maddox's Medicaid program in the state also greatly aided poor blacks and whites by providing needed health care. Likewise he named the first black official to the state's board of corrections and integrated the Governor's Summer Intern Program by bringing in a black student, 21-year-old Morehouse College senior Reginald Lindsay.

Maddox also appointed more than forty African-Americans to the state's county draft boards. In all previous Georgia history, only two African Americans had been appointed to the state's selective service system. "Before I was elected to the state legislature," said State Sen. Julian Bond, one of Georgia's most progressive black leaders and legislators, "I went with all the Negro legislators to see Gov. Carl Sanders. We mentioned a lot of problems to him, including the fact that there were no African Americans on any draft boards in Georgia except in Atlanta. After listening, he said: 'I'll have to study that.'" After being elected Senator Bond repeated his concern to Governor Maddox. Maddox asked if blacks served in the Army and upon hearing that they did agreed there should be blacks on the draft boards. "Just like that," Bond recalled. "He didn't have to study it or anything. He just did it."

Georgia Governor Zell Miller, elected to two terms after serving as Maddox's former executive assistant, said: "No man in Georgia public life has been more maligned, more misrepresented or more misunderstood than Lester Maddox." Many Georgians, for instance, have the impression that Maddox has a distinctive hatred of African Americans, Miller said that is not the case at all. "I have never heard him publicly or privately used the word 'nigger' or slur or demean the black race in any way. The proudest I ever was of Lester Maddox was when he led other politicians off the platform during one of [arch-segregationist] J. B. Stoner's racist speeches. And it was done from basic instinct."

1. The official portrait of Lester Maddox that hangs in the State Capitol alongside other former Georgia governors is quite unusual, in that it contains a photography of the governor's wife Virginia, two peaches, and a fish wrapped in a copy of the Atlanta Constitution. There is also a state seal and the words "In God We Trust" in the portrait. (*Courtesy of the Georgia Department of State Archives.*)

2. Lester and Virginia Maddox.

3. This is the official state photograph of Maddox. He used it to accompany his press releases and made it available to visitors to the governor's office and the governor's mansion, the official residence of Georgia governors. (*Courtesy of the Georgia Department of State Archives.*)

4. Former Texas Governor John Connally (left) sips punch with three prominent Georgia Democrats at a Democratic Party function: (L–R) Governor Lester Maddox, US Senator Herman Talmadge, and former Governor Carl Sanders. (*Courtesy of the Georgia Department of State Archives.*)

5. Driving halfway across the country, this family wanted to introduce their dog "Pickrick" (named after the Governor's restaurant) to Governor Lester Maddox. (*Courtesy of the Georgia Department of State Archives.*)

6. Alabama Governor Lurleen Wallace poses behind the desk of Georgia Governor Lester Maddox (right rear) during the Wallace's visit to address the Georgia Assembly in 1997. Maddox's wife, Virginia (left) and Maddox's friend, George Wallace (center rear) make the photo a family affair. (*Courtesy of the Georgia Department of State Archives.*)

7. Lester Maddox prepares to ride a bicycle backwards during a gathering of businessmen. Although often severely criticized for his antics in public, Maddox enjoyed entertaining audiences and was widely known for his unpredictable behavior. (*Courtesy of the Georgia Department of State Archives.*)

8. Governor Lester Maddox congratulates Atlanta entertainer Graham Jackson (right) who Maddox named the first African-American member of the State Board of Corrections as *Atlanta Constitution* reporter Sam Hopkins looks on. (*Courtesy of the Georgia Department of State Archives.*)

9. Peyton Hawes (right) and Governor Lester Maddox enjoy a light moment during Hawes' tenure as Commissioner of the Department of Revenue. (*Courtesy of the Georgia Department of State Archives.*)

10. Governor Lester Maddox admires the medals earned by General Lewis
Truman (left), who served with Maddox as Director of the Department of
Industry and Trade. Maddox's Adjutant General, Bo Hearn, looks on.
(*Courtesy of the Georgia Department of State Archives.*)

11. Country singer Johnny Cash joins Governor Lester Maddox while he entertains two young supporters during Cash's visit to assist Maddox with his early release program. (*Courtesy of the Georgia Department of State Archives.*)

12. Georgia's legendary Secretary of State Ben Fortson was a reliable Maddox ally during the Governor's terms as governor and lieutenant governor of Georgia. (*Courtesy of the Georgia Department of State Archives.*)

13. Outgoing Governor Carl Sanders (right) greets newly elected Governor Lester Maddox and his wife, Virginia, shortly after Maddox was elected by the Georgia General Assembly in January 1967. (*Courtesy of the Georgia Department of State Archives.*)

14. Maddox and Reverend Ed Kendrick (right) during one of the Governor's morning worship services in the Governor's office. (*Courtesy of the Georgia Department of State Archives.*)

15. Governor Lester Maddox and Virginia congratulate Morgan (Bucky) Redwine (left) upon his appointment as the new Governor's Executive Secretary in 1967. (*Courtesy of the Georgia Department of State Archives.*)

16. Governor Lester Maddox displays a nice string of north Georgia trout during one of his rare outings in the great outdoors. (*Courtesy of the Georgia Department of State Archives.*)

17. Always a colorful campaigner, Lester Maddox, seen here with his wife Virginia, felt at home among Georgia's rural voters, who were the fountain-head of his political support. (*Courtesy of the Georgia Department of State Archives.*)

Chapter 9
Lieutenant Governor Lester Maddox

"He [Jimmy Carter] was very angry, mean and cold. Until then, I did not realize that a person who conducted himself as an honest, kind and gentle person before the public could then act like an animal in private."
—Maddox on Carter laying down "Carter's Law."

On 11 September 1970, Governor Lester Garfield Maddox was probably the happiest man in Georgia. The previous day, as a candidate for the Democratic nomination for lieutenant governor, he scored a resounding, no-runoff victory against popular incumbent George T. Smith and several other candidates. In the polling, Maddox compiled a record number of votes and was undoubtedly the most popular politician in the state. Although he still had to face Republican State Senator Frank Miller in the general election, most political observers agreed that Maddox would become the first Georgia governor in history to later become lieutenant governor.

In the same election, Democratic gubernatorial candidate Jimmy Carter, despite amassing an impressive plurality in the primary, found himself in a run-off election with former governor Carl Sanders. Several weeks later, as expected, Carter easily defeated Sanders and was scheduled to face Atlanta newsman, Republican Hal Suit, in the general election in early November. Suit surprised almost everyone by handily defeating

Talmadge protégé and former State Comptroller General Jimmy Bentley
in the Republican primary. Most political observers believed that, despite
having changed parties, Bentley would win the Republican primary
because of his close ties to the conservative Talmadge and his popularity
among Georgia Democrats. Bentley expected to poll enough Democratic
votes to put him over the top. Suit, however, emerged the victor and was
to face Carter in the November general election. This series of events
meant that Jimmy Carter and Lester Maddox were running mates on the
Democratic ticket. As a result, the two men formed something of an
alliance.

Several days before the general election, Carter appeared before a
group in Columbus and said: "Governor Maddox is a friend of mine and
a good governor. He is the essence of what the Democratic Party is all
about and I am proud to be on the ticket with him and am looking forward to serving with him if you elect me your governor."

At that time in Georgia politics, Maddox was undoubtedly the most
popular politician in the state. He proved his high standing among the
voters by totally demolishing the field in his quest to become lieutenant
governor. Thus, Maddox had little to gain in an alliance with Carter.
Carter, however, saw an opportunity to appeal to the public with
Maddox. By merely associating himself with Maddox as a fellow
Democrat, Carter served notice to Maddox's supporters that he desperately wanted their votes. His strategy was to use Maddox's popularity for
his own benefit, regardless of how he might have felt about him personally.

In early October 1970, Carter and Maddox continued their alliance
as Democratic running mates. In one speech, Carter praised Maddox and
declared "He has brought a high standard of forthright expression and
personal honesty to the governor's office and I hope I measure up to that
standard." Carter also stated publicly that a close friend suggested that he
adopt as his campaign slogan: "The statesmanship of [United States
Senator Richard B.] Russell and the honesty of Maddox."

Several days later in the general election, Carter defeated Republican
Hal Suit by a comfortable margin and Maddox handily out-polled his
Republican opponent Frank Miller by a 2-1 margin. The top leadership
positions in Georgia government for the next four years had been filled.
Jimmy Carter would run the state from the governor's office while Lester
Maddox would run the state senate.

During the lame duck period from the general election until 1 January, Maddox's spirits soared higher than ever. Maddox had not only lived out his dream of being governor of Georgia, but he was now assured a new spot in state government for another four years. He could not have been happier. Before leaving the governor's office to assume his new job, he entertained visitors with newfound energy and humor. He accepted offers from state senators to help him learn the ins-and-outs of the operation of the state senate and traveled around the state fraternizing with them and making speeches. He enjoyed the role of being lieutenant governor-elect. His political high, however, would be short-lived.

Only days after the general election, a delegation of pro-Carter state senators called upon Maddox in the governor's office. They told Maddox that the purpose of their visit was to inform him of Carter's choices for Senate President pro tempore and committee chairpersons. With the announcement, they reminded Maddox that every previous governor had selected the house and senate leadership. After patiently listening to the senators, Maddox made it clear he did not agree with their argument. In fact, he said, he would not even discuss it with them. As his voice grew louder and his anger rose, Maddox said he would never allow anyone, especially Carter, to tell him how to organize the senate.

Still angry, Maddox immediately picked up the phone and called Hugh Gillis, a powerful state senator and son of the long-time highway commissioner, who was a candidate for the pro tempore office. Maddox asked Gillis bluntly if Carter was "putting someone against you." Gillis confirmed Maddox's suspicion. Carter's candidate for the pro tem spot was Bob Smalley, a hard-working and well-liked senator from Griffin, who was one of Carter's earliest and strongest supporters.

The following day, Maddox called a news conference and tore into Carter, claiming that the governor-elect had lied to him. Maddox charged that, in an earlier meeting, Carter had promised he would not interfere with the organization of the senate while Maddox was lieutenant governor. Further, Maddox charged, Carter's broken promise was just another one of his "lies." Maddox said, as governor, he had not named his friends to senate posts and that he was not aware that it was common practice among previous governors to do so. In the same press conference, Maddox criticized Bob Smalley, while endorsing his own man Hugh Gillis.

Carter, meanwhile, quietly backed Smalley until he realized that Smalley could not beat Gillis. He then turned to Frank Coggin, who was Governor Maddox's floor leader, in an effort to defeat Gillis, who he knew was livid with him for firing Gillis's father, Highway Department Director Jim Gillis. However, Coggins, who earlier might have been interested in the job, was already committed to Gillis.

Fearing more Carter interference with his management of the Senate, Maddox and his aides moved quickly to fill vital committee assignments with friendly, not necessarily anti-Carter senators. At the same time, he began removing hard-core Carterites from their chairpersonships. Obviously, Carter was very disappointed. His power was being threatened and it was generally acknowledged that resisting Carter promised reprisals. "If you cross Jimmy," said one insider, "then rest assured you will live to see the day you regret it."

Between his election and his inauguration, Carter proved he knew how to use power. He had forced Jim Gillis out as highway director and replaced him with his own man, Bert Lance. Maddox was no fan of Carter or his tactics and said so.

And Carter had his reasons for hating Maddox.

In a 1997 television interview with CNN's Larry King, Jimmy Carter said the biggest disappointment of his political life was losing the run-off spot in the 1966 governor's race to Lester Maddox. Fresh out of a stellar navy career, was on his way to the political top. After serving effectively as a state senator, Carter was so confident of winning the governor's race that abandoned an almost certain seat in Congress to run. In the primary, however, he lost the run-off spot to Maddox.

Three days after assuming his duties as lieutenant governor, Carter called Maddox and asked him to meet with him. Upon arrival in the governor's office, Maddox said he was very cordial and positive toward Carter. He said he wished him a successful term and stated that they would be fighting for many of the same goals. Once his greetings were over, Maddox said he had expected to receive in-kind cordialities from Carter. Instead, he was shocked at the response. Maddox recalled recently:

"Gov. Carter stood up and, while standing less than two feet from me, he pointed his finger in my face and said: "'Governor Maddox, I didn't call you to my office to find out when and how you are going to support me. I had just one purpose in calling you here—and that is to tell you that if you oppose me even on even one issue I will meet you head-on and fight you with the fullest resources of my office.'"

Maddox charged later that Carter made the glowing statements about him before the general election only because he wanted to ride Maddox's popularity into the governor's mansion. In truth, Maddox contended, there was no sincerity to the statements and, once Carter was elected, he said the new governor had no further use for him.

Unfortunately for the people of Georgia, Carter picked the wrong person and the wrong approach. Lester Maddox was not a sailor on a nuclear sub who must obey the orders of his commanding officer. He was a hard-scrabble street kid from poverty-stricken Home Park who learned his own form of vindictiveness. The stage was set for the most vicious fighting between a governor and lieutenant governor the state had ever seen. Maddox said, "Little did I dream at the time that, for the next four years, there would be no letup in his fighting to destroy those he could not totally control. Carter was so intent on controlling the Georgia senate that he even authorized office space in the governor's office for state senators so he could entice them to join his lustful fight for power."

During his campaign, Carter promised a wholesale reorganization of state government. He contended that the current bureaucracy was so bloated and disorganized that neither services to taxpayers nor the departments themselves could expand. The only solution, he contended, was to reorganize, streamline and economize state government from top to bottom.

Thus, when the 1971 session of the General Assembly opened, House Bill 1 contained the legislation that would allow Carter to implement his reorganization plan. Carter enlisted the help of several knowledgeable and well-known Georgians to help him craft his re-organization plan. He also carefully selected legislative leaders with clout and the ability to compromise to guide the plan through the General Assembly. In the lower chamber, House Majority Leader George Busbee the measure to an easy victory. Once the bill reached the Senate however, Maddox rose up in arms against it. Bob Smalley of Griffin, Brooks Pennington of Madison, Paul Broun of Athens and Ford Spinks of Tifton—Carter's braintrust from his 1966 unsuccessful race for governor—would handle the bill in the state senate.

A key provision of the bill, as approved by the House, was a stipulation that allowed any of Carter's reorganization proposals to become law unless the General Assembly could muster enough votes to veto them. Maddox strongly opposed that provision, contending that such an approach was the reverse of the normal legislative process and that as governor, it gave Carter far too much power over the legislature. Carter meanwhile, charged that killing the veto provision "would effectively kill the bill and I don't intend to let it be killed."

On the evening of Sunday, 8 February 1971, Maddox called a special press conference at the capitol during which he charged Carter with a "secret deal" with key state legislators to gain support for his reorganization bill. Maddox further claimed that Carter promised legislative leaders that, as a reward for their reorganization support, he would support a bill to raise their pay.

In making the charges, Maddox criticisms against Carter were particularly scathing. Maddox claimed that the "deal" had been hatched by "cowardly and conniving politicians...special interests and the 'in' crowd... persons who engender fear and cowardice and lust for power who conceived the plot in defeat and nurtured it in iniquity, in raw and rotten collusion...they would set up a dictatorship, a monarchy....they would sell their souls for a mess of porridge."

On the heels of the charge, Maddox launched his own campaign in the state senate against Carter and reorganization. In lobbying against the measure, Maddox told other senators that the bill was "a monstrous thing." According to one newspaper article, Maddox said the bill was "'ungodly' and "those who didn't understand [it] might find themselves being duped Communists."

Once legislative leaders and governmental officials became aware of the impending Carter-Maddox polarization, they feared the resulting political quagmire and some attempted to avert the coming conflict. "This is an awful thing," Senator Harry Jackson of Columbus said. "What if the astronauts got into a fight right after they blasted off...the country would have been in terrible shape. Well, for the state's two chief executives to fight and put us in the middle is terrible for Georgia."

Three days later, when the reorganization bill came up for a senate vote, Carter's forces scored a narrow, but critical victory against Maddox. Although the senate vote was 53-3, Maddox's attempt to remove the reverse veto provision failed only by one vote. This refusal assured passage of the measure. Maddox called the defeat "a loss for the people" and not himself and stated his intention to continue his fight against the bill and seek its repeal.

Over each of the succeeding three years, Carter implemented the recommendations of his Carter Commission on restructuring state government. Within the framework of the plan, the state's sixty-five budgeted departments were reduced to twenty-two. Also, under the plan, more than two hundred unbudgeted, commissions, agencies and boards were reduced to nine, with their functions being transferred to one of the twenty-two budgeted departments. When Carter left office in January 1975, his new design for state government was in place almost exactly as he had originally planned it.

In the 1973 General Assembly session, the truth of Maddox's claims of a "secret deal" between Carter and key legislative leaders unfolded exactly as he had predicted two years earlier. In January, a $1.9 million salary increase bill was presented which would increase legislators' salaries from $4,200 a year to $7,200.

While the salary bill sailed through the house, as did the reorganization bill, everyone expected the measure to meet stiff opposition in the senate, especially from Maddox. A year earlier, the lieutenant governor had taken a vehement stand against the salary bill and even won praise in an *Atlanta Journal* editorial:

> Lt. Governor Lester Maddox is against the proposed pay raises for the holders of top state offices at this time.
>
> The raises have been proposed and in ordinary times they might make sense. But today, when Washington is trying to control both prices and wages, they don't.
>
> The proposed raises for our elected officials are considerably more than the five per cent which is supposed to be the maximum increase.
>
> As the lieutenant governor said, it would be a "shameful" thing for him and other constitutional officers to get a big increase while their office staffs are limited to five percent.
>
> Right on, Lester. You're earning your keep on this one.

From the very start, state senators wished to avoid a roll call vote on the salary measure. A roll call vote would result in a senate record on how each member voted and all those who voted themselves a raise would have to answer to their constituents. A show of hands however, would absolve legislators of individual responsibility in the matter since there would no permanent record. Thus, Carter forces in the senate who wanted to pass the salary raise bill could only prevail by a voice vote. A roll call vote meant certain defeat.

Former legislator Bobby Rowan of Enigma, who was a state senator at the time, recalled that the Carter forces in the senate were always looking for an opportunity to catch Maddox off-guard and when the salary bill came up for a senate vote, the opportunity presented itself. When a motion was made from the floor for a roll call vote, it appeared that sufficient Senators voted affirmatively. Quickly, however, several members stormed the rostrum, demanding that Maddox call for a recount.

In a moment of indecision, Maddox called for a second show of hands on the motion for a roll call and, again, the motion failed. During the recount, however, Senate Secretary Hamilton McWhorter remembered several pro-Carter Senators moving from one member to the next urging them to vote no, by forcibly pulling down their upraised hands. Thus, when the salary raise bill itself was considered several minutes later, it was overwhelmingly passed by a show of hands.

Later, in defense of not ordering a roll call vote when the second motion for one had failed, Maddox said, "There was no way I could order a roll call after that," he said. "If the motion hadn't been made, I could have gone ahead and called one." Thus, the "shameful" bill Maddox had vehemently opposed over the past year was passed in spite of all his efforts against it. In a moment of weakness, Maddox had allowed the Carter forces to use an ingenious parliamentary maneuver to slip it past him.

Maddox's failure to stop the salary bill would remain with Maddox for the rest of his career. Many detractors, in fact, blamed the passage of the bill on Maddox. A June 2, 1973 editorial in the Atlanta Journal reads:

> Lt. Gov. Lester Maddox, who consistently denies his responsibility for the senate vote without a roll call which produced the most controversial pay raise for legislators in Georgia history, now is going to set everything straight.

He will propose a general bill requiring a recorded vote on every issue to come before both houses of the General Assembly from now on....

The bill is just another exercise in futility. But so is the lieutenant governor.

During his term as lieutenant governor, Maddox was forced to fight off one attempt after another by Carter forces to strip him of his power. First, they tried to change Senate rules which would prevent Maddox for breaking tie votes. Next, there was an attempt to bar him from voting on proposed constitutional amendments. The big push by the Carter forces, however, was to take away Maddox's ability to appoint committees which was, in effect, a fight over control of the state senate.

Carter allies, led by Senator Bob Smalley of Griffin, planned to make their move following the general election in 1972. Their object was to join forces with Senator Bobby Rowan's group, which also wanted to strip Maddox but for a different reason. Rowan and his supporters were seeking "legislative independence." Since the lieutenant governor was not a member of the senate, merely its presiding officer, Rowan believed that members of the senate, not the lieutenant governor, should name committees. Thus, while neither pro-Carter nor pro-Maddox, Rowan's goal was to corral enough votes to oppose the Maddox forces and he quickly found himself in the same corner with Smalley and Carter.

When Maddox assessed his chances of holding his power, he counted twenty-seven solid votes, two short of the majority he needed to win. With no chance to take votes from Carter or Rowan, Maddox realized that senate Republicans, a total of six uncommitted votes, held the balance of power. Should the Republicans vote with Maddox, he was assured victory. Should they go with Carter or Rowan, defeat was inevitable. Realizing their value, all sides dangled choice committee assignments to the Republicans as rewards for their votes. Minority Leader Armstrong Smith of Atlanta, a friend of Maddox, warned his colleagues that they should be careful in choosing sides. "If you choose the wrong side," Smith reminded his fellow state senators, "You might end up on one of those committees that never meets."

When the vote was finally taken, Smith himself sided with Maddox, and the beleaguered lieutenant governor obtained sufficient votes to ward off his opposition. Although Maddox had won, the anti-Maddox movement had refueled the Carter-Maddox feud and the name-calling on both sides continued, this time with renewed vigor.

By the fall of 1973, the ongoing feud between Carter and Maddox was so widely known throughout the state that voters and public officials were making jokes about it. At the Georgia Dairy Association's annual convention near the Atlanta Airport, Lieutenant Governor Maddox found himself seated at the opposite end of the head table from Governor Jimmy Carter. The Mistress of Ceremonies, an attractive young lady from Cartersville, told the audience she had perfected a recipe for peanut butter: "You take freshly roasted Georgia peanuts," she said, looking at Governor Carter. "Then, add fresh Georgia creamery butter," she added, glancing at the President of the Dairy Association. "Next," she continued, turning to look at Maddox, "you beat the devil out of it with an ax handle."

Interestingly, during the last three years of his term as lieutenant governor, Maddox harked back to his "Pickrick Says" days with a paid advertisement newspaper column which he dubbed "You Ought to Know." Obviously, Maddox had hoped the "You Ought to Know" columns would win him support in his fight against Carter.

In August 1972, Maddox launched the column with a preface: "This column 'You Ought to Know' is planned as a regular weekly column. It is dedicated to the cause of good government and designed to reach the people of Georgia with truth and news often denied them. Fence-straddling public officials who deceive the people and refuse to be honest and major Atlanta news media that work to manage rather than report the news because of their bias, unfairness and dishonesty, will not like this column..."

In one column, Maddox launched into a spiteful tirade on how Jimmy Carter and his legislative allies had tried to destroy him and "abolish the office of lieutenant governor" after he "exposed the fact that reorganization of state government was being demanded in violation of the Georgia Constitution..."

In January 1973, Maddox continued the attacks against Carter with an article stating, "I have never initiated a squabble with governor Carter and I never will. Whoever the governor of Georgia may be at any time, I will do my best to help him with every program which promotes honesty, efficiency and government of, for and by the people. However, I refuse to roll over and play dead when attacked…"

In March 1974, he tried to defend himself in his stand against ad valorem taxes (supported by Carter and his legislative allies) and provided all his reasoning on the matter. "IF GOVERNOR CARTER vetoes this property tax relief, as he has stated he intends to do… Governor Carter will be forcing an immediate $50 million ad valorem tax increase on the taxpayers of Georgia…."

The "You Ought to Know" columns were hard-bitten, pamphlet-like, political treatises which attempted to report the wheeling and dealing that went on behind the scenes in state government. Where reading the restaurant ads were enjoyable and brought frequent belly laughs, reading the "You Ought to Know" columns was laborious. They were generally nothing but hate and spite-filled attacks on Jimmy Carter and his allies.

In the course of the "You Ought to Know" columns, Maddox did himself more harm than good. In many ways, all the "You Ought to Know" columns accomplished was to publicize his bitter, ongoing fight with Jimmy Carter. This feud with Carter would later do great damage to both men, as polls would show. Carter was extremely unpopular when he vacated the governor's office in 1975. Despite his earlier popularity, Maddox was defeated in his attempt to regain the governor's office in 1974.

During the course of the feud, probably the harshest blow for Maddox came in June 1971 when Zell Miller, his long-time executive secretary, resigned and joined up with the Carter camp. After serving as "assistant governor" during the second half of Maddox's gubernatorial term, Miller had followed Maddox into the lieutenant governor's office in the same job. While Miller had served ably in both capacities, he grew bored and restless with the lack of challenge in the lieutenant governor's office. As the "assistant governor," Miller was constantly on the front line and had to be on his toes to make crucial political decisions. In the "assistant lieutenant governor's" post however, there was little to do other that routine housekeeping chores. After some extensive soul-searching, Miller resigned and shortly afterward went to work for Carter as head of the Georgia Democratic party.

"When I resigned," Miller recalled recently, "I wrote Governor Maddox a lovely letter. It was as loving and sincere as I could make it. He was mad as hell with me because he saw it as Carter robbing him of me. For years, it bothered me that he was so unhappy with me because the man had been so very, very good to me."

Maddox felt that Miller's resignation was the ultimate act of betrayal. During all the years Miller had served as his assistant, the two men enjoyed a father-son relationship. Somehow, in his heart, Maddox felt that Miller would always be loyal. Maddox wept openly when he read Miller's letter of resignation.

In a 1985 interview, Maddox offered these historical footnotes to his term as lieutenant governor:

"The pressure for reorganization and the salary increases may have been the most ever exerted in the state capitol. State department heads, constitutional officers and the courthouse crowds appeared to almost move their headquarters to the state legislature (to fight for passage of the bills).

"Bert Lance, the director of the State Highway Department and later, under reorganization, Commissioner of the Department of Transportation.... spent more time in the capitol than in his office."

Explaining that he worked against Carter during the presidential campaign (Maddox ran on the Independent Party Ticket in the same 1976 election), Maddox commented:..."I knew him to be a fraud and mean and cold. And I know none of us are totally honest, but from my personal beliefs and experience, Mr. Carter was the most dishonest man I ever met in public life."

Regarding Carter's failure to get reelected President in 1980, Maddox said: "I really don't think that people recognized that Carter...was in over his head (as president).... I don't think a perception of his being dishonest was a determining factor in his not being reelected. What got him elected the first time was President Richard Nixon and his (Nixon's) dishonesty and being stupid enough to get involved in the Watergate scandal.... Then too, Governor Carter left the office of governor in poor standing with the people.

"During the latter part of his last year as governor, his favorable rating in the polls was some twenty-five percent. But he was a great campaigner. He outworked, outcampaigned and out-lied his opponents and got elected President of the United States."

A few weeks before he left the governor's office, Carter told a reporter with the Atlanta Journal that his squabbling with Maddox had been the biggest disappointment of his administration. "I haven't been able to achieve the proper relationship with him," Carter said. "As governor, it was my responsibility." Carted admitted that the "damage has been in the disrespect and doubt that has been engendered in the minds of people toward my office and his....Folks remember the arguing more than the achievements."

Miller observed that Maddox "had no interest in the legislative process, none at all. It was something that simply did not interest him....While he was a masterful politician and a good governor, he failed to learn the difference between real politics and legislative politics.

"It was a completely new experience for him," Miller continued. "The art of legislative politics requires a special ability to put together votes, work out compromises, reward your friends for their loyalty and punish your enemies. You might say that being a successful legislative politician requires and ability to manipulate people.

"Governor Maddox was not a manipulating kind of politician," Miller added. "The thing about him is that there is no meanness in Lester Maddox. I can't say that about myself and I can't say it about Jimmy Carter. Neither can I say that about a lot of other politicians.

"I think that the fact he was not mean to people affected his service as lieutenant governor," Miller continued. "The State Senate is a tough place to run and, to be successful, you must be mean to folks sometimes and he simply wouldn't."

Throughout their public lives, Maddox and his old nemesis, Jimmy Carter, have seldom agreed on anything. Their feud had a definite effect on both and, although Carter would later be elected President of the United States, his poll numbers at the end of his term as governor were extremely low. Many observers believed that he could not have won a second term if permitted to seek re-election. The state constitution at that time limited the governor's term to four years.

Chapter 10

"A Work Horse, Not a Show Horse"

"The 1974 campaign for governor was the meanest, the ugliest, the most
expensive and the most dishonest campaign I have ever been involved in."
—Maddox on the 1974 governor's race

The Carter-Maddox feud was the prelude to the 1974 governor's race. All the major forces that had been active in the feud were the same forces that provided momentum to the 1974 election. During the feud, Carter, Maddox and State Representative George Busbee, the house floor leader who guided Carter's reorganization and salary bills through the lower chamber, were the prime players. In the 1974 election, the same characters—Carter, Maddox and Busbee—would play central roles.

From the first, all of the state's political pundits expected the 1974 election to be a donnybrook. Maddox, of course, was sure to make the race since state law prohibited Carter from succeeding himself. Many felt, however, that since Carter could not run again, he would use every means at this disposal to defeat Maddox. As a result, several Carter insiders were considered for the race but the task of beating Maddox ultimately fell to Bert Lance, a Carter confidante who served as his transportation commissioner. For a full two years before the election, Lance angled for Carter's support in the race by using his vast influence as the state's master road builder to further Carter's legislative agenda.

Lance, a wealthy, affable multimillionaire from Calhoun, was modest about neither his wealth nor his intent to spend it. Active in regional development in Northwest Georgia for many years, Lance had hitched his political wagon to Carter's star during the 1966 primary and remained a key advisor during the four years leading up to Carter's successful race against Carl Sanders in 1970. While Lance was popular with the media, he lacked Carter's Kennedy-like charisma and television good looks.

Meanwhile, Busbee, an ally of former governor Carl Sanders, developed a strategy to take on both Maddox and Lance. Sanders, who had not forgotten the defeat he suffered from Carter in 1970, was solidly behind the capable Busbee, who served as his floor leader in the House of Representatives when he was governor. In eighteen years as a state representative, Busbee proved himself to be a hard worker who not only had a sixth sense about needed legislation but also had the political savvy to engineer the back-room deals necessary to make it law.

By the time party qualifying ended, a total of eleven Democratic candidates had announced their intentions for the state's highest office. While Maddox, Lance, and Busbee were considered the front-runners, several other candidates were close behind. Former Lieutenant Governor George T. Smith, whom Maddox easily defeated for the state's second highest office four years earlier, entered the race. So did former United States Senator David Gambrell and former State Senator Bobby Rowan, a South Georgia farmer. Harry Jackson, a former state senator and a successful Columbus businessman, completed the field of serious candidates. The dark horses included Tom Irwin (not to be confused with Department of Agriculture Tommy Irvin), B. J. Parker and Jennings (Jid) Thompson IV.

From the opening day of his campaign, Maddox emphasized his achievements as former governor as the primary reasons he should be elected to a second term. Citing his earlier record of prison reform, revamping the Pardons and Parole Board, cleaning up corruption and forcing competitive bids on state contracts, Maddox promised an equally effective performance during another term. "I did it once and I can do it again," he said.

Calling for sweeping changes in the state's highway system, Maddox explained that Atlanta's traffic network was not only inadequate, but also "deplorable." Maddox promised, if elected, he would support the proposed I-485 route through the Morningside area of Atlanta to ensure "that the motoring public has an integrated highway system."

Earlier, the state highway department had attempted to build the proposed I-485 route through the residential area, but their efforts were repeatedly blocked by lawsuits from residents and environmentalists.

Time and time again, Maddox charged that state highway officials who built the system of interstate highways into Atlanta committed a grave error when they channeled Interstate 75 and Interstate 85 into a single downtown connector. "If elected," Maddox promised, "I will see that another major connector route is built through Atlanta to relieve the traffic congestion."

Maddox's platform also focused on other issues. He called for reducing the teacher-student ratio in public schools and adding more officers to the Georgia State Patrol. More than anything else, however, Maddox promised that he would continue to speak out against corruption, misuse of state property and other abuses in state government if elected to a second term. "God has given me a divine right to speak out," he said, "And I will never be silenced."

Busbee, meanwhile, well aware that the biggest issue in the race was Lester Maddox himself, began to devise a master plan for victory. During the course of his campaign, he and his advisors would identify every one of Maddox's political weaknesses and, in a carefully orchestrated series of personal attacks, use them against him.

First, Busbee leveled the charge that the lieutenant governor, while touring the nation on television talks shows, had left the Georgia State senate to be run by special interest groups. In a speech that kicked off his campaign in early March of 1974, Busbee unloaded a blistering verbal barrage on Maddox:

> Anytime there is a vacuum in leadership in any public office it will be filled by political hacks who could never be elected in their own right. That's what has happened to the lieutenant governor's office over the past three years.
>
> While the man who was elected to that office has been flying to California and Philadelphia and New York to be on national television, back in the capitol the crowd that was actually running his office was turning it into a brokerage house for special interests.

By mid-May, Busbee had identified a second Maddox weakness—his feud with Carter—and exploited it to the hilt. Charging that Maddox was an "ineffective and quarrelsome" lieutenant governor, Busbee told the Northside Kiwanis Club: "The next governor must reopen the channels of communication between the governor's office and the state legislature. Over the past few years, the state has paid a high price for the constant quarreling and bickering on Capitol Hill."

By early summer, Busbee had added an even more powerful weapon to his arsenal by attacking and ridiculing Maddox's famous celebrity image. Of all the others, this charge would hurt Maddox the most. "I'll be a work horse, not a show horse," Busbee told voters again and again. "I may not be the brightest governor or the smartest governor, but I'll be the hardest working governor this state has ever seen."

Busbee's tactics showed a brilliant insight into Maddox's power as a politician. In the past, a huge part of Maddox's appeal to voters was his celebrity status. Riding his bicycle backwards, performing exercises in public, throwing out witty one-liners and unmercifully raking his opponents over the public coals had been a hallmark of every Maddox candidacy. Although Maddox had no experience and little money, he had been able to get elected by endearing himself to voters with his antics. Now, Busbee was using Maddox's primary political strength against him.

In keeping with the "work horse" image, Busbee stressed his record during eighteen years as a ranking state representative, explaining how he spent endless hours introducing and implementing the passage of various important bills. In contrast, Busbee pounded away at Maddox as a "spendthrift governor" during his term and predicted voters would be hit with huge tax increases if Maddox were elected because "the only way he knows to run the state government is to spend and spend." Busbee did a masterful job of keeping the pressure on Maddox.

Meanwhile Bert Lance, Carter's hand-picked candidate to run against Maddox, desperately sought a way to join Busbee and Maddox as forerunners. Despite his hard work and the support from Carter's people, Lance did not get a good start out of the gate. Thus, Busbee and Maddox captured the limelight.

Although Lance maintained a vigorous schedule of campaign appearances, and authored a sensible platform, he failed to capture voter's attention. Like the other candidates, Lance called for lower taxes, raises for schoolteachers and more new highways.

Early on, Lance made a grave error when he released his net worth statement showing him to be a millionaire more than two and one-half times over. He later committed another mistake when he stated publicly that he was spending almost $1 million on the race, half of which had come out his own pocket. The net worth statement and the campaign expenditures statement led several of his opponents to charge that Lance was trying to "buy the governor's office."

During the primary campaign, leaders of the state's black community demanded that the state merit system be restructured so that more African Americans could get jobs.

As a result, during the primary campaign, they invited each candidate to appear before them for an interview and respond to the demand. Though Maddox enjoyed meeting with the panel of black leaders, he balked at some of their suggested changes to the system. "I stated that I would not support the lowering of state requirements for employment, explaining that to do so would be unfair to the better qualified white and black Georgians and those of other races. I explained that, by lowering the level, we were cheating the qualified and at the same time discouraging the unqualified to become better qualified....What [they were] demanding is that state government hire the less than qualified on purpose and I [could not] go along with that."

Maddox's refusal to consider lowering state employment qualifications had a direct impact on the election results. "Other gubernatorial candidates did agree to the demands, including representative Busbee and he got their votes and I didn't... and he kept his pledge to those people," said Maddox after his defeat by Busbee.

Although there were eight others in the race, only three—Maddox, Busbee and Lance—were viewed as serious candidates. The others made little headway and their campaigns fizzled by election day. Both Gambrell and Smith were familiar names in Georgia. Carter appointed Gambrell to the United States Senate upon the death of Senator Richard B. Russell. Gambrell's name appeared on the ballot in 1972 when he was defeated in the Democratic Primary by Sam Nunn. Smith served as speaker of the house during the Sanders administration and as lieutenant governor during Maddox's term as governor. However, neither Gambrell nor Smith was able to get their campaigns in gear.

On the night of Monday, 12 August 1974, all of the major candidates were scanning the polls trying to determine which way the political winds might blow. From the start of campaigning, pollsters predicted that Maddox would lead the pack with an estimated 27 percent to 37 percent of the vote. They cautioned, however, that many voters were still undecided. Busbee, meanwhile, was expected to poll about 25 percent to 30 percent and narrowly edge out Lance for the run-off spot against Maddox. All pollsters agreed that Maddox would finish first. Whether Busbee or Lance would be his opponent in the 3 September Democratic Party runoff was the largest remaining question.

Most observers agreed that the weather and voter turnout would determine the actual outcome. "If it rains in South Georgia, Lance will win," said pollster Claiborne Darden Jr. "If it rains in North Georgia, Busbee wins."

On the night of 13 August, as expected, Maddox took a commanding lead once the results started coming in. By 8:00 P.M., an hour after the voting booths closed, Maddox was already the projected winner.

Maddox was supremely confident.

Flashing a victory sign to his supporters, Maddox said: "Run-off or no run-off, we will win. You're the greatest."

Shortly after 10:00 P.M. that night, Maddox, his wife and a retinue of children and grandchildren arrived in the ballroom of the campaign headquarters to the rousing cheers of several hundred campaign workers and supporters. "You're walking on water, governor," said a middle-aged man wearing a Maddox straw hat.

Three days later when all the votes were counted, Busbee beat out Lance by a narrow margin. Former senator David Gambrell finished fourth.

Two days after the primary, Maddox's first move resulted in making race an issue. In a morning press conference, Maddox charged that Black State Rep. Julian Bond "owns" and "controls" Busbee. "The fellows I'll be in the run-off with are the two Bs—Busbee and Bond," Maddox told reporters.

Bond, a widely-respected state legislator, was a prime mover in for Civil Rights Georgia for many years. At the time, he was serving as point man for the orchestration of the state's black vote.

Busbee, openly courted black voters in the primary. Some believed his success among the state's black electorate accounted for second place finish and his defeat of Lance. He responded to Maddox's accusation with a vow to "not interject race into this campaign."

"I have read the myth of the bloc vote and the black vote, yet the returns I have seen indicate the votes are evenly distributed," he said, promising to seek black votes "only as I do those of other Georgians."

During the campaign's first week, both Maddox and Busbee charged and countercharged that each had lined their own pockets as a result of being in public office. "My opponent is so desperate for power and a fat retirement check that he would almost sell his soul to get it," Maddox said. Busbee countered that Maddox had used the employees in the lieutenant governor's office to conduct "a full-time witch hunt" against him.

In the same statement, Busbee read the official record of the state senate in which the pay raise proposal was approved. After reading the 1973 Senate Journal record, he charged that Maddox used a parliamentary maneuver on advice of his aides to get the salary bill passed without calling for a recorded vote in the senate.

This was a smashing blow to Maddox and his true position. In the statement, Busbee had made it appear that Maddox supported the salary bill and used a subtle parliamentary trick to get it passed. Maddox countered that he fought to stop the salary measure with all his might because he believed the legislation was part of Carter's "secret deal" with leaders of the General Assembly.

On 28 August, a week before the runoff, Maddox and Busbee faced off in a statewide television debate. From the first, the primary bone of contention was who did and who did not support the controversial 1973 salary bill.

Busbee admitted he voted for the house version of the salary increase bill, but voted against the "Pickrick bill" Maddox passed in the senate without a roll call vote.

Maddox explained that he had never supported the salary bill and was only living up to the letter of the law when the bill passed the senate without a roll call vote.

Repeatedly, Maddox charged that Busbee had been "dishonest" during the campaign.

"You're a lawyer who represented special interests while being a member of the General Assembly," he charged, and then added that Busbee was "a tool of the Atlanta newspapers, an agent of the czars of finance, a captive of the major corporations and a lackey boy of special interests."

During the debate, each candidate tried to pull a personal stunt on the other. Midway through the debate, Busbee pulled out a Maddox "Phooey!" tee shirt and a Maddox alarm clock, souvenirs from Maddox's Underground Atlanta gift shop. Once they were in public view, Busbee explained that, if he were elected, he would not be "moonlighting" like Maddox. At the time, it was well known that Maddox was operating the shop while away from his duties as lieutenant governor.

Near the end of the debate, Maddox stood up and offered his outstretched hand to Busbee and said, "Mr. George, I want to congratulate you…" As Busbee stood up to shake his opponent's hand, Maddox finished the sentence with "to have gone this far without a platform." This ploy was Maddox's payback to Busbee's earlier charge that he, Maddox, had no platform until after the 13 August primary.

On Monday, 2 September, the day before the runoff election, the lead story on the front page of the *Atlanta Journal-Constitution* declared, "Busbee Says Lester's Hand in Cookie Jar." In the story, Busbee charged that Maddox's staff had somehow obtained a copy of the mailing list of defeated candidate Bert Lance and was denying it "to muddy the waters to distract voters."

Maddox replied by admitting that his campaign workers were using a major part of Lance's mailing list, but explained that Busbee had received the youth portion of the list himself.

An angry Busbee countered that Maddox's charges were "completely false" and claimed that "we did not receive any list from the Lance campaign, youth portion of otherwise. We haven't even used any direct mailing in the run-off campaign."

Meanwhile, Lance's former campaign manager, State Sen. Beverly Langford, charged that the mailing list was removed "without authorization" from Lance's headquarters and the Maddox campaign was using it to distribute pro-Maddox flyers to Lance supporters. Langford, who was working for Busbee in the run-off, further claimed that the list was discovered missing on 14 August and "has been used in an unethical, outrageous and completely unauthorized manner."

Maddox and his supporters contended that the list was not taken directly nor unethically from Lance's headquarters. "Many of Mr. Lance's key workers came to our headquarters [after the primary], wanting to help us and we welcomed them with open arms. These people gave us lists of the names of persons that we could invite to join us," responded Maddox. Ned Young, a Savannah businessman who managed Maddox's campaign office, confirmed Maddox's story about the Lance lists: "We did receive several lists from the Lance campaign, but nobody stole them. Disgruntled Lance workers who were angry with Busbee for beating their candidate brought them to us. They wanted Maddox to win and thought the lists might help us reach other Lance voters who shared their feelings."

Though the mailing list controversy turned out to be a non-issue, Maddox supporters believed that the Atlanta newspapers printed the story in a last ditch effort to harm Maddox and his candidacy. The only possible benefit Maddox could have received from the mailing list would have been to identify Lance supporters so that his workers could contact them, if time allowed. Despite the fact that political lists are relatively easy to obtain and are often "pirated" from one candidate to another by malcontents, the tone and temper of the article made Lester Maddox appear to be a thief. "It was a low blow," commented Young.

Both Maddox and Busbee worked to close out their respective campaigns with a series of frantic, last minute speeches and hand shaking. Each was supremely confident of victory. "Tomorrow the people of Georgia are going to bring down the curtain on the 'Pickrick' follies and the Lester Maddox show which has been going on for eight years," Busbee told a group of American Legionnaires in Columbus. Meanwhile, Maddox took time out from campaigning in Fort Oglethorpe to predict a landslide victory with between 55 percent and 65 percent of the vote. "My supporters tell me that my performance in Wednesday night's TV debate earned me a lot of votes and I think we're going to have a great win."

In Fayette County earlier in the day, Maddox showed reporters what he claimed was a Busbee-funded letter from State Rep. Julian Bond, which had been mailed to about 250,000 Georgians, mostly blacks. Maddox also showed reporters what he called "trick literature," a picture of him outside his Pickrick Restaurant on 3 July 1964, with a pistol in his hand. The photo had the caption "Lest We Forget," an obvious reminder of Maddox's famous stand against blacks trying to eat at his restaurant.

In the letter, Bond expressed his support for Busbee and warned voters, if Maddox won the run-off, they would be faced with a general election choice "between an ax-handle and a machine gun," referring to Republican candidate Ronnie Thompson, Mayor of Macon. Thompson had become famous in the state after threatening to use machine guns against criminals.

The Busbee forces accomplished one of their campaign's major strategic goals: to corral and turn out black voters against Maddox. Busbee's agreement to use the state merit system to ensure more state jobs for Georgia blacks was a huge vote-getter. That, coupled with Maddox's conduct at the Pickrick was a powerful issue with black voters and Julian Bond, without a doubt, was an excellent choice to present it to the electorate.

The headquarters of both candidates were excited on election night. The Maddox campaign workers were eagerly anticipating a huge celebration, confident that the former governor would roll up a big victory. Busbee's campaign hotel was likewise lively, filled with a host of South Georgians who made the trip to Atlanta to share in their favorite son's climb to the top of the political ladder.

Shortly after the polls closed at 7:00 P.M. , computers which sampled key precincts around the state projected that Busbee would not only win, but he would put together a larger majority than even his most enthusiastic supporters had hoped for. Over the course of the night, Busbee not only polled strong in areas where he had shown strength in the primary, but he pulled huge numbers of votes in several areas normally considered Maddox strongholds. In his victory speech, an obvious reference to the "work horse, show horse" theme, Busbee repeated the pledge: "I may not be the brightest governor or the smartest governor, but I will be the hardest-working governor this state has ever seen."

Maddox, meanwhile, choked back tears when he told reporters that the loss represented "a staggering defeat" and noted that "the name of Lester Maddox may never appear again on a ballot." Throughout the fifteen-minute speech, with Virginia weeping at his side, Maddox repeatedly referred to God and, at one point, called for a national revival of faith. Finally, his voice cracking with emotion, he concluded the speech by singing a solo of "God Bless America."

Meanwhile, political pundits claimed that overexposure was the primary reason Maddox lost to Busbee. People, they argued, viewed him as an incumbent and a celebrity. Whether a voter liked Maddox or not, he had been in the political limelight for two decades and voters were ready for a new player on the stage. Former Governor Marvin Griffin summed it up with a comment that Maddox never had much of a chance to build the sort of political dynasty that Wallace had in Alabama. "George Wallace," said Griffin, "Doesn't play the harmonica or ride a bicycle backwards." Even former governor Ellis Arnall was there to get in one last stab at Maddox: "This election means a lot to the state," he said. "It means we're going to be rid of Lester Maddox for a long, long time.... People are just tired of his antics."

The 1974 gubernatorial election was particularly notable in Georgia politics. This election was the first time that a candidate, in this case Busbee, openly courted black voters. Also, while the race issue would go underground in future elections, no other major candidate would ever again publicly espouse racial division. It was also the first time that a Talmadge or a Talmadge-allied candidate was not a major factor in the governor's race.

Of the loss, Maddox himself later attributed it to two overriding factors. First, his refusal to lower the state merit system standards so blacks could get more state jobs, giving Busbee a leg up on an important black issue that Julian Bond used effectively throughout the state; and, the Busbee-Carter charge that Maddox was personally responsible for passage of the controversial salary bill. "Their [Busbee and his allies] charge, which was false, was that Lester Maddox was responsible for the passage of the salary increase bill; then Jimmy Carter got out on the campaign trail and made the same false charge. In truth, it was their bill, introduced and passed by them.... They deceived enough Georgians to benefit them on election day 1974."

Chapter 11
Life After High Office

"After my term as lieutenant governor, I missed politics bad. Real bad. I was just never really happy unless I was in politics."
—Maddox on his non-political life

For almost thirty years, politics had been the driving passion in Lester Maddox's life. From the early days of the Pickrick advertisements down through his terms as governor and lieutenant governor, the very fiber of his being had been wrapped up in politics. It had challenged him and his abilities in a way that no other undertaking ever had. Now in early 1975, after the heart-breaking defeat by George Busbee, he was out of politics and would have to discover some new occupation, which would engage his energies as thoroughly as politics.

On the financial front, he was straining under a huge $300,000 campaign debt left over from the 1974 race. His political undertakings also strained his personal finances. While local rumors held that several Georgia governors became instant millionaires after leaving office, Maddox was a glaring exception to the rule. One of the most progressive governor in the state's history had little to show for his eight years of public service.

With the lingering campaign debt always on his mind, Maddox set out to remedy his financial crisis. But, try as he may, nothing seemed to

be "Pickrick" while he was out of public office. He truly missed public life and longed for an opportunity to re-enter public service. But that must be saved for later, he decided. Now, the time has come
To concentrate on the business at hand–dealing with a financial crisis.

Maddox was first and foremost a businessman. Since the job of lieutenant governor is not a full-time one, holders of the office are free to pursue other avenues. So, in 1970, the same year he was elected lieutenant governor, he opened the Lester Maddox gift shop in trendy Underground Atlanta. The souvenir shop did a brisk business selling an extensive line of Lester Maddox novelties. These included autographed pick handles, watches, tee-shirts, clocks, pictures and numerous other notions bearing his likeness and famous name. A month after the loss to Busbee in 1974, he opened a Pickrick restaurant in Underground Atlanta, and in early 1975, another Pickrick in Sandy Springs. Perhaps, Maddox thought, now that he was no longer a public servant, he could throw himself into the three businesses, turn some handsome profits and retire the 1974 campaign debt. Achieving that goal, however, would be easier said than done.

In the fall of 1975, Maddox found some solace for being out of the limelight when he teamed up with local musician Bobby Lee Fears to form a song and dance act they dubbed "The Governor and the Dishwasher."

Maddox had first met Bobby Lee Fears in mid-1973 while he was serving at lieutenant governor. At the time, Fears was serving a sentence at Reidsville prison for possession of $30,000 worth of heroin. Fears, a native of South Atlanta who was raised by his grandmother, had been told that Maddox was sympathetic toward African Americans and wrote him a long letter asking his help in getting an early release. Maddox, upon reading the letter, provided the requested help and Fears was freed. After leaving prison, however, Fears was unable to find employment. He looked for a job, but employers were not eager to hire an ex-convict with a rap sheet that included drugs. Having exhausted all other avenues, Fears approached Maddox and the former governor hired him at a dishwasher/cleanup man at the Sandy Springs Pickrick.

While mopping floors, Fears would often listen and watch while Maddox played his harmonica for patrons. Finally, he went to Maddox and told him that he was a professional musician himself and they should put together an act. After Maddox agreed, the two men did several jam sessions together, then auditioned for an agent and signed a contract to put their show on the road.

Maddox and Fears played nightclubs in Florida, Beverly Hills and New York's Riverboat Lounge in the Empire State Building. They also made appearances on the popular syndicated television comedy show "Laugh-in." "Governor Maddox would dress in a three-piece suit," Fears recalled in 1985, "And I would be dressed in trousers with pants legs rolled up to the knee and a busboy jacket with mustard and ketchup smeared on it. I didn't think it was degrading. I thought it was comical. We made people laugh."

The burlesque-style act folded in the summer of 1977 after Maddox and Fears had a disagreement. About losing Maddox as a partner, Fears would later say, "It left me out in the cold for awhile. It took me five years to get it together again."

In May of 1976, Maddox announced that he was closing the debt-ridden Pickrick Restaurant in Underground Atlanta because his business was no longer profitable. The previous March, the Georgia State Building Authority expanded its cafeteria in a park across the street from City Hall. Immediately, Maddox's business—mostly lunch counter patrons—began to plunge. Before the expansion, Maddox said the restaurant had been bringing in about $40,000 a month. After the expansion, the figure dropped to $15,000, he said. "This has been the saddest business experience of my life," Maddox said at the closing. "It's sad that my business has been destroyed by my own state government."

Now that Maddox was no longer in the entertainment business and had lost one of his restaurants, he opened the Lester Maddox Realty Company in downtown Atlanta. "I have been in real estate off and on since 1948," he told a reporter when he opened the tiny office. "If I hadn't gone into politics, I would probably be retired, rather than just tired, right now."

In September of 1977, Maddox was trimming ivy from a brick walkway in the back yard of his Mount Paran Road home when he was suddenly felt a sharp pain in his chest. "I fell to the ground," Maddox recalled. "Then I got back up and started to the car. By the time I got to the car, Virginia saw me and she came running."

Once fire department paramedics arrived, Maddox was given first aid, then rushed to the Kennestone Hospital in Marietta. Later that night,

doctors told Virginia that the vessels of the left carotid artery at the back
of his heart were blocked and he needed immediate surgery to clear the
blockage. After an emergency operation that night, Maddox remained in
intensive care for eight days.

"My stay in intensive care was longer than it should have been
because they got a call from some guy in California who said he was coming to Atlanta to "finish me off for good," Maddox said. "Shortly after the
threat, hospital officials put a Cobb County security guard at my hospital
door around the clock."

The threat never materialized. "Thank God he never made it,"
Maddox said, "but I did!"

By March of 1978, Maddox had returned part-time to his real estate
business. Much thinner now than when he was as governor, doctors
allowed Maddox to work a few hours, then rest.

"If I took a rest in the morning, then another in the afternoon I did
pretty good," he said at the time. "But I knew I couldn't push myself too
much."

Meanwhile, the huge 1974 campaign debt was still hanging over
Maddox's head. Although he had managed to whittle it down consider-
ably with profits from his various businesses, it was still over $200,000.
Due to the heart attack, recovery period and his inability to work, anxious
creditors were circling his tiny real estate office seeking their money.
Maddox was once again feeling a strain in the pocketbook.

When the state's top political figures learned of Maddox's financial
plight, they decided to form a "Get Well, Lester" committee which was
designed to help the former governor deal with his remaining 1974 campaign debt as well as personal finances which had mounted since the heart
attack. The group, headed by former Senator Herman Talmadge,
Governor George Busbee, Lieutenant Governor Zell Miller and Senator
Sam Nunn, sent out letters to their largest campaign contributors and
asked then to make $1,000 contributions toward a Maddox fund. Over
the next two months, money started pouring into the fund from sources
all over the state.

By early May, Maddox's health was growing progressively stronger.
After the heart attack, doctors had instructed him to pay close attention
to his eating habits if he wanted to avoid another coronary. As a result,
Maddox's diet had consisted of a strict, low-fat diet mostly of raw

vegetables, brewer's yeast and carrot juice. Over a meal with a *Journal-Constitution* magazine writer in which he meticulously peeled the skin off his chicken, Maddox observed, "I thoroughly believe if a man born with a healthy heart would just watch what he ate, he'd never have a heart attack.... You know, once you peel the skin off chicken, that meat won't hurt anybody.

The following month, Maddox went back to his real estate company full-time. Although he was regaining his health, Maddox was anxious to sell properties and make money. Despite his enthusiasm, it would be almost a year before the firm started turning a profit again.

By late June 1978, Maddox had reunited with his musical partner Bobby Lee Fears. Once they were jamming again, Maddox said he wanted them to perform for a memorabilia auction in Underground Atlanta to raise sorely needed cash. At the time, Maddox said he still owed $125,000 in campaign debts and planned to use the auction's proceeds to reduce that bill as well as others. "If I had been dishonest just one day while I was governor," he said. "I could have all these debts paid off now with lots of money to spare."

Although Maddox still had not fully recovered from the heart attack, at one point, he launched into a brief series of strenuous exercises for the crowd to show how good he felt. Then, with sweat beading across his brow, he made the rounds shaking hands.

By late July of 1979, the fund-raising efforts of the "Get Well, Lester" committee had whittled his 1974 campaign debt down to $80,000, but he was still fighting a horde of creditors. The previous month a Fulton County Court Judge ordered Maddox to pay $15,000 to two Tift County campaign investors within six months. "I'm going to be able to make it," Maddox said. "Business is picking up. I'm not earning enough to brag about yet, but I'm out of the red and into the black."

While the Miller-Nunn-Busbee-Talmadge effort knocked a huge hole in the debt, an estimated $40,000 still remained. At that point, Agriculture Commissioner Tommy Irvin, Maddox's former executive secretary, stepped in and called upon wealthy farmers throughout the state to attend a special benefit for Maddox at the farmer's market in Forest Park. At the event in early 1980, attended by Former Senator Talmadge, Senator Sam Nunn and several other dignitaries, more than enough funds were raised to retire the 1974 debt with some money left for Maddox's personal expenses.

But Maddox newly-found happiness was short-lived. In late 1981, Maddox was diagnosed with prostate cancer. For several weeks, his energy loss had become so severe that he was unable to drive back and forth to the real estate office. On the days he had the strength to reach the office, he was exhausted and spent the rest of the day sleeping in an office recliner. After surgery to remove the malignancy, Maddox returned home and spent three weeks in bed recuperating. Finally, shortly after New Year's day in 1981, he was out of bed and felt like he was recovering well.

Two weeks later, however, he developed bleeding in the urinary tract. Fearing that the cancer might have recurred, Maddox called his old friend Dr. Larry McDonald, a urologist and US Congressman, and told him of the new development. "You should see a doctor as soon as possible," Dr. McDonald counseled. "The cancer may be back." Maddox followed McDonald's advice and was diagnosed with a grade one malignancy. McDonald then urged Maddox to go to the Immunology Research Center, a controversial cancer treatment center at Freeport, Bahamas.

Although Maddox wanted medical help and wanted it fast, he was hesitant. While its director, Dr. Lawrence Burton, had a loyal following of satisfied customers, his treatment was unlicensed by the US Food and Drug Administration and listed by the American Cancer Society as an unproven method. Despite this, several Georgians who had been treated by Burton called him a "miracle worker."

One convert was 67-year-old Cullen C. Davis of Conyers. In October of 1982, the retired contractor was diagnosed with lung cancer and given a year to live. As a last resort, he went to Dr. Burton. "I think there's a cure for cancer and he's got it," Davis said. "He keeps the cancer from spreading, and if it doesn't spread, it won't kill you. I think he saved my life."

In the controversial treatment, a patient's blood sample was analyzed to determine which proteins were deficient. Next, the patient was subjected to repeated injections of serum that combined the patient's own blood and healthy blood to supply the immune factors that were lacking. Dr. Burton said the technique boosted patients "into a super-immune state."

An initial visit to Burton's center usually lasted six to eight weeks and cost between $4,250 and $5,150 for therapy alone. Airfare and living expenses were additional. Once patients returned home, they were required to continue the injections, usually six to eight a day, at a cost of $45 a week.

With Maddox's ongoing financial situation, he was hesitant to try the expensive treatment. At the last minute, McDonald provided Maddox with $3,000 to help defray the cost of travel and the first visit's treatment. McDonald explained that the money was a gift from an unnamed wealthy woman who wanted to help him.

In the spring of 1983, Maddox and Virginia journeyed to the Bahamas for Burton to begin the controversial treatment. After several lengthy stays at clinic, Maddox later enrolled in classes in the anti-cancer macrobiotic diet school in Brookline, Massachusetts, then returned to Atlanta where he continued to receive the injections.

From May 1983 until late June 1985, Maddox had received some 6,000 serum injections. In July 1985, Burton's controversial clinic was shut down after it was revealed that the serum showed exposure to the AIDS (acquired immune deficiency syndrome) virus.

Immediately, upon learning of the new development, Maddox went to the Atlanta Internal Medicine Group and was tested for the deadly AIDS virus. When the test results were returned, Maddox proclaimed: "Good news! Wonderful news! Marvelous news! I'm clean as a whistle. I can tell you now, God's not finished with me." Shortly afterward, his cancer went into remission.

On 17 May 1986, Lester and Virginia were the guests of honor at Atlanta's Georgia Plaza Park where 500 friends—and former foes— gathered to help them celebrate their half-century of matrimony. In attendance were former Senator Herman Talmadge and Fulton County District Attorney Lewis Slaton. Other dignitaries included Lieutenant Governor Miller, former governor Ellis Arnall and Secretary of State Max Cleland. Even the presence of sitting Governor Joe Frank Harris was made known through a proclamation read by Lieutenant Governor Miller.

After a meal, several dignitaries gave testimony to the resilience of Lester and Virginia's marriage. Once the testimonials were over, Maddox and his wife took the podium to a resounding roar of applause. "The reason she looks so young," Maddox quipped, holding his arm around her neck, "Is that I married her when she was 12, and he hasn't aged a day since."

"You know what's better than being governor, better than being president, better than anything else in the world?" he asked the audience. "That's sticking it out for fifty years."

Although Maddox tried to make the best of the sixteen years since the 1974 governor's race, it had been an agonizing series of business failures, health problems and the inability to achieve his goals. Things just didn't seem to work out for him when he wasn't in politics. Throughout his life, more than anything else, Maddox had been a people person, a man who was happiest when he was close to his fellow man. Serving, pleasing, making people laugh, making people stand up and take notice of him. That was what he loved most. And the ultimate expression of that need was politics. Finally, in November of 1989, an upbeat Lester Maddox could no longer resist the temptation to return to his beloved public life and announced to the media that he would run in the 1990 governor's race.

Chapter 12
The Last Hurrah

"The 1990 governor's race was something I had to do. I wasn't sure if I could measure up to the younger politicians who were in their prime, but I had to try. I just had to try."
—Maddox on the 1990 race

In mid-December 1989, almost sixteen years after his agonizing 1974 defeat at the hands of George Busbee, Lester Maddox was once again in search of the governor's office. Following his announcement a few weeks earlier, he hit the campaign trial in earnest. His first few stops were at old haunts in Lawrenceville, Winder and Statham where he had canvassed regularly during the 1960s and 1970s.

Outside on the street in Lawrenceville, Maddox greeted several passersby, then went into the Lawrenceville Barber Shop. As he opened the door, a small bell rang and all eyes turned to him. "Is that Lester Maddox?" an older man asked. "Can I shake your hand?" "That's why I brought it in," Maddox quipped, then walked over and vigorously shook the man's hand.

Later in Statham, as Maddox continued his rounds, shaking hands, cracking jokes and asking for votes, one careful observer noted that all those who recognized Maddox were age 40 or more. Most of those under that age peered curiously at the flurry of activity. They had never seen or heard of this man that their elders were making a fuss over.

Maddox was a throwback to another age, an age when Georgia and Georgians were totally different. Over the past sixteen years, the state had undergone sweeping social and political changes. During that same period, Maddox had remained the same. It was a new Georgia, but not a new Maddox. How well he fared in the race would be a measure of those changes.

As before, his signs read, "This is Maddox Country! Reelect Maddox!" Also, as before, he was traveling across the state in a 1986 station wagon and nailing up signs. All the other campaign chores, Maddox did them himself. He wrote his own press releases, stuffed his own envelopes and wrote his own speeches.

In preparing a campaign brochure, Maddox took a package of material to a trusted, former aide and asked him to put together an "attack piece" that not only pointed up his previous record, but also represented a challenge to his opponents. Once the former aide examined the material, however, he could see it contained the same old positions Maddox had espoused in the 1960s: the fight against Communism, school integration and the "socialist, power-mad politicians in Washington." This was 1990. Communism was dead but not quite buried. There was no "one world government," as Maddox once predicted. There was no threat of black revolution. The integration of Georgia schools was now a fact of life. The campaign strategies, which had worked in 1966, were no longer viable in 1990.

As diplomatically as possible, the former aide tried to convince Maddox of this stark reality. "Run on local issues," he suggested. "Talk about giving Georgia children a 'world class education'; about a new generation of industrial development, of lower taxes and better use of those that are already being collected. Tell the people how honest you were when you were governor and what you did to bring about improvements in schools, prisons, industrial development and how you worked to clean up corruption in places like Ludowici and McIntosh County. Those issues will get you votes."

Your opponents are calling for a lottery and increased trade with third world countries....Zell Miller wants to install a state lottery and use the proceeds to provide college educations for all those students who have a B average."

Andrew Young wants to sell Georgia products in Africa and other underdeveloped countries and that's mighty appealing to farmers, manufacturers and folks in the chicken business."

Although numerous friends and former supporters hoped that Maddox would realize his difficulties and withdraw, none had the nerve to counsel him. Even if they could convince Maddox that he had no chance, it would have been useless. He missed politics too much. He was back on the campaign trail; he was back in his element and he intended to stay there.

When one reporter asked Maddox why he was doing it, Maddox replied, "Two years ago, I stated that, unless a conservative candidate with statewide recognition came forth, I would be that candidate. Nobody did, so here I am."

When questioned about his segregationist views, Maddox knew immediately it was no longer a viable issue. "I don't think the racial issue ought to be part of this campaign," he said. "And I don't think it will be unless it is promoted by the media itself."

In the contest, the earliest polls indicated that Zell Miller was the man to beat. For the first time in recent Georgia history, a black man, former Atlanta Mayor Andrew Young, was in the governor's race and held a solid grasp on second place in the polling. Bringing up the third and fourth positions in the five-man field were State Senator Roy Barnes of Mableton and state representative Lauren McDonald of Commerce. Maddox was listed last in the poll. What Hoke O'Kelley was in the 1966 primary, Maddox was in 1990. To make matters worse, Maddox's campaign budget was a mere pittance when compared to the other candidates. As of 2 June 1990, he had put together only $58,503, most of which had come out of his own pocket. That figure represented less than 1/60 of the amount raised by his opponent Zell Miller.

The previous fall, one newspaper columnist projected that Maddox would play the spoiler's role in the contest and referred to him as the "cockroach candidate."

Before anyone gets offended, that's not a personal aspersion, but a description of the kind of impact such a candidate has: it's not what he eats, it's what he messes up, he wrote.

Maddox, in less colorful terms, isn't a serious contender, but in a percentage game like the Democratic primary, he could hurt somebody else. Not Andrew Young...maybe Zell Miller, on the theory that one guy with name I.D. hurts another. But judging by last week's poll, Miller's [the poll's front-runner] the only other candidate who could afford to be hurt.

Miller himself, when informed of his former mentor's candidacy, agreed with the columnist's assessment: "Oh, that's fine (Maddox's entry into the race) with me," he said. "All he will do is help me by taking votes away from my opponents."

Despite the criticisms, the lack of a cohesive platform, a severe shortage of campaign funds and the fact that segregation was a dead issue, Maddox pressed on in his quest. As always, he said his biggest enemy was the press and he referred to the *Atlanta Journal* as the "blue streak fish wrapper." Also, reminiscent of old, he took some shots at his opponents, especially his former pupil Zell Miller. At an Atlanta Optimist Club luncheon in March, Maddox commented that Miller was "the first lieutenant governor in history to get a state bank charter when other people paid a million dollars and couldn't get one."

Although Maddox had said from the outset that race had no place in the campaign, reporters refused to let him forget his segregationist past. During one interview, after Maddox recalled his earlier days as a member of the John Birch Society, a reporter asked: "How many blacks and Jews are Birchers, a group that has long fought being labeled racist and anti-Semitic?" Suddenly Maddox's face started to take on the color of Georgia red clay. "What has that got to do with my campaign?!," he shouted, louder this time. "You promote this racial thing in the media, and black and white political leaders use it as a ploy. And not for the benefit of blacks and whites! I don't want it to be part of my campaign!"

In another question-and-answer session, a reporter asked Maddox: "Gov. Maddox, as you look back, do you think that segregation has or ever had any merit, and did you think that you would ever live to see the day in which Andy Young would be leading you 7-to-1 in a statewide poll?" Maddox didn't explode this time. "That's a question you probably aren't going to ask the other candidates," he noted. "I was born...in a segregated society. The city of Atlanta licensed my restaurant to serve whites only, and I abided by it, and the president of the United States and the Supreme Court said that we had the right to be 'separate, but equal.' I didn't create it. I was born into it. The media keeps talking about race, race, race. It doesn't have anything to do with my candidacy, but the news media keeps bringing it up…. It was wrong when whites practiced it; it is wrong now when you have affirmative action and job quotas in the other direction."

In the race, front-runner Zell Miller consistently called for a state lottery to help finance education improvements, a merit raise for the state teachers and a trust fund for the university system's construction program. Miller explained that his campaign strategist James Carville had suggested a poll, which showed most Georgians, wanted a state lottery to provide non-tax revenue. "I polled and [Carville] was right," Miller recalled recently. "The people of Georgia wanted a lottery and they didn't care what the money was used for. I found my new source for education programs and I found an issue that would set me apart from the other candidates…. With the lottery, I had the issue I was looking for."

Andrew Young, assured of the vast majority of the state's black votes, hammered away at economic issues and called for new jobs and industrial development for the state's depressed areas. A familiar line in his campaign speeches was "I'm the only candidate who can create the economic growth that will hold down taxes…."

Roy Barnes played the role of the progressive and called for environmental clean up, reducing the teacher-student ratios and cutting waste in government, especially in the state's pension system. "The policies and politics of old will disappear only when you decide you have had enough and are ready for a change," he said.

Meanwhile, Lauren McDonald called upon voters to elect a man who would give Georgia a new name. McDonald said, if elected, he would give Georgia the reputation of being tough on crime, soft on senior citizens and bullish on new industrial development. "I want Georgia to have the reputation of having a governor who does what he says he'll do," McDonald told prospective voters.

An *Atlanta Journal-Constitution* poll released on 29 April projected that Maddox would receive an estimated 3% of the likely votes, while Miller and Young remained in first and second places respectively. One of the people polled, a 70-year-old Sylvania woman who asked to remain anonymous, mentioned Maddox as her favorite in the race. In explanation, however, she added, "I only said his name because it came to mind. I don't know much about politics, but he seems like a nice man."

Others in the state were not so kind. Billy McKinney, a black house member from Atlanta, commented that the only votes Maddox would get would be his old segregation cronies. "The only people who will vote for him are the Ku Klux Klan, the White Citizens Council and people looking to take the state back to the 50s and 60s," McKinney said. Martin Luther King III, at the time a Fulton County Commissioner, said of Maddox's candidacy: "The Pickrick incident showed what the heart of the person really is." Finally, the Reverend Joseph Lowery, president of the Southern Christian Leadership Conference, commented, "He's a part of Georgia's history and I think that's the way it ought to remain."

When Georgians went to vote in the 17 July primary, the polls proved to be right on target. Miller came out as the top vote-getter and was thrown into an 7 August run-off with Young. The two conservatives, Barnes and McDonald, placed third and fourth. Maddox, as predicted, had no effect on the outcome.

After reviewing results of the primary, political pundits were quick to conclude that the race issue had assumed a totally new role in Georgia politics. Most agreed that, while racial divisions still existed, the old crude, segregationist name-calling days were gone forever. In early August, only three days before the Miller-Young run-off was scheduled, Young confirmed this view in discussing his experiences in the 1990 race before a group of black ministers. "I haven't had anybody call me any name, and I haven't had anybody shoot me a bird. That's represents a new day in Georgia."

Probably the best measure of the state's racial division in 1990 grew out of a comparison between the votes Maddox and arch-segregationist J. B. Stoner had each received in the 1990 primary and its 1974 counterpart. In 1990, Maddox as a gubernatorial candidate and Stoner as a candidate for the lieutenant governor's office, polled about 31,000 votes each in their separate races. Both ran strongest in the rural areas of north and South Georgia. In those same areas, Young polled the poorest. In the 1974 primary, however, Maddox garnered more than 300,000 votes while Stoner won 74,000 in an earlier bid for the lieutenant governor's office. The segregationist bloc vote had shrunk dramatically in sixteen years.

From a historical perspective, the 1990 race placed Maddox within a gallery of colorful southern politicians who had attempted to re-win the state house after long absences. This gallery included Alabama's James Folsom, Mississippi's Ross Barnett, Louisiana's Earl Long and Arkansas' Orval Faubus.

With his 1990 run, Maddox was trying to become only the third governor during the twentieth century to re-win the state house after holding it twenty years earlier. The only two who actually accomplished the feat were Kentucky's "Happy" Chandler (in 1935 and 1955) and Oklahoma's Henry Bellmon (1963 and 1986). Faubus had won an astounding six consecutive two-year terms (1954-1967) as governor, but failed in 1986 to re-win the state house in a poorly financed attempt.

Recently, Zell Miller, the former Maddox pupil who won the first of his two terms as governor in the 1990 race, commented, "It was sad seeing Governor Maddox in the 1990 race. It was like seeing a good athlete that was past his prime. After it was over, I think that way deep down he wished he had not run again."

Chapter 13
Maddox for President

"I never had a better friend in elective office than Alabama Governor George Wallace."
—Maddox on his alliance with Wallace

For almost one hundred years after the Civil War, the concept of segregation—separation of the black and white races as different social, political and cultural groups—was firmly embedded in the hearts and minds of most white southerners. From the earliest days of Reconstruction through the Jim Crow era of the late 1940s and early 1950s, segregation was as integral to white southern culture as collard greens, cotton fields and magnolia trees. Each generation passed on to the next a set of values which taught that blacks were ignorant, lazy, socially inept and generally inferior to whites. African Americans had their own way of life and their own set of values, fathers taught their sons, and they were forever destined to remain separate from white people. These teachings were part and parcel of what many historians referred to as "the Southern Burden."

By the early 1960s, however, thousands of young baby boomers—offspring of the New South's post-war, well-to-do middle class—returned home fresh from college with a host of hawkishly-liberal ideas. Among them was the belief that African Americans and deserved a higher place in

Southern society. In spite of such "radical" ideas, most old guard southerners—forever faithful to the teachings of their forefathers—refused to
be swayed and, for the next twenty years, found expression for their
beliefs in a long line of segregationist politicians.

As the two best-known segregationists of the 1960s, it was only natural that Lester Maddox and George Wallace would become personal
friends and political allies. Long before Maddox ever ran for governor of
Georgia, he was a great admirer of George Wallace. Maddox liked
Wallace's fiery oratory, his formidable courage, and his sense of rightness
and justness which he brought to the segregationist cause. In virtually
every case, he found Wallace's outlook on government totally identical to
his own. They both wanted to "send 'em a message," as Wallace proposed
in his campaigns for president.

During his 1964 presidential campaign, Wallace's fiery speeches on
what's wrong with America echoed what Maddox had been saying for
years: the common man was fed up with the federal government and its
repressive ways. No longer would middle America, the "silent majority"
which later elected Richard Nixon, stand idly and except whatever their
federal government handed them. They deplored the Great Society and its
endless give-away programs. They were tired of seeing their children
bused to classes far from home and angry when their schools were closed
as a result of forced integration. In Maddox's eyes, Wallace was the man
history had decreed to get the federal government of the backs of
Southerners.

A full two years before the Pickrick closed, Maddox had become a
member of the extreme ultra-conservative White Citizens Council and
voiced his views on government frequently at the organization's various
events throughout Georgia. A persistent theme of his speeches was
"...What Georgia needs is a George Wallace in Atlanta and the state capitol and in the state as a whole." In May of 1964, when President Lyndon
Johnson came to Atlanta to speak, Maddox was one of three men who
hired a plane to fly a banner overhead which read: "Wallace for
President."

By late 1964, Maddox had channeled his pro-Wallace sentiments into
more mainstream political forms. While Wallace campaigned in the 1964
presidential primaries in Wisconsin, Maryland and Indiana, Maddox
founded and headed up a group called Georgia Democrats for Unpledged

Electors. After Wallace bowed out of the race, however, Maddox swung his support to Republican Barry Goldwater and renamed the group Democrats for Goldwater. Maddox knew exactly what his political ideals were. He was looking for someone to champion them.

Shortly after the 1964 presidential election, Maddox lobbied the Georgia General Assembly for an invitation to have Wallace address a joint session. Governor Sanders, however, noting that the legislature was in special session to amend the constitution, argued that politics should not become a part of the proceedings and actively moved to block the Wallace invitation. Afterward, Maddox charged that Sanders "future effectiveness as governor is nil" and launched a second effort to obtain an invitation for Wallace to speak, this time for a breakfast speech to the legislature.

When Wallace canceled out on the breakfast address, Maddox formed still another pro-Wallace organization which he dubbed "The Patriotic Americans." Once founded, Maddox announced that the new group's first festivity would be a Fourth of July political rally at Atlanta's Lakewood Park with the Alabama governor as keynote speaker. This time, Wallace accepted and, flanked by a bevy of the South's foremost segregationists including Maddox, Ross Barnett, Roy Harris and leaders of the Alabama and Georgia KKK organizations, Wallace delivered a fiery speech denouncing forced integration and federal oppression.

During the following spring of 1965 when the civil rights unrest in Selma was at its height, Maddox picketed the old Atlanta federal courthouse to protest federal intervention in the south Alabama town. One of his signs read, "Treason is the Reason! DOWN with Johnson, the Justice Department, Socialism and Communism—UP with Wallace, Free Enterprise, Capitalism, Liberty, Private Rights and America."

By the fall of 1966, however, while Maddox campaigned for governor of Georgia as a Democrat, his pro-Wallace stance began to raise questions among party loyalists as to where his true sentiments lay. In September, while Maddox was campaigning against Callaway in the general election, a group of Fulton County Democratic nominees asked Maddox who he planned to support in the 1968 presidential race. "I'm going to support the [Democratic] ticket," Maddox answered. "I will not support George Wallace if he is not the nominee."

Maddox's announcement would be the first in a long series of reversals on the loyalty question between Wallace and the Democratic party. On one hand, he wanted to give every appearance that he was faithful to the party under whose aegis he had been elected. On the other hand, he could never totally renounce his love of Wallace's down home ideals.

After being elected as governor in January 1967, Maddox was now imbued with political clout. No longer was he a side-line player. He had a "bully" pulpit, one from which he could make things happen. He moved quickly to ally himself and the Georgia governor's office with his hero George Wallace.

On 16 January, less than two weeks after he was elected governor, Maddox sent a delegation of five Georgia legislators to Montgomery to attend the inauguration of Lurleen Wallace, George Wallace's wife, as Alabama's new governor. Since Alabama law prohibited a governor from succeeding himself, Mrs. Wallace became a candidate and was elected as a stand-in for her husband. During the inaugural festivities, Wallace welcomed the Georgia delegation with open arms and, according to most observers, the Georgia representatives received a warmer reception than all the other out-of-state attendees.

Slowly but surely, the Maddox-Wallace bond was being cemented, but the national Democrats had no intention of letting it go unnoticed. When Governor Maddox visited President Johnson in the White House on 2 February 1967, they spoke privately for some fifteen minutes on several issues. When Maddox emerged, he told reporters the "national Democratic party is big enough for all views," and, with that comment, Georgia Democrats cheered with the hope that Maddox's heart and mind was now with the Democratic Party rather than Wallace. But it would be a short-lived hope.

Three weeks later, on 28 February, Maddox proudly invited Governor Lurleen Wallace and her husband to speak to a joint session of the Georgia General Assembly. Earlier, he had pleaded with legislators for a Wallace appearance. Now, as governor, his will carried the weight of political power. After Mrs. Wallace delivered a short, mild speech, Wallace himself took to the podium and poured forth a fiery oration denouncing a host of mutual Wallace-Maddox enemies including the Atlanta newspapers, the US Supreme Court, school desegregation guidelines and unrelenting federal oppression. Party loyalists were confused again.

Two weeks later, the state's true Democrats were heartened again when Vice President Hubert Humphrey came to Atlanta to meet with Maddox. At first, Maddox refused to meet with Humphrey. He distrusted anyone that close to Lyndon Johnson. Besides that, Humphrey was a regular target of Maddox's Pickrick ads and speeches. Finally, an aide who knew and was sympathetic to Humphrey convinced Maddox that it would be bad political form to snub the nation's vice president and, after extensive coaxing, Maddox finally agreed to meet with Humphrey. The meeting took place, not in his office, but at the governor's mansion. Following an hour-long chat on the mansion's porch, the two men strolled across the mansion grounds while photographers snapped photos of Humphrey holding Maddox's arm as if he was the Georgia governor's high school escort. After the meeting, Humphrey reiterated for reporters the same Democratic party line which had grown out of Maddox's earlier meeting with Johnson. "The Democratic Party is like a big house," Humphrey said. "There are plenty of rooms for everybody…"

The Humphrey visit had been an obvious attempt to bring Maddox within the National Democratic Party's fold, but two weeks later, he was back to his old Wallace ways. In an interview with *Meet the Press*, Maddox said, as a third party candidate, the ex-Alabama governor could possibly win all twelve of Georgia's electoral votes in 1968. Maddox explained however, he had a definite distaste for splinter political parties and noted that, if the Wallace-Maddox brand of conservatism was strong enough to win an election, "then we're strong enough to be a dominant voice in our present party."

Maddox, as ever the rebellious outsider, was secretly excited about a third party movement with Wallace as the candidate. In his speeches, he repeatedly reminded voters that he had not supported a Democrat since Harry Truman. In fact, he openly admitted that a Republican, Dwight Eisenhower, was the best president in modern times. As a young man, he cut his teeth on Roosevelt and the Works Projects Administration and found it not to his liking. Johnson and his Great Society was nothing more than a repeat of Roosevelt and the New Deal. He bemoaned the fact that, in the Democratic party, nobody recognized "his" issues. As a result, Maddox took an even harder stand for Wallace while giving the appearance of loyalty to the Democrats.

Finally, at a 1967 Christmas party for Democrats, an Atlanta newsman, trying to pin down Maddox's true loyalty, baited him with: "You
intend to go to the national convention and fight for what you want.... If
you don't get something you can support, barring a bizarre development,
you plan to come home and keep your mouth shut...." "That's my
plans," Maddox said flatly, adding "If they put little Bobby (New York
Senator Robert Kennedy) on there, I don't know what I'll do."

Although the third party movement that swept the country in the
1960s has its origins in the South, it was not without support in other
parts of the nation. George Wallace's admonition to Americans to "send
'em [Washington] a message" was a popular theme in the wheat fields of
Nebraska, the auto assembly lines in Detroit, the shrimp boats along the
Atlantic coast and in the tobacco fields of North Carolina. There was a
definite appeal for Wallace ideals outside the South. Wallace proved that
during the 1964 primaries. He fooled the experts when he rang up surprising totals in Wisconsin, Indiana and Maryland. Maddox was
confident that Wallace was the candidate to bear their standard in 1968.
The question was whether Wallace should do it as a Democrat or an
independent.

In the spring of 1968, Wallace, Maddox and Mississippi Governor
John Bell Williams met secretly in a Montgomery motel room. While the
actual facts of the meeting may never be known, one newspaper reported
that the three men agreed to go to the Democratic convention in August
and place Wallace's name in nomination. The plan, as reported, was for
Williams to make the nomination and for Maddox to second it. The
Atlanta newspaper article that reported the meeting dubbed the plan the
"southern strategy" for the 1968 Democratic convention.

On 2 April 1968, apparently as part of the plan's design, Maddox
launched a move to draft Wallace for a spot on the national Democratic
party ticket. "I want to call upon the American people this morning who
would like...a restoration of constitutional government...a return to
common sense government...and quit financing communism around the
world...to call on their Democratic leaders to name George Wallace as a
candidate on the national Democratic ticket." Wallace is the "only hope
of the Democratic Party to stay in the White House," Maddox said.

A month later, Maddox began to openly wear a "Wallace" button on
his lapel. Maddox had third party petitions for a Wallace presidential run

spread out on a table in the Governor's mansion for those who wanted to sign.

If a visitor saw the button, however, and commented, "Oh, are you supporting Wallace for President?" Maddox would quickly flip the Wallace button over and answer, "Oh, no, I'm not supporting Wallace." He would then wink and change the subject.

The months of May, June and July 1968 were the test period for the Wallace-Maddox-Williams "southern strategy." During those months, the political facts indicated there was nowhere near sufficient grass-roots support to get Wallace on the Democratic ticket at the convention. While the former Alabama governor would run well in the South and show surprising strength in the North and Midwest, the mere suggestion that he could ever be on the national ticket was little more than wishful thinking. The earlier "southern strategy," therefore, was out the window.

In early August, Wallace announced that he would be a candidate for president on the American Independent Party ticket. After Wallace's not-so-surprising announcement, Maddox announced that he was considering a run for the Democratic nomination himself. Their joint efforts had failed to gain momentum; now they would try their luck separately. This fall-back move, however, would result in a new wrinkle in the Wallace-Maddox relationship.

Two days after Maddox announced his candidacy, Wallace publicly stated that Maddox's chance of winning the Democratic nomination was "virtually nil." Well aware that, as a segregationist, he was politically stronger than Maddox, Wallace commented, "If Governor Maddox could get the nomination, I probably already would have been drafted by the Democratic Party. "In the final analysis," he added, confident of Maddox's ultimate loyalty, "Governor Maddox and I will be on the same side in November."

When asked if Maddox could possibly be his running AIP running mate, Wallace said no. The former Alabama governor told reporters that he and Maddox had discussed the matter and both agreed that his running mate should be someone outside the South.

On 19 August 1968, two days after Wallace's discouraging words, Maddox called a morning press conference at the capitol and announced he was indeed offering himself as a candidate for the national Democratic ticket. In a speech which accompanied the announcement, Maddox lashed out at "social experimentation," "law-defying criminals," and "special interest groups." The pronouncement was met with shouts of approval from staunch Maddox supporters. The media and most mainstream Georgians, however, greeted the announcement with shock and dismay.

The very same day, an editorial appeared In the *Atlanta Constitution* which was one of the most momentous occasions in Maddox's political life. Eugene Patterson, the newspaper's editorial director who had lambasted Maddox numerous times as a "racist bigot," rushed in to defend the former restaurateur against the Wallace statements.

"...The snake oil pitch of George Wallace may be stripped of some of its overlay of cunning before his good friend Maddox finishes telling it like it is..."

"The governor of Georgia possesses little of the Alabamian's silken shrewdness and deceptiveness in debate. Old Lester didn't just stand in the Pickrick door. He got a gun, and his boy got an ax handle, and he didn't care who took a picture of him defying the law..."

"So an element of undoubted honesty is introduced with the Maddox candidacy. He is no slick southern demagogue with eyes like a water moccasin and tongue like a fork. Naked of camouflage, he faces 1968 television like a naughty child, severely limited in his capacity to understand what's cooking, but mischievously willing to get in there and make mudpies..."

The editorial concluded that, while Maddox's candidacy was "crippled," in the final analysis, his chances of getting the Democratic nomination were equally as good as Wallace's. Never before had either of the Atlanta newspapers tried to defend Lester Maddox. With phases like "uncalculated clowning," "with the shuck off" and "one who does not disguise his limitations because he cannot," the newspaper showed true honesty toward the man.

As promised, in late August, Maddox put together a group of hand-picked delegates and set off for the Democratic Convention in Chicago. Before leaving Atlanta, he said he was very concerned about the imminent nomination of Hubert Humphrey and he wanted to send a message to the "socialists and power-mad politicians who control the Democratic party."

From the very first, the seating of the Maddox-led delegation was in doubt. In briefs filed at a subcommittee meeting of the Democratic Party Credentials Committee, the Maddox delegation was challenged on the basis of racial composition, bias against urban party members, loyalty to the national party and the method by which the delegation was selected. The challenges were filed by the Democratic Party Forum and a group led by Georgia State Representative Julian Bond which called itself "Loyal National Democrats."

The Forum's petition stressed doubts about the party loyalty of the Maddox delegation. Bond's group questioned both the method by which the delegates were selected as well as its racial make-up. First, the Bond group explained, the Maddox delegation was appointed rather than elected. Secondly, its racial make-up was only 2 percent Negro while blacks represented 23 percent of Georgia's electorate. On the loyalty question, Maddox himself, as well as six other delegates were challenged for allegedly supporting either Republican Barry Goldwater or Independent candidate George Wallace in the past.

While Chicago police battled violent demonstrators outside the convention walls, a series of bitter charges and counter-charges were exchanged before the convention's credentials committee between leaders of the three groups. After two days of wrangling, the Maddox delegation was about to be turned away from the convention.

On Sunday, 21 August, Maddox told reporters that, if his delegation leaves, it would be pointless to continue his quest for the party's nomination. "I can't foresee carrying on without our delegation even being here," he said. The following day, seeing that the delegation had no chance of being seated, Maddox resigned as a delegate and as a candidate. Later, Maddox said of the experience, "I never felt for an instant that my candidacy would meet with success, but I felt strongly that in failing I would cause the socialist and power-mad politicians in charge of the Democratic party...to react in such a manner as to let all America see how ugly, prejudiced, cowardly and deceitful the [party] leadership... is. In that sense, my effort was a success."

After the convention, exactly as Wallace had predicted, Maddox campaigned hard for him as an independent candidate. In Oklahoma City, Maddox told one group, "By following the blood-and-tear-stained path charted by socialists, Communists, anarchists, draft card burners, traitors, flag desecrators, looters, rioters, punks, pinks and polished politicians, these 'great leaders' of our two major parties have made it possible, even probable, that on January 1, 1969, George Wallace will be sitting in the White House." In early November, however, when Americans cast their ballots, Wallace finished third with 9.9 million votes.

From its inception, Maddox's attempt to win the Democratic nomination for president had been a source for jokes among the nation's political elitists. In the fall of 1968, Maddox's notoriety as a possible presidential candidate inspired an absurdist play titled "Red, White and Maddox." The production, which featured Maddox as the main character, was an irreverent take-off on Maddox and his down-home, ultra-conservative political philosophies. At the play's conclusion, Maddox has been elected president and he announces to God he has "finally gotten rid of all them vermin. All them hippies and yippies and race-mixing agitators." The production was so popular that, in the spring of 1969, it ran for forty-one performances on Broadway.

By the summer of 1971, Maddox desperately wanted Wallace to send more than a "message" in the 1972 presidential election. He knew, however that, as an independent, Wallace could never possibly get elected. With that in mind, Maddox designed a new plan for Wallace, one that would return him to the Democratic party. Soon thereafter, Maddox placed an urgent call to Wallace and asked to meet him at the Montgomery, Alabama airport.

The following day, after Maddox's plane touched down at the Montgomery airport, his security people whisked him across the tarmac to a limousine where Wallace was sitting with his new bride, Cornelia Wallace, a niece of former Alabama Governor James Folsom.

After greetings and introductions, Maddox turned to politics: "I explained to Governor Wallace that, in his 1968 bid as an AIP candidate, he had not only received very little press coverage, but most of it had been negative. If he ran again as an AIP candidate in 1972, I explained that it would be the same way again." Wallace emphasized that he had no intention of leaving the American Independent Party, but urged Maddox to continue. "If you leave the AIP and seek the Democratic Party's nomination for president, you'll get more attention and more press in one month than you received during a year as an AIP candidate. As a Democrat, you would almost assuredly win several southern states, including North

Carolina, Florida, Georgia and Alabama. Already, you've proven you have strong support in Indiana, Maryland and Wisconsin...." After a moment of silence, Cornelia, who had been listening to the conversation, turned to her husband. "George, I think it's an excellent idea," she said. "I think we should do it."

Despite his wife's urging, Wallace remained hesitant. He explained to Maddox that he needed time to consider how best to withdraw as an AIP candidate. He did not want to alienate the supporters who had followed him to the AIP. During the spring of the following year, Wallace took Maddox's suggestion to heart and announced that he would indeed seek the Democratic nomination for president and, in mid-April, he and his wife Cornelia took to the campaign trail. The following month, while campaigning in the Maryland primary, Wallace was felled by an assassin's bullet in the parking lot of a Laurel, Maryland shopping center.

When Maddox heard of the assassination attempt, he, his wife and a former aide who lived in Washington, rushed to the Silver Springs, Maryland hospital where Wallace had undergone emergency surgery. The former Alabama governor was in critical condition, heavily sedated, and under 24 hour surveillance. Outside Wallace's hospital room, Maddox was met by Cornelia Wallace and the Wallace children. After Maddox and Mrs. Wallace talked for some minutes, Maddox sought admission into Wallace's room to visit his political ally, but Wallace's condition was too tenuous to permit visitors. "Tell him we're praying for him," Maddox told the governor's wife. "The country needs him. He's got to pull through."

As Maddox boarded a plane at Washington National Airport to return to Atlanta, he reminisced about his close friendship with Wallace. As the last two last Southern segregationists, they had spent the almost ten years trying to bring their cause to the national political arena. They had pooled their resources, compared notes and conferred endlessly to the achievement of that goal. Now, with Wallace laying paralyzed and near death, Maddox knew that their joint efforts were, in all likelihood, at an end.

With the arrival of spring in 1976, Wallace, who had endured more than ten operations, was functioning again as a full-time politician and acting like a possible national candidate. The previous year, he had been elected to an unprecedented third term as governor of Alabama and was so popular in his native state that his political foes no longer bothered to oppose him. Although both legs were paralyzed and he was in constant pain, Wallace felt that he still had a huge Southern and national following and promised the American Independent Party he would be their candidate in the 1976 presidential race. Wallace asked AIP officials to schedule its convention later than usual so he would have time to prepare himself for the rigors of a nationwide political campaign. Party officials agreed and began formulating a campaign and fund-raising strategy geared to Wallace.

Sometime in late July, however, Wallace changed his mind. He felt physically unable to meet the strenuous demands of another presidential campaign. The AIP, of course, was disappointed. The membership had put all its hopes and resources on Wallace's candidacy and, with their champion out of the race, had no standard-bearer.

The party looked strenuously for a replacement for Wallace. Finding none, they turned to Lester Maddox. After several discussions with party leaders, Maddox offered himself as a candidate and, at the party's 27 August convention, he was nominated. During his acceptance speech, Maddox likened the American Independent Party to the signers of the declaration of Independence and said, "It's not how our campaign will go, it's that I hope I don't disappoint you."

At a news conference afterward, Maddox said: "I'm a segregationist, and you are too, most likely. A segregationist is a man who has enough pride in his own race and other races to want to keep them from being desegregated."

Shortly after the nomination, Ned Young of Brunswick who was serving as Maddox's unpaid AIP campaign manager, told newsmen that his long-time friend faced an incredible uphill battle. Young said Maddox had set off on the campaign trail with a budget of only $35,000, two telephone lines, an office on Atlanta's 14th Street and several boxes of American flags. "We don't have a first-rate campaign here because we don't have a first rate budget," he told one reporter. "I was looking through the contribution cards the other day and the single biggest contribution we have is $500."

Maddox's campaign would have been much easier, Young noted, if Wallace had not reneged on his promise. First, the AIP convention was set late at Wallace's behest, causing Maddox's to enter the race much later than usual. Also, the party's strategy had been geared to Wallace, not Maddox, and once the campaign began, their new candidate was left to his own devices. "So there we sat with nothing," Young said. "No money, no organization. No office. No staff. Nothing." In a last-minute flurry after the nomination, therefore, Young said he and Maddox had thrown together the campaign the best way they knew how. Even the campaign's pleas for Secret Service protection of Maddox were ignored.

Despite the problems, Young anticipated that Maddox would have a measurable effect on the race. "They started this election with everybody thinking the South was going for Carter because he was from Georgia," Young commented. "But Lester Maddox is also from Georgia and he might take some of the votes Carter is counting on."

Over the next few months, the relationship between Maddox and Wallace would be changed forever. In late September, George Wallace endorsed Carter, Maddox's arch-enemy, for president. Maddox viewed this as the ultimate betrayal of their long-standing alliance and wasted no time in attacking his old hero. "It's sad for him [Wallace] because he'll be miserable spending the rest of his life around people who hate him," Maddox said of the endorsement. "If he lost a tire on his wheelchair, those people wouldn't put it back on."

In the presidential election the following November, Carter squeezed out a narrow victory over Gerald Ford. As an Independent, Maddox polled slightly more that 170,000 votes, a far cry from the 9.9 million Wallace received in 1968. In many ways, though, Maddox's 1976 AIP campaign was part of his revenge on his old enemy Jimmy Carter. Again and again, Maddox had launched personal attacks on Carter who, he felt, mistreated and abused him during his term as lieutenant governor. In exacting his revenge on Carter, however, he had lost his relationship with Wallace.

The true historical significance of Maddox's 1976 presidential run was that it signaled the death of segregation as an political issue, not only in the South, but also in America culture. In Georgia, segregation politics died as an issue during the 1974 governor's race. On the national level, Maddox's defeat in the presidential election of 1976 marked the final time a segregationist's name appeared on the ballot. The surviving American Independent Party continued as a force in American politics, but its officials and its candidates no longer flew a segregation banner. Maddox would be the last national politician to call for racial separation.

Many observers say Wallace's terrible injury and subsequent confinement to a wheelchair threw him into a state of introspective soul-searching that eventually caused him to recant his deeply-held segregationist beliefs. Despite the conversion of Maddox's long-time ally, Maddox never renounced his own views on segregation. To this day, he espouses the benefits of segregation regardless of its political death as an issue.

Although years have passed since the Maddox-Wallace alliance ended, Maddox still has a certain nostalgic fondness for the Alabama governor. More than anything else, he feels personally responsible for Arthur Bremer's bullet that struck Wallace's spine and left him paralyzed for life. "My thoughts, since the horrible attempted assassination," Maddox said recently, "has been that had he not switched parties, his lower profile as the AIP candidate may not have attracted the gunman."

"Life has a funny way of coming back to haunt you," Maddox said recently. "As long as I live, I'll always feel bad about it."

Chapter 14

The Loss of Virginia

"And we did love and honor and obey until death did us part..."
—Maddox eulogizes his beloved Virginia, July 1997

For more than sixty-one years, Virginia Cox Maddox lived in the shadow of her famous husband. During the first two decades of their marriage, she had given birth to two daughters and two sons for him. While he was out politicking and serving in public office, Virginia was the family CEO for whatever business or businesses they owned at the time. During his term as governor, Virginia served as his first lady, acted as hostess at official functions, played the mother role and still found time to serve her family. Even after his eight years in public office, Virginia continued to be there to mind the stores and play wife, mother, housekeeper and cook while he had the heart attack, dabbled in real estate and toured with musician Bobby Lee Fears.

Throughout those sixty-one years, Maddox intuitively sensed that his wife had some sort of mysterious medical condition, which her doctors failed to diagnose. "After our first daughter was born in 1938," Maddox recalled recently, "Virginia developed a kidney infection and started seeing doctors and taking drugs. Every few months she would go back to the doctor for the kidney infection and get a new prescription. Before I knew it, she was taking seven or eight different medications. When the second daughter was born two years later, she went into a deep depression and doctors prescribed still more drugs.

By 1959, she was taking 11 different drugs for a long list of ailments ranging from a kidney infection to headaches and depression. Besides the prescription drugs, Maddox said, she was constantly taking BC Headache Powders. "After the doctor looked at all the drugs she was taking, he said several of them were lupus-inducing. Despite that information, none of the doctors who were caring for her suggested she might have lupus," Maddox said.

In the fall of 1984, a friend of Maddox at the capitol, a photographer named Bill Birdsong, told him about a woman he knew in Carrollton who had lupus. When Birdsong described the woman's illness to Maddox, he revealed that Virginia could be suffering from he same disease. Several days later, he took Virginia to her doctor and asked him to test her for lupus. He did. The results came back positive.

Lupus is an autoimmune, degenerative disease, doctors explained, which strikes specific organs, especially the joints, skin and kidneys, and causes severe injury to body tissue. At the time of the diagnosis doctors warned Maddox that, over the succeeding years, the disease would slowly but surely cause Virginia's body to waste away. The doctors proved all too correct. Maddox recalled, "Her last public appearance was on September 30, 1995, when Zell Miller pitched that 80th birthday party for me at the governor's mansion. By that time the disease had taken its toll. She was losing weight. She had little energy and her physical strength was down to almost nothing. When I told her that Zell had planned the party for us, she didn't want to go but she agreed to do it for me. Finally, I managed to get her dressed and down to the governor's mansion. When we got back home, she was so exhausted she slept almost twelve hours trying to regain her strength."

Over the years, Maddox watched his beloved Virginia waste away. "At the time of the diagnosis, the disease was already in her kidneys and her joints. Then, as time went on, it moved into her stomach and liver and intestines and other organs. Finally it broke her body down from 155 pounds to 70 pounds. It broke her arms, pelvis, shoulders and ribs down to almost nothing. The muscles fell off her bones. The skin on her arms, legs and elbows would break at the slightest touch."

By 13 November 1990, as doctors had predicted, Virginia's condition had deteriorated to the point that she was an invalid. Immediately, Maddox prepared himself to begin taking care of his wife full-time. "It was then that I started canceling all of my speaking engagements and only on rare occasions would I accept one. I wanted to spend as much time as I could with Virginia. I also discontinued virtually all of my business, civic and social activities so that I could become her round-the-clock nurse, cook, housekeeper and shopper."

Despite the tremendous physical and emotional commitment, Maddox took up the role of caretaker gladly. "What a blessing I was given to be able to care for the person I loved most on this earth. She had cared so well for me in the past when I was sick or injured. It was during those years that our love and affection for each other grew to new depths and new heights and our commitment grew stronger than it had been at any time during the previous years of our marriage."

No sooner had Maddox fallen into the routine of being his wife's nurse, cook and housekeeper than a new tragedy struck. One night just before Christmas of 1990, Virginia awoke in the wee hours and told her husband she smelled smoke. Once out of bed, Maddox started inspecting the house and discovered smoke billowing out of electrical junction box in the basement. Quickly he moved to get Virginia out of bed and into a wheelchair. "By the time I got to the front door, the heat was so intense that the glass was popping out," Maddox recalled. "Once I got Virginia out on the porch, I ran back inside to call 911."

"Virginia was scared to death out on our porch with the fire so close. I was afraid she was going to roll out of that wheelchair and off the porch. I should never have left her out there. Anyway, when I got back outside, a passing motorist who had stopped helped me get her and the wheelchair off the porch. She was bare-footed in her gown when I finally made it out into the yard with her." Six minutes later, firemen arrived and extinguished the blaze. Damage to the ranch-style home was estimated at $80,000.

After the fire, Maddox and his wife lived with one of their sons for a week, then moved into an apartment. In April 1991, after the house had been repaired, the couple moved back into the family home. Maddox recalled, "I didn't want her to go to a nursing home and neither did she. So I cooked for her, dressed her, bathed her, touched her, talked to her, loved her and fed her. Instead of buying orange, carrot and apple juice, I would make it fresh and give it to her. She was supposed to get Ensure seven days a week three times a day, but lots of times she didn't want it. Once a week, she wanted to go out and I would take her out to eat. Then I would take her to the beauty parlor as long as she was able to make the trip."

Maddox said he didn't realize she was having as serious brain problems. She got to the point she couldn't transpose figures on her checkbook. She couldn't write letters. She couldn't address envelopes. Sadly, she reached the point when she asked her doctor to recommend a physician who could help her improve her memory.

By mid-April of 1997, Virginia's health declined even further. Her children brought food, but she wouldn't eat it. She ate and drank only after Maddox pleaded with her to do so. She had lost so much weight, he was afraid she might die from starvation.

Ever the caring husband, Maddox went into the kitchen and started making juices for her. He knew there was something wrong, but not what. About midnight, Maddox carefully tucked his wife into bed. She went immediately to sleep. "Then, about three that morning, I felt something trembling in the bed, then it quit. I thought that maybe she was just turning over. About five minutes later, she started trembling again, then I realized she was having seizures. I got up and called the doctor, then I went back to check on her. Some thirty minutes later, she had another seizure, then another and another," Maddox remembered.

Shortly afterward, Maddox himself was admitted to the hospital. While he was gone, Virginia stopped taking her medication, stopped drinking her juices, and stopped eating her food. When Maddox returned home, she was so weak and infirm that she could not raise her head off her chest.

He immediately carried her to the hospital where she was examined and tested. The tests were not encouraging. Virginia's doctor told Maddox that he should not take her home. In late April 1997, he moved his wife to a nursing facility near their home so that she could receive around-the-clock nursing care.

Knowing that the first few nights away from home would be the hardest, Maddox remained at her bedside all that night and most of the following day. On the second night, before he left, he knelt by her bedside. "Babe," he whispered. "I want to thank you for marrying me all those years ago and for having stayed with me during all our years together." For a moment, Mrs. Maddox opened her eyes and smiled. "Thank you, Lester," she said softly. "We've had a wonderful life."

While Virginia remained in the nursing home, Maddox made daily visits to her bedside. He was there to attend to her personal needs, such as helping with her letters and arranging her biweekly beauty appointments. "A few weeks later, me, Virginia, her beautician and our minister had a circle of hands prayer at the nursing home," he recalled. "After the others had finished praying, Virginia continued. 'Dear Lord,' she prayed, 'please do something for me so I won't hurt my husband any more.'"

Over the next week, her condition grew worse and worse. She couldn't hold her head or her arms up. She pleaded with Maddox to take her home. She became disturbed when heard other people in the nursing home wailing and sobbing. She feared that she would finally reach that stage. On May 9, their 61st wedding anniversary, Maddox told the nurse he was taking her home. The nurse agreed.

Maddox bought a hospital bed and brought Virginia home, where he fed her liquid food every day and night. He even ate it myself because he didn't want to ask her to eat something he wouldn't eat. He had to grind up her medicine and mix it in her food to make it more palatable.

Over the next few days Virginia's condition worsened. One night, Maddox recalled he tried to help her out of a chair, but she was limp. She became less and less lucid. She cried as she fought the unbearable pain. Finally, Maddox said, he took his wife back to the nursing home because he could not care for her.

Back at the hospice, Maddox was asked to give his permission by signature to allow her to die. It was a terrible time for him. Five days later, Maddox told a reporter: "Virginia and I celebrated our 61st wedding anniversary last week. We'll never have another one."

On the night of 23 June 1997, Maddox and his children knew that the end was near. All afternoon and all evening, Maddox stayed by her bedside, talking, remembering old times and seeing that her needs were met. Finally, when he was ready to leave, he bent over her bed and said, "Babe, I've got to go, but I'll be back tomorrow morning as always." With that, he bent over and kissed her on the cheek.

As Maddox straightened up, his wife reached up a frail hand. He gently clasped it in his own. "I want you to do something for me," she said softly. "I want you to remember that there is someone in this place that loves you, always has and always will. Don't ever forget that."

At 10:35 the following morning, Maddox arrived back at her bedside. He knew her time was near. Her breathing became heavy and labored. Maddox said, "Finally I raised up and stepped back because I wanted to hide my grief. As I buried my face in my hands, she drew her last breath. She had waited for me to return to her before she died. She wanted me to be there when she passed away."

Doctors pronounced Virginia Cox Maddox dead at 10:39 A.M. "Heaven has gained and I have lost," Maddox told an Associated Press reporter during an interview that afternoon. "I'll never fully recover from it. I loved her from the first day I saw her sitting on the bicycle eating the ice cream on McMillan Street...."

Several weeks after his wife's death, Maddox wrote a short history of their marriage.

"Our marriage was not an easy one. Had it been, I honestly believe that we would have lost it. She was the kind, soft-spoken one, a gracious and gentle lady...and smart! She did a spectacular job of keeping her nose out of everybody's business but mine. That's where it should have been, although at times I questioned whether she might have been overdoing it.

"During all the years we lived and loved together, Virginia's first and foremost goal was to protect and love her family and home. I must say I purposely became the passive partner in matters relating to our home. It was her turf and I respected that. At home, she had the active, outgoing role while I played the reserved one. Away from home however, the roles became reversed and I played the outspoken extrovert while she assumed the role of the quiet, reserved one.

"Those differences did create some problems and disagreements, but nothing ever threatened our marriage. Throughout the marriage, I never mentioned the word divorce and certainly never sought out an attorney to implement one. I had made the commitment when we were married that, in sickness and in health, for richer or poorer, I would be with her until death did us part.

"Even on the few occasions my "Babe" mentioned divorce and talked of seeing a lawyer, I never paid her any attention, because I knew she really didn't believe in what she was saying....

"She had every reason in the world to leave me several times, but she stayed. She suffered as a result, but she never complained. After I left Atlantic steel, she followed me to Birmingham.

"My Virginia went through hell on earth leaving her family, her mother, her father, her sisters, church friends, neighbors to follow me to Birmingham. She rode in the moving van with our two daughters because I didn't have the money to send her on the bus. After we moved back to Atlanta, she was a single parent again while I traveled for the Navy department. Again she didn't complain and she stayed with me. She stuck with me during those times and I'll always love her for it. Thank God kept her vows because most of the problems in our marriage originated with me, not with her...."

In the past, Maddox was able to fight everything that stood in the path of his happiness. Now, when dealt the most crushing blow of his life, there was nothing he could do to defend himself from the sense of loss and overwhelming grief. A full month after her death, the still-distraught Maddox said, "She was my wife, my partner and my best friend for sixty-one years, one month, fourteen days, fifteen hours and forty-one minutes. That was the time that death needed to separate us."

Maddox's second love—politics—had been lost twenty-three years earlier. Now he had lost his first love—his precious Virginia. "The feeling he had for Virginia was very real and sincere," said Maddox friend J. O. Partain. "He absolutely worshipped her. And I think it bothered him that he knew he was taking too much time away from her. He told me in his later years that he often looked back with deep regret because he spent so much time in public service and so little time with her."

Whatever regrets Maddox may have about his marriage, he still struggles with the loss of his partner. "I do believe that all of us have reasons for wanting to live, but now my number one reason for wanting to live has been taken away. Presently, I am living in the most difficult and the saddest time of my life...."

Chapter 15
In His Own Words

"I'm the only person who ever picketed the White House and became governor."
Lester Maddox on picketing Lyndon Johnson and the White House in 1964

On 18 April 1997, Lester Maddox called the news media together in the rotunda of the state capitol for a rambling conference that centered on his health. The 81-year-old former governor said he had recently survived yet another operation, this one to relieve an intestinal blockage, and wanted to use the occasion to respond to the many inquiries he had received about his health.

Maddox handed reporters a six-page detailed chronology of his medical record, dating back to his youth. Among Maddox's maladies are cancer, a serious heart attack, stroke, intestinal problems, several other serious illnesses and an accident at his job in Birmingham that severely injured him. "I've been in a hole, in a ditch, a lot of times and I've always worked my way back up," he proudly announced to a bevy of reporters, television cameras and radio microphones.

Despite his misfortunes, Maddox remains physically strong and mentally alert. He often displays his strength by lifting his greeters off the floor and, much to their amazement, holding them aloft for several seconds.

Today, Lester Garfield Maddox spends his days quietly and alone at the Maddox home on Johnson Ferry Road in Marietta. The street on which Maddox lives is a busy suburban thoroughfare where traffic is heavy and highway noise very noticeable. In the front yard, Maddox has erected a hand-painted sign paying tribute to his beloved wife, Virginia, reminiscent of past signs deploring the death of free enterprise, and other exhibits that expressed Maddox's dislikes.

Sometimes, Maddox journeys downtown to visit friends or run errands. Since Virginia's death, he has applied himself to the job of running the household, grocery shopping, preparing his meals, and performing other household chores. Although it has been a decade since Maddox shared the political spotlight, he continues to receive scores of cards and letters from friends and supporters. He insists on responding to each individually, as opposed to acknowledging mail with form letters. He has found the task insurmountable, so he says he does the best he can to keep up with his correspondence with an old, outmoded typewriter he has owned for years. Some of his friends passed the hat at a luncheon celebrating his eighty-third birthday to purchase him a new computer.

Many years have passed since Maddox started his paid advertising column, "Pickrick Says" in the *Atlanta Journal.* But Maddox continues to use that method to communicate with his public. In February 1998, Maddox began a new paid advertising column in the Atlanta newspapers entitled, "STAY MARRIED." The ad reads, "Dear Moms and Dads. Help save lives, families and the USA. 'STAY MARRIED! (signed) Lester Maddox."

The former governor says the ads are a crusade to help save broken marriages and to persuade couples to adhere to their commitment. "If I can save one family and it doesn't cost but a few thousand dollars, then it's worth it," Maddox said.

Maddox also continues to send his friends periodic reports bearing Christmas messages, reports on his health and, sometimes, his comments on current events. In one such communication, Maddox wrote,

> Being tired, weary, worn, aged, diseased and alone, I seldom leave my home other than for trips to my physicians, the hospital, pharmacy, grocery store and to a cafeteria when I am unable to cook. But when I do get out I appreciate the number of people who say, "You sure look good."

However, when I hear it I usually think, "I hope and pray that they never look as good as I do" and feel they are probably hoping and praying the same. Then, there is another untruth never before objected to, and that is, whey you ask most old people how they feel, they seldom tell you the truth. It is usually "good' or fine."

Neither Maddox's personality nor his philosophy has changed over the years. He remains a racial segregationist, a critic of what he calls "socialistic" government and a proponent of "honesty, efficiency and morality" in government. He continues to abhor former presidents Lyndon Johnson and Jimmy Carter. He has also lost the love and admiration he once had for the late George Wallace, whom he once called "the best friend I've ever had in politics." But, despite his age and infirmities, Maddox has maintained his strong work ethic, his ornery independence, his devout religious beliefs and his unshakable faith in the American free enterprise system.

In an interview in his Marietta home, Maddox relived some of the incidents that marked his business and political career. Naturally, the conversation began with his experiences at his famous fried chicken restaurant, the Pickrick, not only his first real business success, but an enterprise that also launched his political career. He immediately launched into a detailed explanation of how he arrived at that name for his restaurant and why the name has endured for these many years:

One night, after I had been trying for months to find a name that nobody else had used, I found the term "pickwick" which was used in England about a lamp or something.

Picric is a bitter acid and, well, I couldn't use that. So I found the word "pick" which means to fastidiously pick out, to choose or select, and "rick," which means to pile up, to heap or to amass, like a hay rick. And so, I named my restaurant "Pickrick," advertised it as such and said, "If you'll picnic at the Pickrick, you pick it out and we'll rick it up," and that's what we did.

"Why did you run for Governor of Georgia in 1990," I asked. "Times had changed, you were no longer in the limelight."

The aging War Horse took a deep breath, paused to search for words and replied:

"Uh, I still had the same thing about wanting open and clean government," he said. "Some of the things that happened then really disturbed me.

"I had observed that, in order to pick up thirteen million dollars for pork barrel projects in the Senate," he continued, "they changed financing on bonds from five years to twenty years. And, just to pick up thirteen million dollars, it cost the taxpayers an extra seventy nine million dollars. They were just going wild with bonded indebtedness."

Maddox paused, then added, "You know, I tried to get a sales tax increase during the latter part of my term as governor. The legislature condemned me for wanting to increase the sales tax, but, if I had gotten it, and used it like I planned (for cities, counties, education and to relieve ad valorem taxes) Georgia would be much further ahead today."

No discussion with Lester Maddox would be complete without a conversation about the former Georgia governor's relationship with long-time segregationist and Southern folk hero, George Wallace.

"Tell me about George Wallace," I requested.

Maddox quickly responded with a reply that made it perfectly obvious that the two old friends and political pals were not close when Wallace passed away earlier.

"If George Wallace came into your living room today, what would you say to him," I asked.

Maddox paused to collect his thoughts.

"I would be friendly and gentlemanly to him," he said, "but I would let him know that I was disappointed that he campaigned for anything he didn't believe in.

"That's what got me campaigning for mayor of Atlanta [in 1957]," Maddox continued, "People campaigning one way and living another. I would never have campaigned for anything if that had not happened."

He referred to the reason he opposed Mayor William B. Hartsfield in his first attempt at political office. The reason for his entry into the race, Maddox said at the time, was because he watched his friend Archie Lindsey run on a reform platform only to observe no reform once he took office.

Wallace, who like Maddox was a staunch segregationist and states-righter, endorsed Maddox's political nemesis Jimmy Carter when Carter sought the presidency in 1976. The Alabama governor also revoked his segregation beliefs before his death.

"More than anything else," Maddox said, " I was disappointed with Wallace that he campaigned for something he didn't truly believe in. He gave up his ideals and joined his enemies.

"Suppose Lyndon Johnson walked into the room where we sit. How would you greet him?" I asked.

"Lyndon Johnson was nasty," Maddox quickly replied. "He wouldn't answer my letters or my telegrams. I'm the only person who ever picketed the White House and became governor. I'm the only person who picketed the Supreme Court and became governor."

Over the years, Maddox has taken to the picket line when he felt he and his message were ignored. He picketed outside the Democratic National Convention in Atlantic City in 1964 when Johnson won the nomination by acclamation. He picketed the White House while Johnson was president and he carried protest signs on the street on which the Atlanta newspapers are located many times.

"And, what would you say," I asked, "if Jimmy Carter came in and sat in that chair over there. Would you shake his hand and say, 'hello, Mr. President?'"

"I would shake his hand and say 'hello, Mr. President,' then I would immediately ask him if the emotional trauma he admitted he had during that campaign [when Maddox and Carter faced each other in the 1966 Democratic primary] is the reason he refuses to be honest with the American people.

Maddox obviously referred to Carter's continuing criticism of him thirty years after the two combatants squared off in the 1966 primary.

Since then, Carter has been critical of Maddox on several national television shows, including Larry King Live and the PTL Club, hosted by evangelist and politician Pat Robertson. Maddox, likewise, seldom passes up an opportunity to get in his digs at Carter.

"It's awful what he's doing," Maddox said of the former president. "And, it's deliberate."

Maddox said he believes Carter agreed to appear on Pat Robertson's show (PTL Club) to admonish Robertson (a Christian conservative) for "not being the same kind of liberal Christian he [Carter] is and to hit me."

Maddox said Carter remains angry because he did not win the governor's election in Georgia in 1966.

"He said [on the PTL Club] the biggest disappointment in his life was when they counted the votes (in 1966) and racist Lester Maddox was governor and he was not.

"When they counted the votes," Maddox continued, "Lester Maddox was governor and Ellis Arnall wasn't. I didn't beat Jimmy Carter. He ran against a former governor, another liberal. (Actually, Maddox defeated Republican Bo Callaway to become Governor.)

"You may not agree with me but it's a fact. Two liberals and Ellis Arnall had been governor and was best known. He's the one who beat Jimmy Carter. When they had the runoff, I didn't beat Jimmy Carter, I beat Ellis Arnall. He [Carter] said I beat him. He wasn't even in the race. He was beat by another liberal."

Maddox defeated Arnall in the Democratic party runoff election but failed to defeat Republican Howard (Bo) Callaway in the 1966 General Election. Although Callaway received a plurality of votes, he did not reach the required majority and lost to Maddox in a vote by the Georgia legislature.

"I think Jimmy Carter is the most dishonest, coldest and most cruel person I ever met," Maddox said, echoing the statement he has made many times over the years.

Lester Maddox is in his 83rd year. He has lived through some good times and some bad times. He survived a tough childhood, health setbacks, two world wars, a great depression, a losing battle against the nation's civil rights legislation, exploration of outer space, landing a man on the moon and many other historical events. Yet, he clings tenaciously to a philosophy rooted in the status quo and fails miserably in recognizing that, as time marches on, so does prosperity and with it a change in the attitudes and mores of the American people.

"What do you think of modern society?" I asked. What have computers done or television. What effect have they had on us?"

He again paused, took a deep breath, and carefully measured his response.

"I don't understand any of them enough to say what I think, he said, but said it anyway.

"I believe there are plusses and minuses. The plusses are communications and educational benefits.

"Without computers, we'd be a third world country.

"The man who said around 1900 that everything that could be invented has been invented sure missed it, didn't he," he said with a chuckle.

"I thank God for them [computers]."

"People blame our problems today on government," Maddox volunteered. "I think they're outside government.

"It's our society in general [which is to blame] or we wouldn't have that type of government. Our people are approving of it.

"You can't clean up government," he continued, "until you clean up outside of government. And, that's not likely to happen, unless its done by the clergy.

"That has been a part of my crusade in life," he said. "It can't be done by the Democrats or Republicans, by the United Nations, by the United States, by the czars of finance, scientists, labor, industry or the media.

"There'll be no turnaround unless something is done to restore families and if it is not church led, or synagogue lead, it simply can't happen," he said.

Feeling that Maddox didn't understand my question, I again asked for some examples of what he thinks is right or wrong with modern society. He again blamed governmental action.

"We have used public housing to cripple this nation, said the man who has opposed such programs since first offering for public office. "Millions of people have turned to crime and drugs who might otherwise own their own homes and could have been law-abiding citizens.

Sensing that Maddox might tear off on a rampage against other government programs, I abruptly changed the subject.

"If you could swap lives with any politician who ever lived, who would it be? Truman? Washington? Who?"

"Well," came his Regeanistic reply, "me and Truman had a lot in common. We were on our own. We both came from free enterprise and we were free to be our own men. Truman exercised that freedom to a great extent.

"I liked Eisenhower," he continued. "The last Democrat I voted for was Harry Truman. If all the presidents since Eisenhower had started no more programs than he did, we'd be out of debt.

"Eisenhower didn't do a whole lot, thank God," he added.

Since the Clinton-Lewinsky affair was front page news and a vast majority of Americans indicated through opinion polls that character was no longer a political issue, I asked Maddox what he thought about today's moral values.

"Isn't it awful to hear that, that character doesn't matter," he answered the question with a question.

"What has happened to make us feel that way," I asked.

"The church," he said. "The church has failed. Most ministers follow the media like most politicians.

"The Methodist minister last Sunday didn't want to get after Clinton's morality, he thought we ought to get after [Kenneth] Starr for investigating him! If I were a member of that church, I would have called for him to get out!"

Maddox appeared to be tiring so I quickly asked him two questions that are fundamental to his life and times.

"You're a segregationist and not a racist, " I said, "echoing a position Maddox has defined over the years.

"Amen," he quickly responded.

"You know what I think a segregationist is?" he asked.
"Someone who has racial pride and racial integrity that want their races preserved and the races of other people preserved.

"My segregation includes opposition to amalgamation, which would wipe out the races. My fight at the Pickrick was for the right or private property, the right of free enterprise for every human being in this country. The same position the Supreme Court had taken and all the presidents."

The other fundamental question was this:

"Deep down in your heart and soul, how do you feel about black people?"

His response:

"I feel that they're a part of the human race and I'm proud of them when they succeed. Or white people, or orientals, when they are productive and law-abiding and I am opposed to them when they waste their lives and follow the will of a socialistic government that makes failures out of people who otherwise would be producers."

With that, the interview ended.

Lester Maddox, now aged and infirm, is a political icon. Those who know him, like him. Those who do not, give him the benefit of their doubt. They think him honest, if too outspoken. He has not, nor will he ever, make believers of his dissenters.

Will his last stand at the Pickrick restaurant spoil his place in history? There are those, including former Maddox confidante and Georgia governor Zell Miller, who hope not. After all, they say, Maddox was no more guilty of racial division at the time than other Atlanta restaurants, hotels and places of business. They point to his political successes —becoming governor, then lieutenant governor — as proof of his acceptance by the people. His tenure as the state's chief executive is given high marks by most political observers. He acted forthrightly to correct many of the abuses and misconduct in state government, made excellent appointments to various offices and judgeships which pleased many critics and astounded others. Several of his key appointments remain in the state's political leadership. Former governor Zell Miller, his chief aide, completed a remarkable career in state politics, first as lieutenant governor for sixteen years, then governor for eight. Agriculture Commissioner Tommy Irvin has served in that position for 32 years, gaining national recognition in the process. Former aide Mac Barber served terms on the Public Service Commission twice and was narrowly defeated in the 1998 Democratic primary for lieutenant governor. Former legal aide Jack Gunter became a Superior Court Judge in his native Cornelia and served with distinction for many years. Lawyer John Blackmon, who Maddox appointed to replace Revenue Commissioner Peyton Hawes when Hawes was named to the Georgia Court of Appeals by Maddox, has retired after a successful legal career in Atlanta. The late Bill Burson, Maddox's welfare chief, became State Treasurer. Maddox's floor leader in the Georgia House, Tom Murphy of Bremen, later became speaker of that body and has served longer in that position than any other speaker in the history of Georgia. His Senate leader, Frank Coggins, went on to enjoy a successful law practice in Hapeville, an Atlanta suburb. The quality of Maddox's associates was exemplary and serve as a perfect example of his desire to have a successful administration. But, despite best efforts, Maddox was too often the victim of media assaults, many of which were self-inflicted. His sudden and vicious attacks on racial integration, the "socialistic" federal government, political opponents and even friends often muted his good works.

Some Maddox sympathizers feel that three decades of racial progress should have erased the cruel deeds of earlier generations. Americans and Georgians, for the most part, are living in racial harmony and like it that way.

As hard as he may try, there is nothing Lester Maddox can do to change things. In a 1990 poll, only 3.3 percent of those Georgians surveyed said they still believe in strict segregation of the races. Sixty-two percent said they supported integration and another 30 percent said they favored something in between.

Maddox looks back on his political life philosophically and with rare pride.

"I think I've had an unusual life," he said. "I was an outsider... and I'm the only governor ever elected lieutenant governor [in 1970]. And, I'm really not a Democrat or Republican. I'm just Lester Maddox.

"That's kept me in trouble most all of my life. And that's what I want to be remembered for, being true or real as I can."

Appendix A
Maddox Anecdotes

Governor Maddox and several aides made a surprise visit to a prison in South Georgia when one of the inmates recognized him. Maddox ordered a nearby guard to open the cell so he could talk to the inmate. Inside the man talked briefly with Maddox, then presented him with a miniature piano—complete with forty-four white and forty-four black keys. Lester expressed his amazement at the tiny piano and chatted with the prisoner for several minutes.

As Maddox and his aides walked back down the prison corridor, admonished the governor for entering the cell. "That man is a savage killer. He brutally murdered seven people in Florida in cold-blood." Lester calmly looked at the guard and responded, "That's funny. He seemed like a pretty nice fellow to me."

During the early eighties, the cancer-stricken Maddox received 8,000 blood serum injections from a last-resort clinic in the Bahamas. Doubters charged that the injections were useless and its doctors were nothing more than quacks.

Finally, after his cancer went into remission, Maddox commented: "All I know is I got my health back. I can't prove that the injections helped me, but nobody can prove that they hurt me either."

Throughout his political life, Maddox was at constant war with the *Atlanta Journal* and its sister publication, the *Constitution.* During the summer of 1968, the sensative governor felt the newspapers had treated him especially unfairly and he ordered all of the *Journal/Constitution* vending machines removed from the capitol complex. Then suddenly, a week later, he was stricken with kidney stones. While recuperating, he summoned long-time Atlanta Constitution reporter Bill Shipp, to his bedside at the Mansion. "Tell your circulation department they can come and put their vending machines back on the capitol grounds," Maddox said.

Shipp did not understand. "What made you change your mind, governor?" he asked.

Maddox, looking pale and weary, raised himself up on his elbow to face the reporter. "I wanted to clear my conscience before I go on to meet my reward."

During a watermelon and ice cream party at a state representative's house, Governor Maddox teamed up with African American accordionist Graham Jackson (one of Franklin Roosevelt's favorite entertainers) to sing "You are my Sunshine," "Shine on, Harvest Moon," and "Old Shanty Town." The two harmonized so well that Jackson commented to Maddox later: "People in Atlanta would pay big money to hear singing like that." Maddox laughed and commented, "Lots of people in Atlanta don't like what I been singing already," he said.

Throughout the first year of his governor's term, Maddox fought with the federal government about their school desegregation guidelines. Each time Maddox took action to resist, the government threatened to withhold the monies due the state's education system.

After a fiery speech against the guidelines, Maddox said he would like to see 100 more private secondary schools in Georgia and, if possible, he would use state money to help fund them. "...As for the money the federal government says they will withhold from us..." Maddox said angrily, "They can take it and ram it!"

In a dress-code memo to his office staff, Maddox made it clear that he wanted "skirts down to the knees and hair up to the ears (apparently referring to male employees). No man has ever had nice thoughts about a woman he saw half-dressed."

After only a month as Georgia governor, Maddox was formally invited to visit President Lyndon Johnson in the White House. When a reporter asked how he felt about the invitation, he said it was a perfect example of just how two-faced professional politicians were. "Two years ago," he quipped, "they wouldn't even let me in the driveway," referring to his picketing the White House in 1964.

While campaigning for lieutenant governor against incumbent George T. Smith in the fall of 1970, Maddox, his wife and several aides went to Athens for a University of Georgia football game.

When Maddox's state trooper-driven car pulled up to the stadium, a security blockade stood in their path. Upon seeing the obstacle, Maddox immediately jumped out of the car, opened the gate and began to set the orange pylons aside. As he did, several fans on the upper deck watched. Once the car passed through, Maddox closed the gate and replaced the pylons while the football fans applauded loudly at seeing their governor doing things for himself. Back in the limo, Maddox quipped to his aides: "Now Ole George T. ... He would have been too uppity to do that!"

It was well known that Maddox would not accept a political contri-bution if there was any hint that a political pay-back was expected. After one such man approached Maddox with a contribution, he tried to play on Lester's religious beliefs to get him to accept it. "Mr. Maddox," he said, "The Lord told me I should give you this money." Maddox looked at the man and replied: "Well, the same Lord told me not to take it!"

Maddox was very sensitive about his religion and he took offense when NBC's Douglas Kiker wanted him to do some make-believe praying for publicity purposes. During a parade in Bainbridge, Georgia, Kiker told Maddox "If you'll stop for a minute and kneel down at the curbing as if you were praying, I can guarantee you will be on every NBC station in the country tonight." Maddox replied angrily, "If we were not already on TV, I would pop you in the mouth."

While trying to make the inmates at a south Georgia prison under-stand that he sympathized with their plight, Maddox explained, "I know it's not an enjoyable thing to be in prison. I feel the same way about polit-ical cartoons. They're pretty funny unless you're in 'em."

A portrait of Lester Maddox hangs next to his bitter rival, Jimmy Carter, in Georgia's State Capitol. In it, Maddox, clad in a seersucker suit (he wanted to look southern, he explained), stands with his wife, Virginia. In the background is the state seal of Georgia with a man standing next to a Maddox-trademark bicycle hidden inside. There is also a fish wrapped with the *Atlanta Constitution*—known always as "the fishwrapper" to Maddox—resting on a table behind the former governor. "The artist wanted to put it out front," Maddox explained, "but I wanted the fishwrapper near my rear end because that's where it belongs."

Maddox always seemed to enjoy jousting with the news media. At the Georgia Press Association's Eighty-Third annual convention in Savannah on 4 July 1969, he began his remarks by saying, "It's good to be back with my good friends in the Georgia Press Association—both of them."

Appendix B
Selected Speeches

Inaugural
11 January 1967

The emotions of this moment are many and mixed.

But that which is uppermost in my heart...is a deep sense of humility.

I am humbled by the honor you do me...by the magnitude of the task you have entrusted to me...by the gravity of the responsibility you have vested in me and—most of all—by the confidence you have thus demonstrated in me.

For this I shall be eternally grateful...But, more than gratitude, I pledge to you my fullest energy and every effort for the next four years...to measure up to your honor...to fulfill your trust...to discharge the responsibility you have delegated to me...and to merit your confidence.

And in setting out this noon...to labor toward those ends I do so with the prayer of Solomon of old:

...Oh Lord my God...Thy servant is in the midst of Thy people whom Thou has chosen...give Thy servant therefore an understanding mind to govern this Thy people, that I may discern between good and evil; for who is able to govern this Thy great people?"

We meet today at the end of a long and tortured trail…from the political platform, to the ballot box, to the courts and into the legislative forum. It has been a journey which has tried the public patience and has tested the procedures of democracy.

There were issues that divided us and there were inconclusive results…which brought us several times to the brink of despair.

But because of the vitality of our institutions…because of the adherence of our people to the processes of law an order…and because of the faith of Georgians in the ultimate triumph of their will…continuity of government has been maintained and an orderly transition of leadership effected.

We have reason to be proud of the restraint of the partisans of all sides…of the forbearance of the electorate as a whole…of the dispatch and dignity with which the courts resolved the points at issue…of the statesmanship of our able and respected outgoing Governor, Honorable Carl Sanders…and, most particularly, of the courage and responsibility with which the members of this General Assembly faced up to, and discharged, the difficult duty imposed upon them by the constitution of our state.

One step yet remains to bring a satisfactory conclusion to our year of searching and indecision.

And that, my friends, is for all of us—those gathered here and the remainder of Georgia's four and one-half million people who are elsewhere—to unite in the cause we all hold in common esteem.

That cause is the building of a greater and more prosperous Georgia with expanded horizons of opportunity for all.

That is a cause which is greater than one or group of us.

That is a cause which transcends all differences of philosophy and politics.

That is a cause which requires the help and support of all Georgians —young and old, poor and rich, farmer and city dweller, and Democrat and Republican, regardless of race, creed, color or national origins.

I seek that help.

I ask that support.

The great architect of our democracy—the revered Thomas Jefferson—faced division when he assumed the presidency. And the words with which he dealt with that subject in his inaugural address are as vital and as apropos to our situation now, as they were to his then.

Let us," he declared, "restore to social intercourse that harmony and affection without which liberty and even life itself are but dreary things. And let us reflect that having banished from our land that religious intolerance under which mankind so long bled and suffered...we have yet gained little if we countenance a political intolerance as despotic...as wicked...and as capable of as bitter and bloody persecutions."

Mr. Jefferson then went on to state that "difference of opinion is not a difference of principle." And he concluded that "error of opinion may be tolerated when reason is left free to combat it."

More than a century and a half have proved the Jeffersonian concept of government—that the people, when given the facts and the opportunity to act upon them, can be counted upon to decide public matters wisely.

I subscribe to the principles of Jeffersonian democracy with its emphasis upon unity in the pursuit of common goals...upon the free interchange of ideas in areas of differing opinion...and upon final determination of issues by the people themselves.

That is the American way.

That is the Georgia way.

That will be the way of the Maddox administration.

Much has been said and written about there being no mandate for anyone in our primaries and general election.

I dispute that.

I consider the people to have spoken loudly and clearly...not only about what they want and expect from their new administration...but also about they do *not* want and will not tolerate from it.

They want a public school system equal to the best in the nation,...and they want every child regardless of his circumstances or where he lives to be prepared to compete on an equal basis...with every other child in the country.

They want a system of higher education adequate to the needs of today and of the twenty-first century just ahead...and they want that education made available to every youth capable of profiting by it.

They want swift completion of our interstate highway system...a solution to the traffic and transit problems of our cities...and an end to slaughter on our highways.

They want dignity, comfort and adequate facilities and treatment for the mentally ill…the retarded and the aged…and they want a decent, modern correctional system dedicated to rehabilitation.

They want training for the unskilled and unemployed…and they want a vigorous, effective industrialization program to assure jobs now and in the future…for all that can and will work.

They want aid for our strangling cities and our struggling smaller communities and they want to be allowed to solve local problems on the local level.

They want all citizens to be safe in their homes and on the streets…and for private property to be protected from the thief…the hoodlum and the mob.

They want their state government to continue to be operated on a sound, economical, businesslike basis…with morality and honesty scrupulously enforced in all its agencies and activities.

Those are the positive aspects of the people's mandate.

On the other hand, we have been told:

The people do not want any undue changes in the direction or policy of their state government.

They do not want a single school closed or the right of a child to be educated or a teacher to teach to be impaired.

They do not want riots in the streets or breaches of the peace in public places or institutions.

And, above all, they do not want any extremist organization or group to have any voice or influence in any state programs.

These points, my fellow Georgians, constitute the mandate I read into the returns from the ballots you cast in 1966.

It is a mandate for progress and responsibility…which I accept wholeheartedly and without reservation…as your servant and as the instrument of your will.

It is a mandate which the Maddox administration will follow as the chart of its course over the next four years.

It is a mandate which be will be carried out in accordance with the advice from the best minds in Georgia…and the wishes of the people as expressed thorough their elected representatives.

No one realizes more than I that the administration of four years of multi-million-dollar budgets...and the formulation and implementation of complex policies...is not a one-man job.

Immediately following this ceremony, I will announce my appointments to key offices of the executive branch. I have called upon people I believe to be capable, competent and committed to no interest except that of Georgia and its citizens...to serve you in these jobs. I have impressed upon all of them that I shall expect their services to be in accordance with the yardstick set by Henry Clay when he said:

Government is a trust, and the officers of the government are trustees, and both the trust and the trustees are created for the benefit of the people."

As soon as possible I shall name a number of task forces to make specific recommendations for legislative and administrative action in fields of major interest and concern.

I will call on leaders in all areas of endeavor throughout the state—women as well as men—to serve on these groups.

These men and women will make thorough studies of all aspects of our problem areas. In some cases, they will hold hearings to ascertain public thinking and to get citizen recommendations. And in all cases they will be requested to present detailed programs dealing with how as well as what...for my consideration in time for presentation to the 1968 session of the General Assembly.

There will be task forces in the fields of education, mental health, highways and highway safety, industrialization, corrections and law enforcement, and perhaps others where the need for studies in depth is evident.

We will take steps to avoid any further repetition of the confusion and controversy caused by the primaries and general election last year.

First, during the coming months,...I will study and evaluate the State Election Code in light of our experience since its adoption in 1964...consulting election officials as to means to strengthening and improving our election machinery in Georgia...and such changes that might be needed will be prepared for submission to the earliest possible session of the General Assembly.

And, second, I will ask the General Assembly to submit to the voters for ratification in the 1968 general election a constitutional amendment to require a run-off election for governor between the top two candidates...in the event no candidate receives a majority in the general election.

The people have made it very clear that they want to do the electing of their governors themselves. That this is their right is a conviction I have long held and expressed often...and the assurance of that right under all circumstances is a priority goal of the Maddox administration.

The Maddox administration will not shirk its responsibility in the matter of legislative apportionment.

Georgians believe, as I do, that the states should have the right to apportion one house on the basis of population...as in the United States House of Representatives...and the other on the basis of geography...as in the United States Senate.

But Georgia is under federal court order to reapportion the General Assembly in accordance with the "one man—one vote" principle by May of this year. The only alternative to acting ourselves is to let the federal courts do the job for us. And such a course is wholly unacceptable to all of us who believe in states' rights and states' responsibilities.

It would be unwise to complicate the deliberations of the regular session of the General Assembly now underway with this complex and controversial task. Therefore, I have decided to call a special session next spring for that sole purpose. And, at an early date, I will confer with the lieutenant governor and the speaker of the house to reach agreement on a date for a special session.

Believing...as I do...in separation of powers of government, I will make no recommendation as to how reapportionment should be accomplished...unless it becomes evident...that a majority of the members of the General Assembly cannot agree on an acceptable plan. I am confident that they will meet their responsibility in this regard and will enact a plan the federal courts will approve.

The Maddox administration will address itself to another grave need of our state—that of a new, modern constitution.

It is all too obvious that we cannot expect our state and its government to continue to be responsive to the demands upon them under our present patchwork constitution. The multiplicity of amendments on which we have to vote last fall was proof of its failure.

We cannot legislate at the ballot box so we must have effective home rule and local self-government for our cities and counties. And the only way we can get them is through writing a new constitution attuned to a modern, growing Georgia.

I will ask the reapportioned General Assembly to call such a constitutional convention. This will be done with a view toward submitting a new constitution to the people before the end of this administration.

We will not hesitate to meet head-on these and whatever other problems subsequently may arise and endeavor to resolve them in the best interests of the people.

Of this one fact, all Georgians may be assured: we will solve Georgia problems in Georgia and channel change to the benefit of the people of our state while Lester Maddox is governor.

There is no necessity for any conflict to arise between federal and state authority. We should—and we can—solve any disagreements under the framework of the Constitution—respecting the authority of the national government…and being ever mindful of protecting the rights of Georgia and Georgians.

That will be true because the Maddox administration will do its utmost here at home…within the framework of law and order…to solve those issues and problems which must be solved at home.

I say this to you: I will keep my eyes fixed awarely on the proper conduct of state business and service to all the people of Georgia. Our single goal is that of restoring the voice and involvement of the people in determining their own destinies through solving local problems at the local level.

The Maddox administration will support and provide increased financial assistance to cities and counties…in solving their own problems locally, or, where those problems are state-wide in scope or beyond local capacity to solve,…we will act promptly on the state level to deal with them realistically and effectively.

Law and order will be upheld in Georgia during the Maddox administration.

The first responsibility of government is protecting the lives and property of all its people. That responsibility will be met!

No person need counsel others to engage in riots and disturbances because there will be no need for any person or group to take grievances or problems into the streets.

Should any person or group in the State of Georgia have any problem or grievance, the place to take it is to duly-constituted authority on the local level, if a local matter, or to me, as chief executive, on the state level, should it require a state solution.

There will be no place in Georgia during the next four years for those who advocate extremism or violence.

Peace and tranquillity will prevail in this state while Lester Maddox is governor.

The Maddox administration will be one of compassion and concern. Those Georgians who cannot help themselves will have a friend in the governor's chair for the next four years.

That goes for the school child that will be the product of the kind of education we give him.

That goes for the bright youngsters with the potential of greatness who cannot afford a college education.

That goes for the unfortunate victim of mental illness and for the forgotten and abused inmate of a correctional institution.

That goes for the poor fellow who has lost his job and would work if only he could find another or learn another skill.

That goes for the high-minded mother of the slum family who would inspire her children to a better future if only she could break the chains of poverty that bind her and them.

My friends, you now have a governor who knows what it means to be poor,…to want an education and be denied one,…to toil for a living and to meet a payroll the hard way.

I will not forget those lessons of the past but rather will do everything possible to apply them in a constructive way so as to spare the children who come after us some of those agonies and hardships.

In this moment of beginning and dedication, I would emphasize my total commitment to the proposition that there is room for everybody in our great State of Georgia.

There is room enough for every faith, every ideal and every shade of opinion—and room enough for full freedom to express them by the individual citizen…as well as by the press and communications media.

There is room enough for the right of dissent as well as the right to conform.

There is room enough for the right to pursue one's honest livelihood without fear of oppression, for the right to live at peace with one's neighbor and for the right to be left alone, secure an unafraid, by one's own fireside.

There is room enough for honest, effective, efficient government at all levels,...each acting within its proper sphere of authority...and for the right of each person to speak out and to act when, in his conscience, he feels there are things which must be set to rights.

Liberty!

Freedom!

Those are the watchwords of American democracy and the foundation stones of the Georgia philosophy of government.

Georgians love their freedom and they believe with Daniel Webster that:

God grants liberty only to those who love it, and are always ready to guard and defend it."

Thus, on this solemn occasion, I pledge myself and your new state administration...not only to protection and preservation of these inalienable rights we hold so dear...but also to the responsible exercise of them.

My deepest and most heartfelt desire is to weld all Georgians together into one unified force to improve our state and the opportunity it affords our people, particularly our children.

Georgia belongs to all of us.

She belongs to every citizen.

Her interests and welfare are the interests and welfare of all.

As I promised you as the people's candidate, I promise you as the people's governor; ours shall be a people's administration.

Accordingly, the governor's office will be set aside specifically the first and third Wednesday afternoons of each month for the people to meet their governor and for their governor to confer with them.

As I had the opportunity to shake the hands of Georgians during the campaigns of last year, so I look forward to shake them again during my administration as your governor.

When the record of this administration is written four years hence, let it be said that the conduct of daily affairs of the office of governor the people's interests were protected first, last and always.

Let it be said that bold, courageous leadership was offered.

Let it be said that in all state dealings, they were handled honestly.

Let it be said that the rights of the state and her people were guarded jealously and protected fully.

Let it be said that, in these four years, emphasis was put on the true values of government and of life.

Let it be said that those who worked in this administration did so with sweat, toil and prayer in dedication to get the job done.

Let it be said that there was full citizen participation in the state government during these years.

Let it be said,…notwithstanding the fact that the goals set at the outset were high, that they were achieved in the realization…that no worthwhile accomplishments can be attained without setting great goals.

Let it be said that we did not seek things merely because they were easy to accomplish.

Let it be said that we recognized the challenge and met it.

Let it be said that we were not content with being average but rather sought and achieved nothing less that leadership in all areas.

The task is before us.

Our duty is clear.

Georgia's destiny is in our hands.

Toward its realization I ask for your advice, your support, your help and your prayers…and, in turn, pledge to you my best and my all.

Thank you and God bless you!

State of the State and Budget Message
13 January 1967

On Wednesday we inaugurated out administration and defined its goals.

Today, we meet to roll up our sleeves and to get on with the task at hand.

I am pleased to report to you that, although the problems we face are many, *the state of our state is excellent.*

And, working together—you and I—we shall over the next four years make it better.

At the outset there are several fundamental facts I wish to outline and to emphasize.

First, honesty and morality in government will be the watchwords of the Maddox administration.

Second, efficiency, sound economy and good business practices will characterize all state activities for the next four years.

Third, prudent expenditure of all public funds to assure maximum return for the common good from every tax dollar spent will be our constant policy.

Fourth, every state employee in his or her job is important in carrying out our mandate to serve the people and each will be expected to give his or her best at all times.

Budget System

For four years now, the State of Georgia has had in operation a modern budgeting system. It has worked well. The success in administration of several budgets serves as proof that Georgia's new budget law are fulfilling a need long felt in this state.

We meet here today to chart a course of fiscal integrity for the next two year period.

We are fortunate, indeed, that our new budget machinery assures a smooth transition from the old administration to the new. This allows a continuity of sound fiscal policy as Georgia approaches the challenges of the future.

Under Georgia law, it is the duty of the outgoing governor to have a budget report printed and transmitted to you within five days of the organization of the General Assembly.

This has been done and that document is now on your desk.

The law also provides that the governor-elect shall be thoroughly conversant with the budget report and that the budget bureau shall give the incoming governor every assistance in acquainting himself with it.

This has been done. The assistance which has been provided me has been invaluable in familiarizing myself with the intricate operations of the various departments of state government. It has afforded me a sound basis for making decisions as to what I am recommending to you in connection with the appropriations bill which you will consider during this session of the General Assembly. This bill has been introduced today for your study and analysis.

Assembly Cooperation

First, in consideration the allocations for the various operations and functions of the state government, I want to say to you as clearly as I know how that the Maddox administration expects...intends...and is determined to work in the closest harmony with members of the General Assembly to enact into law a biennial budget bill which is sound in its inception...which is commensurate with the state of our economy and reasonable revenue estimates of anticipated collections and, which will meet the essential and growth needs of a vibrant state which is on the move.

Our jobs, yours and mine, is to enact a bill along the lines I have stated...one that does not appropriate...on one hand...an inordinately excessive amount of money far beyond all reasonable revenue expectations...and, on the other hand, one that does not appropriate too little which would result in curtailment of services and not meeting the needs of our state.

I am confident that you will work with me and with budget officials in finding this sound middle ground upon which we can build a fiscally responsible budget and enact a sound appropriations act.

The budget laws of the State of Georgia authorize the General Assembly to appropriate anticipated revenue together with whatever portion of the anticipated surplus might be required to meet the upcoming needs of the state.

Revenue Estimates

After conferring with budget officials and economic analysts, it is our considered judgment that total state revenues and income for fiscal 1968 will be $734,000,000 and for fiscal 1969, $806,000,000.

You will note in the green budget document on your desk that the revenue estimates for the remainder of fiscal 1967 and for fiscal 1968 and for 1969 are approximately $14,000,000 higher than estimates in my supplemental budget document, also on your desk. Let me emphasize to you…and reemphasize…that these estimates were made last fall and were based upon information available at that time, and they are too optimistic in view of the current national economic conditions and in view of the trend of receipts coming into the state treasury. I will point out to you specifically that the percentage increase in collections during the month of December over December of 1965 was only four and one-half percent. Likewise, the percentage increase in revenue collections for the current fiscal year projected to the end of the year will not show as great a percentage increase as was shown in fiscal 1966 over fiscal 1965.

Last Tuesday night, the President of the United States called for a tax increase in the form of a 6 percent surtax on net income tax liabilities of both individuals and corporations.

All of these things suggest prudence and caution to me and, I know, to you. And these are the reasons I have reduced revenue estimates.

During the past five years, we have been in the midst of a rising economy. We hope this condition will continue. But we do not know that it will. We are confronted with what kind of year 1967 will be. We know that we are entering an era of uncertainty where there are contradictions among fiscal experts as to what is in store and many are predicting a leveling off in our economy.

You and I are familiar with the budget laws. We know that if we appropriate too great an amount of money and income does materialize, it is necessary that I, as budget director, in carrying out the directive of the General Assembly, apply pro-rata reductions to every agency in state government.

We want to avoid this hazard.

We can do so by writing a sound bill in the knowledge that if additional income is in hand, we can come here twelve months hence with a supplementary appropriations bill and will utilize this accumulated income.

Supplemental Budget

In fact, during this session of the General Assembly, I will present for your consideration a supplemental budget to meet the critical needs of the State for the biennium ending June 30, this year. Detailed descriptions of each agency's needs are contained in information furnished you for your consideration.

By enacting into law the proposed supplemental appropriations, and taking into account the revenue estimates, the State can expect an anticipated surplus on July 1, 1967, of $121,000,000.

New Biennium

The anticipated surplus, together with revenue estimates will permit the enactment of an appropriations act appropriating $785,000,000 in fiscal 1968, and $877,000,000 in fiscal 1969.

This is $1,662,000,000 to finance the services of our state government, to accelerate the growth of our state and to minister to the needs of our people during the twenty-four months beginning next July 1.

In a moment, I will detail to you the recommendations I am making for expanding state services in the major agencies of the state government. These expansions will account for increased expenditures of more than $412,000,000 in the two-year period, above expenditures in the 1965-1966 appropriations act.

This increase in appropriations and services is the greatest ever undertaken by any administration in any biennium in Georgia history.

Schools and Colleges

In every town and hamlet in Georgia, I visited with parents, students and educators last year. I talked with those vitally interested in the cause of education, many times. I sought to acquaint myself with their hopes and aspirations—what was needed to bring to the children of this state knowledge and learning.

Ladies and gentlemen of the General Assembly, no one knows more than I that a Georgia of liberty, progress and prosperity is dependent upon improved education.

That is the goal of the Maddox administration.

The appropriations bill which I have submitted to you is designed as the first step in implementing the Maddox administration's education program.

I am proposing to you an expenditure for public and higher education of $973,000,000 over the next two years—an increase of $252,000,000 over the current biennium.

This represents the largest single increase and the most far-reaching advance in the history of public schools and higher education in Georgia.

Teachers' Salaries

My budget recommendations will provide for:

A salary increase of $700 in fiscal 1968 and $558 in fiscal 1969 for our deserving elementary and secondary public school teachers. These increases are the largest that have ever been proposed for our teachers. Also, I have recommended an increase from $620 in the present year to $750 in the first year of the biennium and $850 in the second year for maintenance, operation and sick leave grants to our 195 systems. I am recommending that funds be provided in this budget to help pay school lunchroom workers and if the object of this expenditure is found to be unconstitutional then these funds will be transferred to the grants for maintenance and operation of our public schools.

I have asked for many new and improved programs in education, such as driver education, increased funds for textbooks, school library materials, public library materials and additional funds for educational television.

I am also asking for increased funds to provide necessary classrooms for the systems feeling the pinch of expanding enrollment.

In the field of higher education, I am proposing the largest percentage and dollars increases to the University System of Georgia in the history of our state.

During fiscal 1968 I have proposed an increase of 39.3 percent over the amount appropriated this year to the University System. For fiscal 1969, I am asking an increase of 70.7 percent over the amount of funds appropriated this year to the University System.

These unprecedented increases will provide for a 10 percent salary increase each year of the biennium for academic personnel and a 5 percent increase for non-academic personnel. I am asking the General Assembly, *for the first time in the history of higher education in Georgia,* to appropriate $5,000,000 in each year of the biennium for improved quality of the University System's program.

An increase in authority rentals of $2,500,000 in each year of the biennium will build approximately $70,000,000 worth of additional college facilities.

These expenditures which I am recommending that you approve for education, will assure every Georgia student a brighter opportunity in the form of better qualified teaching personnel, more adequate classroom and instructional facilities, and in the form of a generally-enriched educational program from beginning grades through graduate levels.

Welfare Services

Now, permit me to move into the delineation of a broad program of social, welfare and health services which will be undertaken during the Maddox administration.

The most significant development in welfare assistance programs since its enactment into law in 1937 will come in the next two years. New additions to recipient budgets under Title Nineteen of the Federal Social Security Act will provide increased benefit payments for all categories of assistance—aged, blind, dependent children and totally disabled.

Another item of great social impact in the proposed appropriation bill is the proposal for an appropriation of $2,000,000 to finance the construction and equipping of a new Youth Development Center to be used for housing and training 150 girls.

This facility will be operated in conjunction with presently established Youth Development Centers.

Early in the next fiscal year we will open six new regional detention centers for youth committed to the custody of law enforcement agencies and the budget I submit today provides funds for their full operation. This represent a long-desired step toward getting children out of the common jails of Georgia and into a wholesome environment for the beginning of their training and rehabilitation.

Concurrent with this, we also will provide $175,000 for each of the two years of the biennium to assist the seven existing county-owned detention centers. This is another first for state assistance in this important field.

Another important new program we will be launching will be known as "Medicaid," and funds are being provided for in this budget contingent upon the expected approval of the Georgia program by federal authorities.

Under this program all recipients of welfare assistance will be provided with physicians, laboratory, out-patient hospital and in-home advisory services.

This is another phase of Title Nineteen of the Federal Social Security Act. Georgia's full participation in this program will mean that the state will receive $35,000,000 from the federal government over the next biennium for an outlay of less than $2,000,000.

That, my friends, I regard to he an excellent investment—one which will pay untold dividends in terms of improved health and increased comfort for the less fortunate of our citizens.

Milledgeville Hospital

In accordance with my promise to the people of Georgia, I have included in the proposed budget an increase in funds for Milledgeville State Hospital which is more than twice as large an increase as that provided in any other biennial budget in the state's history.

It is my recommendation that more than $26,000,000 be appropriated for the 1968 fiscal year and almost $27,300,000 for the 1969 fiscal year. This will make possible many important advances at that institution.

It will mean the hiring of 440 new employees and the placing of all employees on a forty-hour week—an important improvement in working conditions long overdue.

It will provide more that $3,000,000 for capital outlay. And that will be in addition to the construct of an $8,700,000 dollar medical-surgical unit under the authority lease-rental program.

In addition we propose to do something about overcrowding in the institution by quadrupling the patient load at the new Southwestern State Hospital in Thomasville. Funds will be provided to increase the number of patients there to 800 over the two-year period.

During the second year of the biennium, we will open the regional hospitals in Atlanta and Augusta. And during the biennium, we will begin construction on three other regional hospitals at Columbus, Rome, and Savannah.

All of these steps in total will constitute the largest single effort to improve and upgrade mental health facilities and programs in the history of our state.

Retardation Center

We will make a substantial beginning on a needed expansion to care for retardates waiting for admission to Gracewood State Hospital. It is proposed that $700,000 dollars be spent over the two-year period for new housing of patients and staff there. It is anticipated that this will make room for between 175 and 200 additional patients at that facility.

In this connection, we are also proposing the appropriation of $1,250,000 for completing, staffing and opening the new Georgia Retardation Center in DeKalb County to serve retardates.

And we propose to step up our attack on health problems on the local level by increasing grants-in-aid to counties for local health services by more than $2,600,000 over the biennium.

Highway Construction

As you know, the constitutional allocation to the State Highway Department for highways is the total amount of motor fuel tax collections, less cost of collection and refunds. The appropriations bill submitted to you provides for the general operations of the Highway Department, for authority rentals to amortize the cost of bridges, rural roads, and department quarters, for maintenance and betterments; for planning and construction; and for statutory grants to counties as provided under the 1945 act for fixed distribution and the 1951 act based upon a state road mileage ratio formula.

All Georgians are concerned about and inconvenienced by the clogged condition of highways leading into our major metropolitan areas, particularly, the Capitol City of Atlanta. This situation is of special concern to me because of the fact that some $80,000,000 in interstate federally-aid primary and secondary projects are being held in abeyance because of the freeze on federal highway funds.

We cannot afford to stand still in this state or the nation in this vital field. As governor I feel some relief must be given to the states in this matter, and I am confident that other chief executives throughout this nation share this view.

Expressways

It is my intention, therefore to communicate with the president and other appropriate officials to seek a solution and, if necessary, I will call upon him in person to relate to him the urgency of an early release of these road funds.

In my opinion, a release of highway funds will do more to relieve the areas of stress in the economy—particularly here in Georgia—than any single program the chief executive might initiate at this time.

Airport Development

You will note a proposed appropriation for capital outlay—airport development of $1,400,000 during the period. These funds for the first time will allow the State of Georgia to provide aid for major commercial airports. In addition to that, this will provide assistance for twenty communities in building new airports, extending runways, constructing taxiways and aprons. For this state expenditure, with federal aid and local support for this purpose, these projects will total $6,000,000 during the first fiscal year and $2,000,000 dollars in the second.

During the current fiscal year grants to municipalities and total grants to counties are $9,317,000 to each category. In the new budget submitted to you, there are large increases in the first year and even larger increases for both in the second year.

This is but the beginning of an effort by the Maddox administration to carry forth my program for substantial state assistance to help meet the fiscal needs of our cities and counties.

Correctional Reform

In keeping with our mandate to give Georgia a decent, modern correctional system dedicated to rehabilitation, I am proposing that we make the largest single increase in operating funds for the Department of Corrections in the history of this state. Over the biennium, we propose to add more than $1,750,000 or 50 percent above the total for that purpose during the current biennium.

This money will make it possible to place all personnel on a forty-eight-hour work week and to add an additional 219 positions over the two-year period. It will also permit an extensive program of replacement of outdated and worn-out equipment.

During the biennium, we will complete and open the $8,000,000 dollar Butts County Classification and Diagnostic Center which will include a fully-equipped hospital for the treatment of inmates throughout the state corrections system. And we also are including funds for building an honor institution for 500 young offenders at a site yet to be selected.

In an effort to provide more adequate probation and parole services, it is recommended that funds are to be allocated for the employment of fifteen additional probation officers and to raise the salaries of all probation and parole officers to Merit System salary levels.

Toward the goal of reducing the slaughter on our highways in the interest of assuring adequate strength for the Georgia Highway Patrol and the Georgia Bureau of Investigation, we are recommending additional funds to employ 100 new state troopers and sixteen new GBI agents. In addition, we propose to establish a Crime Information Center which will be tied into the national FBI network—making Georgia the first state in the southeast to add this valuable tool to its law enforcement machinery.

Development Proposals

Other major proposals included in the budget I am submitting today include:

—An increase of more than $1,250,000 to expand and strengthen the programs of the Department of Agriculture.

—A contingent cost of living increase of 3 percent per year for all permanent state employees.

—An increase of more than $1,000,000 to enlarge the industrialization and development programs of the Department of Industry and Trade.

—An increase in lease rentals for the State Ports Authority to provide $6,000,000 to build new bulk handling facilities for clay, fertilizers, minerals and ores at the Savannah port.

—An increase in lease rentals for the Parks Department to provide $7,000,000 in capital improvements at all parks including $400,000 each year for acquisition and development of four new park areas.

—An increase in the level of college loans guaranteed by the Higher Education Assistance Committee from $2,500,000 to $6,500,000 by 1969 and an increase from 495 to 1,203 in the number of scholarships issued by the Scholarship Commission.

—Provide funds to construct and equip a 150-bed addition to the Georgia War Veterans Home at Milledgeville and to staff and operate the Veterans Nursing Home in Augusta.

—Provide $250,000 in each of the fiscal years of the biennium to match federal and local funds for Rapid Transit in Atlanta as soon as the authority qualifies for the assistance.

—Provide $350,000 in grants to twenty-eight remaining counties that have not initiated a tax re-evaluation program.

I have presented to you the highlights of the appropriations bill now before you. What I have presented is the executive budget proposal for your consideration. It represents a balanced program designed to meet all of the current and growth needs of the state, to take into account the requirements of all and to utilize the resources of the state to the best advantage in terms of service to the people.

No New Taxes!

I do not ask for any tax increase at this session the General Assembly.

We will finance this budget through utilization of anticipated revenues and surplus, as provided by law.

While I realize that there are some proposed expenditure which have much merit, that should or would have been included had prospective income permitted, I ask you that, in consideration of the budget, you keep in mind our efforts to achieve a proper balance among essential services.

We must look constantly toward meeting effectively the growth challenges of the state consistent with the resources available to us.

By doing so, we can do the best and most effective job for all Georgians.

Ladies and Gentlemen, I am grateful to each of you for your help, support and cooperation which you have given in the operation of state government. I assure you that I will be readily available to you at any time to discuss the details of the budget, as will the budget officer and his staff.

At this session, you and I will make a substantial beginning in implementing a platform which means progress for all Georgians.

To that end, I am dedicated.

To that end, the Maddox administration proudly joins with you.

State of the State
9 January 1968

It is with pride in the past and optimism toward the future that I come before you today.

We have just passed through the greatest year in our history, far beyond our fondest hopes and dreams of a few years ago.

There has been progress on all fronts.

Georgia has moved into a position of solid leadership in many, many areas.

Americans are watching and listening.

They welcome, they appreciate, what they are seeing and hearing here.

They see Georgians strong in their faith and loyal to their country.

They see Georgians who are not afraid to stand up for constitutional processes and who have the fortitude to fight for what made this nation great.

They see a state of peace, progress, prosperity and leadership.

They see a state of harmony and tranquillity.

They see Americanism alive.

These great blessings are ours because of a unity of purpose, a unity of purpose on the part of this distinguished General Assembly, the governor, the constitutional officers and members of the judiciary, other officials and employees of the state, county and municipal governments and the people.

With a deep sense of appreciation, I express to each of you in this honorable body my everlasting gratitude for the friendship, understanding support, cooperation, and counsel which you have extended me in such large measure.

I want to thank you personally on this occasion for I realize, as do the people of Georgia, that the contribution—the tireless contribution—you have made representing your people and your state has made all of this progress possible.

The year I have served with you has been the most rewarding of my life.

You helped to make it so.

I want to thank you for that.

And, too, there is a warm spot in my heart, as I know there is in yours, for the people of Georgia.

People Fountainhead of Governmental Authority

I feel sure that you would want to join me in expressing our gratitude to the wonderful people of our state for the opportunity to serve them, how fortunate we are that they have reposed in us, as their servants, their confidence, their hopes, their ideals, their aspirations, and their prayers.

And you know, as well as I, that as we begin our labors here we are determined to keep their faith and trust and to ever hold it high.

Our duty—yours and mine—is to the people.

They are the fountainhead of governmental authority.

Because of their involvement, their interest and their support, I am encouraged, I am inspired, I am dedicated to meeting the task ahead, to fulfilling my responsibility as governor of this state.

As chief executive, one with enduring faith in our republican form of government, I supporter with all my being the re-emergence of the legislative establishment to perform its full, functioning role as a partner in the progress of our state.

It is my fervent hope and prayer that our national Congress will do likewise.

People Want Independent Legislature and Governor

Believing as I do, having been taught this…feeling it with all my heart, I am a firm supporter of legislative independence, legislative independence with a correspondingly high sense of responsibility, legislative independence coupled with constructive thought and with constructive action.

The people want an independent legislature, one determined to carry out their wishes— *and*, an independent Governor,—beholden to none, free to act with a clear conscience as he has been taught by the word of God in accordance with the directions given him by the people he serves and bound only by his solemn oath of office and his pledge to serve the best interest of the people…all the people…all the time.

This is a task ever with us.

Under this concept, you and I can carry out what the people deserve, what they expect of us, what they demand of us.

During the coming weeks of this legislative session as has been my policy in the past—I will make myself available at all times to render whatever service and help that I can in matters of paramount interest to the growth and development of our state.

As a strong advocate of self-government, I believe that we have proven to the nation and the world that we—as political leaders and as citizens—can identify and solve our own problems in our own way.

We have afforded the entire nation an example of the proper exercise of states' rights and states' responsibility as envisioned by our founding fathers.

And, by so doing, we have given an irrefutable answer to those who seek further consolidation of national power on the grounds that the states and their local political subdivisions are incapable of governing themselves.

Georgia Is Succeeding In Education

We are succeeding with the business of government in Georgia and proof of it is reflected in the record.

Within a few short months, we in Georgia have assumed a position of leadership in education.

At the stroke of midnight on December 31, 1967, Georgia completed its most historic and progressive year in both common school and higher education.

We opened the doors of our public schools to more than 21,000 new students and, have provided more than 1,600 new classrooms.

We have financed a $700 salary increase for public school teachers, enabling Georgia to close the gap on what heretofore has been a critical teacher shortage.

We have expanded and enriched the educational programs within the University System of Georgia by providing, for the first time, special funds to improve the quality of programs at our state's institutions of higher learning.

The appropriations we provided the State Board of Regents this fiscal year amount to an increase of $30,000,000, a 40 percent increase over the previous year, the greatest dollar increase ever in any single year.

This great advance in higher education not only improved its quality but also enabled us to provide a college education for an addition 8,000 young Georgians this year.

I know you share with me great pride in having been a part of this meaningful program for education.

Its end result, I am confident, will mean much to Georgia, our children and their future.

Our success in implementing a crash program in education, however, is but one of the many accomplishments that our partnership has produced.

In the field of mental health, we have made greater strides than ever before in developing in our state a modern program of mental health and mental retardation.

Two new regional hospitals for the mentally ill are now under construction in Atlanta and Augusta. Construction will soon begin on another one in Savannah. Plans are underway to construct similar facilities in Columbus and Rome during this administration.

Each succeeding General Assembly has had to cope with an ever-rising population at Central State Hospital.

I am happy to report to you and to herald to all Georgians the most significant development in mental health in our time—a reversal of this trend, a reduction in the population there in the past year of 2,000 patients.

In agriculture, Georgia farms are producing more than ever before.

Nineteen sixty-seven was truly a banner year for farmers and the services rendered both to the farmer and the consumer by the State Department of Agriculture were expanded and improved.

Our Forestry Department, acclaimed by many as one of the nation's finest, has expanded its program of forest fire protection into every Georgia county, a milestone which has been the goal of professional foresters and forest owners for years.

The prompt and decisive action by you and this administration last year in traffic safety has resulted in the substantial saving of lives—the first annual reduction in the number of fatalities in six years.

Traffic Safety Legislation

Because of my personal concern about Georgia's traffic safety problems, I appointed a specific traffic safety study committee to recommend to me, and to you, solutions to these problems.

This committee will present to you a package of legislative proposals for your consideration during his session. I am sure that each these measures merits your careful study. I want to emphasize, particularly, the need for your enactment of a law imposing jail sentences for those convicted of drunk driving. This, in my opinion, will do more to reduce slaughter on our highways than any other weapon in the arsenal of traffic safety.

I believe that elected public officials, law enforcement officials and the courts have evaded their responsibilities in dealing with this serious problem.

It is a responsibility which we can no longer run from.

We are dealing with a question of life and death and, in my judgment, we have failed to place the proper emphasis on life.

Your enactment of strong and enforceable legislation to deal with the problem of drunk driving, coupled with vigorous enforcement and proper action by the courts can save hundreds of lives annually.

It could well be your own lives or the lives of your families or friends are the ones that you save.

I urge you to give serious thought and immediate action to this matter.

We created the state department of traffic safety, the first in the Southeast, and the second in the nation to receive federal approval.

We have provided for the addition of 100 men to the force of the Georgia Highway Patrol and we are doing a better job than ever of enforcing traffic laws, rules and regulations.

In the overall area of law enforcement, we have strengthened the Georgia Bureau of Investigation and transformed it into a more modern, effective and professional law enforcement agency.

We have also declared war on crime in Georgia and made it known to one and all that crooks, criminals, and influence peddlers are unwanted in our state and while I'm governor they will receive my strongest opposition.

For the first time in history, a special governor's commission is at work examining all aspects of organized crime, as well as law enforcement methods and procedures. This select committee will reports its findings to me and to you and we, together, will determine what is needed to control crime in Georgia.

In wildlife and fish conservation, the State Game and Fish Department has broadened and expanded its operations and has merited the confidence it now has among the sportsmen of the state.

Record of Honesty, Efficiency and Morality

Nineteen sixty-seven saw the Maddox platform of the previous year put into practice.

We promised sound government, responsible, conservative government with emphasis on honesty, morality and efficiency and, with your help, we are providing our people just that.

In keeping with my pledge and my own personal convictions, the Maddox administration has removed the business of government from behind closed doors and from smoke-filled rooms.

We have opened the doors and raised the shades so that the people can see the inside of government...the soiled, as well as the clean...the bad, as well as the good.

This is true in corrections, law enforcement, industry and trade, and all other state departments.

It is a policy we will continue and one which assures Georgians that they will get the kind of honest, progressive, efficient government they deserve.

Record Year in Industrial Growth

Nineteen sixty-seven was a banner year in Georgia for industrial growth.

From a state of disorganization, we have reorganized the State Department of Industry and Trade, just as I promised you and the people of Georgia in 1966.

Georgia now has the most successful industrial development program in the history of our state.

We are moving!

We are selling Georgia to the nation!

Proof of this is found in the year end report of new and expanded industries issued only a few days ago.

Contrary to the predictions in some quarters, this report shows that new and expanded industry last year reached an all-time high of more then $422,000,000, and this figure my friends does not include a $150,000,000 atomic power generating plant which Georgia won as the best location over several competing states.

Not counting this, the total investment in new and expanded industry in Georgia during calendar 1967 was almost $50,000,000 more than in any preceding year.

It is significant, I believe, that more then $327,000,000 of this industrial growth occurred during the last six months of the year, a growth in six months which is far greater than the average annual growth during the past ten years. And, all of this occurred since the first budget of the Maddox administration took effect on July 1, 1967.

With the $500,000 I requested and which you appropriated, along with an additions $400,000 which I made available, we carried the message of Georgia industrial potential and tourist attractions to the nation and the world.

For the first time, we told the Georgia story on television in seventeen major markets from coast to coast. And we are pursuing a massive media campaign projecting the theme that "Georgia's Got It!" in the newspapers, magazines, travel guides, periodicals and highway billboards.

This one-year intensive advertising campaign of selling Georgia far exceeds any other four-year period in history.

Tourism and Recreation Reach New Pinnacle

Tourism and recreation in Georgia today have reached new pinnacles. Visit to our state's seven operating welcome centers almost doubled in 1967 when more tourists than ever visited Georgia.

Park Attendance Up Substantially

Simultaneous with the growth of our tourist trade has been the public use of recreation and camping facilities at Georgia's state parks.

Attendance at our forty-two state parks reached an all-time high during 1967—a total of almost 6,500,000. During the past twelve months receipts received from state parks totaled 28.7 percent over the previous year. This is ten times the income from state parks only six years ago.

Jekyll Island, Stone Mountain Setting New Records

Two of the nation's top attractions—Jekyll Island and Stone Mountain—are undergoing their greatest period of development during this administration and both are setting new attendance records daily.

We extended Merit System coverage to seven additional state agencies with brings to 24,000 the number of state employees now protected by the State's Personnel Agency.

We instituted new purchasing procedures designed to make state purchasing more competitive and assuring that the taxpayers of Georgia receive the best quality and quantity for every tax dollar.

We provided the firstly general increase in state aid for our senior citizens, the blind, the disabled and dependent children since 1963 and the largest since November of 1958.

We moved ahead of many states in implementing Medicaid in order to provide every dollar and every assistance possible at this time under the program.

In the last six months, five regional youth development centers have been opened and a sixth one will soon be ready at Gainesville.

These, along with several urban county detention centers that furnish services to adjoining counties under special arrangements with the Division of Children and Youth, give Georgia the nation's finest system of youth treatment centers.

Every public official who deals directly with juvenile offenders has been fully informed about the purpose of these centers. There is no longer any reason for putting a boy or girl in jail with adult offenders.

We also made significant progress in the construction, improvement and maintenance of Georgia highways.

New Veterans Programs Underway

Benefits for veterans reached new heights in 1967:

It was the first full year of operation of a 572 bed VA hospital in DeKalb County; we appropriated more the $900,000 for the construction of the 150 bed Carl Vinson Building and an occupational therapy workshop at the Georgia War Veterans Home in Milledgeville and 1967 saw the beginning of the construction of a 192 bed skilled nursing home for veterans at Augusta.

Corrections

Georgia, unfortunately, was one of the last states in the nation to lay to rest the infamous "chain gang" concept of corrections with its philosophy of vindictive retribution.

The stripes and the leg-irons came off decades ago but, even so, we have yet to deal a death blow to harmful ideas that punishment, not rehabilitation, is the key to restoring wrongdoers to useful lives.

We all recognize the fact that it is no easy job to administer justice to those who run afoul of the law and those who violently commit crimes against society.

We appreciate the dedicated employees who perform the often dangerous and always thankless task involved in the operation of our prison system. Theirs is a difficult job and they deserve the support and gratitude of all Georgians.

We are determined to provide Georgia with an enlightened and effective penal program.

We're going to begin anew, if that's what it takes, to have a system which helps inmates shape their futures, rather then one preoccupied with reminding them of their pasts.

Such action, in my opinion, is extremely necessary if we are to have the type of prison system which our people want and out state deserves.

Pardons and Paroles

In the whole area of corrections and executive clemency, this administration has not been willing to sweep the dust under the carpet.

We have not been content to sit by while the system imposed such harsh discrimination upon the individual.

This administration has shed the light of day upon conditions which have been existent for a long time by initiating the first in-depth study into the conduct of the State Board of Pardons and Paroles.

I am sure that there is no need for me to explain to you the meaning of recent events as they relate to the operations of that board.

You are familiar with the shocking findings of Attorney General Arthur Bolton. You are also familiar with his recommendations. And I am certain that you are aware of the steps that have been, and are being, taken by this administration toward correcting any irregularities in the granting of executive clemency.

I have requested that the Board of Pardons and Paroles get its own house in order through the adoption of administrative policy and procedures to bring its business out into public view so that people may know and the press of this state may know exactly what action is being taken at any given time.

I was amazed to learn that this board had never had a formal, public meeting at which business is transacted.

I do not believe that we should leave anything to chance but, rather, we should adopt legislation to make it very certain that the parole board will not lapse into loose or haphazard practices.

I am proposing for your consideration a complete program of vitally-needed legislation which will protect the interests of society.

I will also propose to you during this session a number of legislative measures which are necessary to modernize state government and make it more effective.

The first of these are three constitutional amendments relating to the Board of Industry and Trade, the State Game and Fish Commission and the State Board of Corrections.

I am recommending that these three boards be structured to assure the best possible service to the people, and that their membership be consistent with fair representation of the entire state.

Therefore, I propose that:

...The State Board of Corrections be increased from five to fifteen members, one from each of Georgia's ten congressional districts with five additional members to be appointed state at large.

...The State Game and Fish Commission be increased from its present eleven members to fifteen, one from each congressional district and five additional members to be appointed state at large, with one of the at-large appointments coming from one of Georgia's six coastal counties.

...And, that the State Board of Industry and Trade be *reduced* from twenty to fifteen members, one representing each congressional district and five additional members representing the state at large.

I want to make it clear that the present members of the boards affected by this legislation will continue to serve their present appointed terms. This will in no way affect the tenure of any board member presently serving his appointed term.

In all cases, members of boards appointed state at large will serve at the pleasure of the governor, their terms running concurrently with that of the governor.

I shall also propose a bill amendment Code Section 27-101, empowering the governor—upon approval of the Attorney General and the Director of the Department of Public Safety—to offer and pay rewards, not to exceed $25,000, for information leading to the arrest and conviction of the person or persons responsible for any felony committed in this state.

Tax relief by government is always a rare privilege, especially at a time when the people are overburdened by the cost of government at all levels.

I will submit to you two tax relief measures, the first of which will empower the General Assembly to raise the limits of homestead exemption from a low of $1,250 and a high of $2,000 to new limits of $2,000 as a low and $4,000 as a high. This will also provide that homestead exemption be deducted from the value assessed for ad valorem tax purposes and not fair market value of the property.

The second of these provides that all property subject to taxation be taxed at 40 percent of its fair market value. This, of course, will place on the statute books what has already been approved by the courts.

Among other bills to be offered is one designed to put a halt to the obnoxious practice of fleecing tourists and our own people by those resorting to tactics in places referred to as "clip joints."

This legislation makes the practice of keeping, maintaining or carrying on any game for the hazarding of money or other things of value a felony.

I want to make it clear that this legislation is intended solely to rid Georgia forever of clip joint operators and establishments.

I believe that this legislation will encourage the victims of these unscrupulous operators to return to Georgia to testify against them. It is my judgment that the state should provide funds to pay the expenses of witnesses who return to Georgia to testify in these cases.

I also believe that the time has come for us to take a careful look at our laws concerning riots, civic disobedience and insurrections.

I am submitting for your consideration a measure which is similar to those already enacted in other states.

It defines the crime of rioting and makes it a felony.

It makes it prima facie evidence of participation in a riot if the accused were present a the scene of a riot and failed to leave after being requested to do so by a duly authorized law enforcement official.

It makes it a felony to manufacture, possess, transport or use so-called "Molotov cocktails" or any other device designed to explode and cause physical harm.

Workman's Compensation

I will ask you to authorize the largest single increase in workman's compensation benefits in the history of our state.

I will submit to you legislation which increase benefits for total incapacity from a maximum of $37 to $50 weekly; increase benefits for partial incapacity, permanent partial handicaps and maximum burial benefits. I am also proposing that maximum medical payments be increased from $2,500 to $5,000, plus allowances for artificial limbs. These improvements in workman's compensation are the minimum I feel necessary and in my judgment are in the best interests of employers and employees.

Gainful Employment

This administration during the past year has supported the policy of the State Department of Labor in giving training to unemployed persons and getting them into gainful and productive employment in the labor market.

Toward this end, the administration assisted and cooperated with the Federal Bureau of Employment Security in making possible the Atlanta Metropolitan Area Manpower Center at No. 1 Peachtree Street—the first of its kind in America—which will afford counseling and job placement for thousands of workers each year in this area.

When brought to full operation, the manpower center will afford services for industrial and service workers and be of great importance to the youth in this area.

We are determined to do everything possible to bring gainful employment to every segment of our society. It is my conviction that the manpower center here will have great social and economic impact in the years to come.

Unemployment Compensation

Also, in line with my policy of assisting deserving workers of this state I am lending my support to legislation designed to eliminate the one-week waiting period for unemployment insurance. This legislation will be applied only to those workers who are laid off through no fault of their own and will be designed to encourage them to seek employment more rapidly than in the past. Appropriate safeguards will be contained to protect the trust fund. Certainly, if a worker is laid off through no fault of his own, he needs to buy groceries for his family the first week of unemployment as well as the other weeks.

School Consolidation

I have publicly stated my feeling on the matter of school consolidation many times.

The news media have carried statements and accounts of my proposals in this regard for several months.

Therefore, I do not feel it necessary to outline completely my proposed legislation on this matter at this time.

But I want to assure you that the administration's school consolidation legislation will have the full support and backing of this governor.

I believe it is absolutely essential, if we are to provide the kind of education our children must have, that we must preserve local control of education and retain the voice of the people in matters concerning the education of their children.

The exercise of local control of education is democracy in action.

It is the American way.

I have said time and time again that I support consolidation of schools when it is in the best interests of cur children and the future of our state.

But I feel that all of us will be delinquent in our duties if we stand idly by and see our school system ruined and our children deprived simply because a handful of people want to consolidate our schools.

The legislation which I am presenting to you will assure school consolidation where it is needed and protect local schools from unnecessary consolidation.

Election Laws

Last year I made my position clear about the need for adopting suitable measures affecting future general elections.

Now is the time to do that in order to submit it to the people in this year's general election and while election year differences are in the background.

We should provide in our state constitution—the people want us to provide—a runoff general election when no candidate receives a majority of the votes cast in the general election.

So that there can be no misunderstanding, let me emphasize that the general election would be open to all candidates, party nominees, independents and write-in votes would be permissible.

But, if a general election is held, and no candidate receives a majority of the votes cast, the two candidates determined to have the highest number of votes should settle the contest in a runoff general election where only those votes cast for those two candidates would be counted and tabulated.

In keeping with a campaign pledge, I will continue my support of a constitutional amendment providing additional homestead exemption for peace officers, firemen, and members of the armed forces injured in the line of duty, provided that such injuries exceeds 20 percent or more of total disability.

The same benefits authorized by this legislation will also apply to widows of these dedicated public servants so long as they remain unwed.

I am also asking you to provide state scholarships to state institutions for the dependents of peace officers and firemen totally or permanently disabled or killed in the line of duty.

These things for which I ask, for police officers, firemen, custodial officers and military personnel who face grave danger and often lose their lives in providing a safer and better state in which to live, are the least which we can give.

Ladies and gentlemen of Georgia and the Georgia General Assembly, the legislation I will submit to you is vital to the future of Georgia.

I sincerely endorse its enactment into law.

Proposals and legislation I shall offer for your consideration and endorsement, in my sincere judgment, will be in the best interest of Georgia and all her people.

Never, never will I offer special interest legislation for the benefit of a few at the expense of many.

I ask of you now and I shall ask of you in the future for your understanding, your counsel, your cooperation and your prayers.

I ask nothing now, nor will I ever, for the political present or the political future of Lester Maddox.

For, my fellow Georgians, the political present and future of Lester Maddox, or that of any one individual, is of little importance, but the present and future of our beloved state is of great importance.

I am grateful that the Georgia General Assembly is composed of devoted and dedicated men and women like you.

It is a pleasure and an honor for me to be privileged to work with you, and for you, as we launch into the deep and fill our nets with the ingredients that will assure our building a cleaner, greater and more prosperous Georgia. It is my hope that, as we travel together, it will be my good fortune to be blessed with your understanding, confidence and friendship.

You...you...and you...all members of this august body and Georgians everywhere, have my assurance that I shall strive in every thought and action to conduct myself in such a way as to merit your trust and friendship today—and tomorrow.

I am convinced that this General Assembly and this administration have the greatest opportunity ever afforded a Georgia General Assembly and a Georgia administration to be of service to the people, to Georgia, and to America.

It is an opportunity that requires each of us to realize and to accept the awesome responsibility which is ours.

It is an opportunity that demands that we give all we can give, that we be dedicated, determined and resolute in measuring up to the challenge that is ours, a challenge that in truth, we have asked for.

We must pay the price, we must sacrifice, when duty demands it.

In a nation where the crime rate is increasing some seven times faster than our population, this General Assembly can, through its actions, direct America back on the path to law and order.

In a nation which bears the scars of rioting, burning, looting and draft-card burning—the 1968 General Assembly of Georgia can provide the void in leadership and lead Americans back to peace, tranquillity, progress and patriotism.

In times like these, when some insist God is dead, that His name should be removed from our oath of office, from our coins and courtrooms, from the pledge of allegiance to our flag and country, when some insist the name of God and His word must not be spoken or read by, or to, our children in the public schools—members of the Georgia General Assembly of 1968 can, through their actions, say to the nation and to the world that God is *not* dead—He lives—He lives within our hearts, He guides us in our deliberations and we publicly and unashamedly profess our faith in Him.

In a nation blessed with an abundance of material things, but where there is too much neglect for the less fortunate, you and I can lead our nation toward a real concern and compassion for the helpless, the needy and the handicapped, as God and our conscience would have us do.

On every hand we see the soul of America decaying.

Dishonesty, inefficiency and immorality run rampant.

I plead with the members of this distinguished body, and my fellow Georgians everywhere, to lend their support and cooperation to this administration so that Georgia and Georgians can be the state and the people that leads all of America toward honesty, efficiency and morality.

While some are speaking out for socialism, communism, and atheism, let the members of this General Assembly and all Georgians cry out for free enterprise, Americanism, God and liberty.

Let us begin and end our deliberations fully aware of the truism that without God and liberty no society can be great.

Let us be sure that our deliberations and decisions are not partisaned. Let's not think just of ourselves, our own local communities, our own state. Let's think of all America—and God.

Perhaps, some of you say that the task is too tough.

I say to you that the tougher our assignment, the more glorious and the more rewarding our success.

Georgians and Americans are crying out for courageous leadership. I urge you to be the state legislature which provides it.

You say it can't be done? You ask what's the use? You feel it's impossible?

I refer you to the year 1966 when one Georgian faced insurmountable odds, when there was no chance for victory, when on every hand the voices of doom cried out, "It can't be done, what's the use, it's impossible," and were heard throughout Georgia and America.

One man, with the help of God and the people, with faith in America, overcame tremendous odds and won a significant victory.

I am sure that we all realize the total success in reaching the goals which I have outlined will be difficult, trying, often disappointing and always tough.

But your chances for victory are far greater than the chances of the man in 1966 of which I spoke.

One strong, fearless, dedicated and God-fearing patriotic legislature can do the job and return America to its rightful place as the greatest, freest and cleanest nation on earth.

When the annals of history are recorded, let them say to the world that the members of the 1968 Georgia General Assembly heeded the call of Georgians and Americans—that they set the course for out state and country to return to law and order, to peace and tranquillity, to free enterprise, to patriotism, to obedience to God, and yes, that you, more than any state legislature in American history, fought for the restoration and preservation of sensible and constitutional government.

Will you accept the challenge? Will you work to carry out the programs? I am depending on you. But, more important, the people of Georgia and America are depending upon you. Thank you and Godspeed.

State of the State
14 January 1969

It is a truly great experience to participate at this hour in the history of our state and our nation, for we have passed into the beginning of a new age.

A stimulating age.

Full of inspiration.

Posing challenge after challenge after challenge.

It is a time requiring leadership and dedication of the highest order.

A time for us to take off the old, no longer of value, and put on the new.

A time for new approaches to old problems.

A time to reaffirm our enduring faith—the kind of faith that was relayed to us just a few short weeks ago from across the great void of space.

A time to think and a time to pray.

A time for man to expand his horizons, to dream, to plan, to work, and to build.

I am encouraged and full of hope as I look out and see those with whom I have worked so closely over the past months and those who are here for the first time.

I see a blending of experience and youth which bodes well for Georgia.

I come before you on this occasion offering my full cooperation and seeking yours.

I am grateful for the close and friendly working relationship which has existed between the members of the legislative branch and the executive branch.

A relationship that has been characterized by open doors in both branches.

A relationship that has brought Georgia to the zenith of her growth and development.

The governor and the staff of the executive department are ready to work with you in every way to further the interests of the state and her people. I urge that you call upon me when I may be of assistance to you—and I humbly seek your understanding, your cooperation and your counsel as we work to achieve our common goal of making ours a better state in which to live.

I am confident that a deep sense of duty will compel each of us to live up to the great trust and confidence which the electorate has placed in us, both collectively and as individuals.

The issues we face are complex, and dealing with them will be trying. But, the progress we have made should provide the inspiration needed to get the job done.

Let's look for a moment at education.

We are in the best position for qualified teachers since we have been in the business of public education. While children and classrooms in some other states have been without teachers, this has not been true in Georgia.

Rather than being faced with a critical teacher shortage, as predicted earlier, Georgia, according to a survey in September 1968, was the only state in the fifty with an ample supply of qualified applicants.

In this one year alone, some 15,000 new students were added. They required 600 teachers and 600 schoolrooms—the equivalent of twenty new thirty-room school buildings with all the equipment, facilities, staff and books required for them.

All of this is possible because we together had the courage and foresight to make advances in education during the past two years that exceeded any previous four years, and that of any other Southeastern state during this period.

Many said it couldn't be done. But you didn't believe it.

What about higher education?

Nine out of ten Georgians now live within thirty-five miles of a state institution of higher learning.

We are finally competitive in holding and attracting qualified professors in the University System. We have grown from an enrollment of 30,000 students in 1960, to 77,000 in 1968—an increase of some 8,500 in this school term alone, which is more than the equivalent of starting a new Georgia Tech.

We can share full pride that Georgia has won for herself national recognition and admiration from the educational, industrial and governmental leaders of this country.

You helped make this possible, too.

What about industrial development?

With your help, we have been able to do more telling the story of Georgia's industrial opportunities in one fiscal year than in any one previous four-year period and, with the present fiscal year that closes our first biennium, our promotional program in these two years will exceed any previous twelve-year period.

Dollars for new and expanded industry for the fiscal ended June 30, 1968, amounted to more than $625,000,000—exceeding the previous two record fiscal years combined, and the increase in fiscal 1968 alone amounted to the total increases in the past ten years.

In a survey conducted by a national magazine among leading businessmen and industrialists to determine where they would like to locate their plants or make their investments, our own State Georgia received more favorable responses than any other state in the Southeast.

And what about mental health?

Our regional mental health program is well underway with facilities now open in Thomasville, Bainbridge and Atlanta one will soon be opened in Augusta, one is under construction in Savannah, and one each planned for Rome and Columbus. These, together with the new Retardation Center in DeKalb County, which will open this spring, will give Georgia a decentralized mental health program without equal in the nation.

And what about penal reform?

In keeping with the open door policy of this administration, we have thrown open Georgia's backward and benighted prison system to the scrutiny of the press and public of this state; comprehensive investigations of conditions in all areas of the penal system have been conducted and, when we implement the recommendations to be made to this session, there will be true penal reformation and rehabilitation in Georgia for the first time. The time for talking and investigating is past—the time for action is now.

However, in our expression of concern and compassion, and in our zeal to lend a helping hand to those who inhabit our prisons and who have moved in the wrong direction, we must also continue to meet our first responsibility of government, that of protecting the lives and property of the law-abiding citizens and achievers in this state.

It is well-known by the people of this country that there are places where this responsibility has not been met, and the people have suffered accordingly. Thank God, this condition is to a lesser degree in Georgia than in many other places. We have maintained the peace, tranquillity and progress and, so long as Lester Maddox is governor of Georgia, it will continue!

To you young people who are now watching from your elementary, high school and college classrooms—you who are earning, learning and building up—rather than ruining, burning and tearing down, as some do—you, too, are helping to make it all possible—we say thanks. Your governor, the distinguished members of your state legislature and your parents are proud of you.

And what about workmen's compensation?

Advances which had been actively sought for many years in the field of workman's compensation became a reality through legislation advocated by this administration and passed into law by you. These advances represent the greatest single increase since the enactment of Georgia's workmen's compensation laws.

Just as we have made unprecedented progress in these areas, our accomplishments have been equally significant in the Departments of Labor, Veterans Service, Game and Fish, Parks, Forestry, Tourism, Public Safety, Agriculture, Revenue, Family and Children's Services and Highway.

The moral tone of state government has never been higher. Where corruption has been found, it has been cleaned up. Where inefficiency has been discovered, it has been corrected. Where waste has been uncovered, it has been stopped.

With your support, and that of the people of this state, we brought about a new day in the State Board of Pardons and Paroles by requiring the first investigation and reformation of the system since its beginning. There is now hope and opportunity for all prison inmates—black and white, the unknown and those without influence.

This administration not only has preached honesty, morality, economy and efficiency, but it has also practiced them. And it will continue to do so!

As I promised as a candidate, it has been the practice of this administration—and shall continue to be—to make certain that the people of this state have an opportunity to participate in their government in every way possible.

I'm extremely proud that there have been more visitors to your governor's office and the Governor's mansion the past two years than in the past quarter of a century.

Toward this end of involving the people of Georgia in their government, I have gone to the lowlands and the highlands—to the slums and to the suburbs—to the wage earner and to the wage payer—to the deprived and to the provider—to the schoolhouses and to the prisons—to the farms and to the factories—and to the churches and to the homes.

I am grateful for the hospitality the people and the elected representatives have shown me and the confidence they have given me during my administration.

Now, my fellow Georgians, although it has been customary for governors, including this one, to devote practically all of their state of the state messages to lengthy recitals of the accomplishments of their administrations, my purpose here today is not to dwell at length on the past, but to talk to you as candidly and as forthrightly as I know how about the future.

I think it would best serve the public interest and do more toward achieving a general enlightenment to devote the remainder of my remarks to you here today to the subject of where we are in Georgia, financially, how we got there, and where we must go from here.

Prudence and sound financial administration demand that you and I recognize that the day of fiscal reckoning is at hand.

Anyone in or out of government, with but a rudimentary knowledge of finance, and familiar with the budgetary process in this state, knew this day had to come.

It was with full awareness of this that the Georgia house and the Georgia senate, during the 1967 sessions, passed resolutions calling for a thorough tax revision study to be made.

We are confronted with this situation now, and would be, regardless of who might be sitting in my chair or yours. At this hour and at this time, duty demands that we face the issue squarely and meet our responsibility.

So there may be no misunderstanding on the part of anyone—legislator, official, newsman or taxpayer—I wish to emphasize in the strongest terms at my command that the issue is not the future of Lester Maddox or his administration, but the future of Georgia and her people.

If our only concern were the second half of the Maddox term, then I would be delivering an entirely different message to you and to our fellow Georgians today.

And it most assuredly would not be one about raising taxes.

And what brought about this hour of decision?

There are a number of reasons, some of which I will outline now:

Let us first consider inflation. Just as no household, no church, no commerce club, no business, no industry, no farm, no other state government, nor the federal government can escape the ravages of inflation and the endless problems it produces, neither can your state government.

Just and you and others in the American economy must adjust to the problems of inflation, so must state government made the necessary adjustments to assure fiscal soundness and meet its duty to the people.

Another reasons for the position in which we find ourselves is that other people throughout this nation in business, industry and all levels of government are constantly receiving wage increases and in order to be competitive and to keep and attract qualified and able employees to provide the services demanded by the people, Georgia must also be competitive.

Then, too, we should consider that, according to a survey for the years 1965 and 1966, the citizens of forty-three other states pay more state and local taxes per capita than do the citizens of Georgia.

Further, since 1965, forty-six states have undergone tax structure changes resulting in increased revenues, but not Georgia. In addition, in the states of Florida and Alabama, the sales tax is 4 percent; in Mississippi, Kentucky and Pennsylvania, it is 5 percent; and in fifteen states, the sales tax percentage is higher than in Georgia, and less in only seven.

There are many other factors we could cite, but the last one of significance, and perhaps of paramount importance, which I will now refer to, concerns the use of large amounts of surplus funds in annual appropriations.

In the appropriations act of 1965, including supplements later added, the budget for fiscal year 1966 contained surplus funds in the amount of 11.4 percent, and 12.2 percent for fiscal year 1967.

The use of surplus funds has averaged 9.3 percent in each of the annual appropriations for the past four years. These funds accumulated as a result of estimating anticipated revenue far below actual growth. But I am pleased, as I believe that you are, that we had surpluses, rather then deficits, for, because of them, we were able to activate, improve and expand programs that have contributed greatly to the pace-setting progress and leadership that we enjoy today.

However, it was this same practice of appropriating surplus funds to begin and expand existing programs which would entail recurring, and sometimes escalating, costs in later years, which also contributed to our current dilemma.

Those in and out of state government with a sound knowledge of finances and with even a nodding acquaintance with the state budgetary process, knew that day would come when it would be necessary to either replace these funds by a permanent means, or else drastically curtail, bring to a halt, or, in some instances, even reverse our upward trend of progress and prosperity, thereby jeopardizing many of the previous investments and progress already made.

I personally will have no truck with bringing progress to a halt in Georgia. Neither do I believe that you distinguished members of this General Assembly will act in such fashion.

If *NO* is to be said to progress in Georgia, it will have to be said by others—not Lester Maddox.

The Maddox administration could get by. It could keep our state government and its programs functioning within the present anticipated revenue, although at minimal levels. Some would call it a "standstill budget," but in believing that there is no such thing as standing still in education, in government and in business, I call it a "go backwards budget."

As one who prides himself upon being a fiscal conservative and a hard-headed businessman, it would be far more popular for Lester

Maddox to oppose any new or revised taxes and, instead, to make loud speeches about "cutting the fat" out of the budget.

But that would only postpone the day of reckoning and create a crisis of hair-curling magnitude for my successor.

This situation which confronts us is not one of our choosing or our making. It was passed on to us; and duty demands that we face the issue. I, for one, hope that no other administration and no other General Assembly will ever have to inherit a similar burden.

In the interest of preventing the recurrence of this situation, I will recommend, in my budget message to you, the enactment of measures to provide fiscal restraints and safeguards in future budget appropriation matters that, in my judgment, should have enacted years earlier.

One will deal directly with the use of surplus funds and the other with our working reserve. These measures, in my opinion, should have been implemented years ago, and fiscal sanity demands that they be delayed no longer.

To fail to act would betray the best, long-range interests of our state.

It would be turning our backs on our children, our needy, our city and county governments, our property owners and our business community.

It would represent an abdication of our responsibilities as elected servants of the people.

Worst of all—for me, at least—it would be self-serving.

And anyone who knows anything at all about Lester Maddox knows that he takes his stands on the basis of what he believes is right, and not what is popular.

Besides, it just so happens that I believe like Mark Twain that to do what is right is best because it pleases some people and thoroughly astounds all the rest!

So, let everyone be on notice that opposition to tax revision solely on the basis of opposition to Lester Maddox is simply not justified. Opponents will have to come up with a better reason than that.

With that at rest—hopefully for good—let us look at what really is at stake.

At stake is the fact that, under our present tax structure, the local property tax in Georgia will have to be doubled over the next eight years.

At stake is the fact that, under our present tax structure, the property tax rapidly is becoming a major impediment to the location of new and expanded business and industry in Georgia, and is interfering increasingly with the functions of the private free enterprise system.

At stake is the fact that, under our present tax structure, the poor and needy among our citizens—those whom we are trying to help pull themselves by their own bootstraps—are being taxed twice as heavily percentage-wise as are our affluent citizens.

At stake is the fact that, under our present tax structure, the State of Georgia cannot finance any new or expanded programs or services to the people, cannot provide adequate facilities for swelling public school and college enrollments and cannot staff and open the new mental health, penal and other institutions now under construction and planned.

At stake is the fact that our present revenue structure will not sustain the present rate of progress in all fields of which we are all so proud, nor will it provide a sound revenue base upon which we can plan, build and grow to take our rightful place in the twenty-first century, now only a little more than three decades away.

The facts are clear and indisputable.

The property tax in this state has reached a point of saturation, and the already overburdened property owner cannot be called upon to bear an even greater portion of the burden of supporting governmental programs in Georgia.

The regressive nature of our present uncoordinated sales and income taxes is serving as a major deterrent to getting our disadvantaged citizens—those who cannot help themselves—out of poverty and into productive, tax-paying citizenship.

The spiraling local property tax is directly penalizing the establishment, expansion and improvement of capital facilities by business and industry and threatens to halt and reverse the very encouraging economic growth spurt we are now having and which is keeping our revenues under the present structure above maintenance level.

Every authority we have consulted has stated, without qualification, that it is imperative that Georgia act now to devise a tax system which will provide our cities and counties with substantial additional revenue and create a favorable business climate by achieving fiscal adequacy and tax equality.

On Thursday, I will come before you again with bold and imaginative proposals which I have advocated for more than ten years, and which will herald a new day and benefit all Georgians.

I will then offer them to you for consideration, believing that if implemented, they will generate more than $2,000,000,000 in new and expanded industry beyond what we may gain otherwise during the next decade. They will raise per capita income by several hundred dollars; they will help strengthen and preserve our local communities; and they will provide relief for the property owner who, otherwise, would continue to bear the brunt of the tax-load.

The discrimination of our present tax structure against the poor, the property owner, and local governments cannot be justified and, if long continued, likely will set counter forces into motion which will undo all the progress we have achieved in the last quarter century.

Ladies and gentlemen, I began these remarks on a note of faith and I come to my conclusion in the same vein.

The recommendations of your governor can be summed up in that one word:

FAITH—faith in God, faith in our representative democracy and faith in ourselves and our capacity to solve our own problems.

State of the State
13 January 1970

It's good to be back with you for another legislative session.

I am sure that each member of this august body is well aware that this governor always has a hearty welcome for the members of the Georgia General Assembly. I look forward to this time of the year because the beginning of each new session is always accompanied by new hope.

We can now begin anew. We can attack those problems which we have left from past deliberations and resolve to deal effectively and courageously with those new problems which are of vital concern to our people.

It is expected that politicians will sometimes be politicians, but there comes a time in the life of every public official when politics must be set aside and every consideration be given the public good. That time is now.

The power of this free government rests with a free people—the men and women who run the machines, build the bridges, milk the cows, lay the bricks, drive the trucks, fry the chicken and do the other things within the private free enterprise which earn our government a living, and make our government possible.

I think it is well for us to remind ourselves upon occasion that government is not a producer, but a consumer.

Government consumes labor, material and money—a lot of money. State government is like a campfire in the wilderness. As long as the fire is fed adequately, it provides light, warmth and protection. Too much fuel, given without adequate controls, creates a danger to the people. Too little fuel leaves some of the people out in the cold, unprotected. We are the watchers of the fire. It is our job to say, "That is enough, and that would be too much." And it is only natural that we would sometimes disagree.

But there is only one fire, and it must be regulated to serve all who look to it for light, for warmth and for protection...

Ours must not be just a rural state government...

Not just an urban state government...

Not just a poor man's state government...

Not just a rich man's state government...

Not just a white man's state government...

And not just a black man's state government.

Ours must be a state government of all the people, for all the people, and by all the people, bar none.

Of course, this is no great revelation to you. It is because of your recognition of this important principle that we, as servants of the people, in their state government, have been able to make such tremendous accomplishments in the year just passed, and, in those years immediately preceding 1969, enabling me, today, as Georgia's chief executive, to report to you, the esteemed members of the Georgia General Assembly and to the people of the great State of Georgia that the state of the state is excellent.

Such a report should be applauded by every Georgian. Hailed by every Georgia newspaper. And welcomed by every politician, whether Republican, Democrat or Independent.

But, let's recall some of the predictions that were being made back in 1966 and in early 1967 about what the Maddox administration would do for Georgia—or, maybe I should say, do "to" Georgia. Remember this headline? "New South 'Buried,' Maddox Foes Claim." One person was quoted as saying, "I sincerely believe that the image of Mr. Maddox is so negative that even if he does a good job, we won't be able to overcome the effects of a four-year term."

Other prophets of doom said that a vote for Lester Maddox would hold back Georgia's progress for the next four years. One Georgia editor said that "Lester Maddox constitutes a grave danger to all that responsible Georgians hold dear."

Some said that schools would close, industry would move out, new industry would not come in, our economy would roll backwards and Georgia would be engulfed with rioting, looting, burning, killing, chaos and disorder. But, now, I am going to take this opportunity to bring the truth and to bring the facts to you and to all Georgians without any bias, without any editorializing and, yes, without any fear.

Throughout the nation and throughout the world, Georgia today is recognized as one of the finest, most progressive, most dynamic, most peaceful and most promising states in the union. And you don't have to take my word for it. Just look—anywhere. The facts speak for themselves.

During this administration, Georgia finally moved out of its adolescence to take its rightful place as a full-fledged member of this great nation—and not just a member—but a leader. Isn't that wonderful!

The great seal of Georgia has been polished to a luster never before seen in this state by the hands of the people and put out in the light for all to see, rather than for just a special few. Out-of-state visitors are flocking to Georgia as never before. Everywhere we turn, we see more progress and more prosperity. In spite of predictions, conditions are more peaceful and more harmonious than even the most optimistic among us would have thought possible under the circumstances that have been forced upon us.

I sincerely believe that this administration has been tested with more potential crises than any administration has had to face since the Reconstruction days. And, with God's help, we have met the challenge. By showing a willingness and the ability to work with all people, we have paved the way to better understanding among all factions and to more civilized resolutions of divergent opinions.

Let's take a look, now, at what has been accomplished by this attitude of cooperation. Let's look at the record—the real record, and not just the rumors, half-truths and opinions.

During the past thirty-six months, investments in new and expanded industry have exceeded one and one-half billion dollars. The Maddox administration's three years have topped the previous seven years by some $150,000,000 in industrial gains.

As a result of this industrial revolution, Georgians are enjoying a higher standard of living Georgia's percentage of personal income increase places our state fourth from the top in the entire nation, according to the latest available figures.

We have a good momentum going, and there is almost no limit to how much we could build upon it. Our people are staying in Georgia and helping to build a stronger, more prosperous state. And, not only are Georgians staying, but people from other states, and, yes, from other parts of the world, are coning to Georgia, bringing with them new capital, new industry, new job opportunities, new revenue, new ideas, and, yes, new hope.

We promised the people that we could carry the story of Georgia's industrial potential and her tourist attractions to the nation and the world as never before. And, with your help and the help of many other individuals and organizations, that story has been, and is being, told.

During this administration, leaders throughout the nation in education, in government and in industry have been fully awakened to the fact that Georgia is the dynamic, prosperous and peaceful hub of a great region.

Georgia's Department of Industry and Trade, a one-time political dumping ground, has been turned into one of the most efficient and most effective such agencies in the United States. That is a remarkable achievement. When we consider that in 1960 Georgia was at the bottom of seven Southeastern states in dollars for new and expanded industry and was the only state in the nation without an advertising campaign, due to the mismanagement and misuse of funds, the accomplishments of the Department of Industry and Trade appear all the more impressive.

Another factor which I believe has contributed greatly to the progress in our industrialization program and in virtually ever facet of our economy which has been the peace and harmony enjoyed by our state which, when compared to many of our sister states, strikes a stark contrast.

This administration has been recognized for its efforts to bring together industry, labor, government, education and many other private interests into one cooperative unit, working together in harmony for the common good of all, and I am deeply grateful to all who have been willing to put aside personal interests to seek workable compromises which have resulted in a better day for all concerned.

I am especially grateful to you young people who have demonstrated their maturity and responsibility by doing their best to devote the majority of their efforts to getting a good education and taking advantage of the opportunities being offered them by the taxpayers and other supporters of education.

Georgia is richly blessed with just plain outstanding young men and women who, because of their faith in God and love for country and strong moral character, do more than all of us combined in making Georgia the peaceful, progressive and dynamic state that it is. Don't you agree? Georgia is not the "nation's battleground," as some predicted. From time to time, and even now, we have faced difficult moments, but reason has prevailed. Peace has been preserved.

I thank God for this blessing, and I pray that we can continue during the trying months ahead to have the cooperation and support of all Georgia citizens, black and white, rich and poor, powerful and weak, in our effort to reach solutions to our problems which are fair to all. This is the only way. We cannot afford to battle among ourselves. There are many other battles to be fought: The battle against poverty, against hunger, against disease, against ignorance, against injustice, against inefficiency, against immorality, against crime, and, yes, even against boredom.

We have waged a tremendous battle against injustice in the State Board of Pardons and Paroles. For the first time in the history of that department, this administration called for, and received, a total investigation, with the findings open to the press and to the public.

We were determined to clean up this vital operation and to bring a swift conclusion to the old days of secrecy and favoritism. And we have done just that.

Penal reform, too, was something that had been talked about for decades, but very little had been done. So, I went to the prisons, myself, and I saw first-hand, what needed to be done and how these facilities had been neglected. Our duty was clear. We swept out the rats and roaches; we built visitation facilities for the inmates' families; we declared war on fire-traps and health hazards; we put decent, nourishing food on the tables; we established and enforced humane work and recreation standards and regulations; we introduced new programs of education and vocational rehabilitation.

When it was seen that these minimum standards for penal operations in Georgia would not be compromised, many camps found it impractical to remain open. During the first three years of the Maddox administration, a total of twenty correctional facilities have ceased operation, which equals the exact number closed during the entire quarter of a century prior to our thirty-months months in office.

Rather than follow the old policy of discharging a man in rags with eight dollars and a kick, he now gets twenty five dollars, transportation home, a new suit and a handshake.

We have established the first work-release program in the entire history of Georgia's penal system, another milestone which benefits the inmates, their families and the taxpayers.

You might not see our progress reflected in the news stories you read or hear, but the inmates and wardens and other prison personnel who have seen the changes come about during the past thirty-six months will tell you that we have had more real penal reform in Georgia in the past three years than was the case during the previous thirty to forty years.

Everywhere we look, we see evidence of Georgia on the go. In virtually every area of our state, we can see progress being made in highway construction. This accelerated construction is not only providing more convenience and safety for motorists, but everywhere we put down a new yard of concrete, we add to the opportunities of that area.

Although all citizens cannot take advantage of these opportunities, our Department of Family and Children's Services has been doing a good job in helping those who cannot help themselves, but the increases in assistance to the blind, disabled and aged and the families with dependent children have not been sufficient to even keep ahead of the wolf of inflation.

Later this week, I will be asking you for additional protection for those of our citizens who are being left out in the cold. As we all know, to have good government we must have must have good government employees—people who are honest, skilled and dedicated. It has been the policy of this administration to protect the able career employees who are doing a good job, giving a day's labor for a day's pay, and this policy is paying off handsomely for every Georgia taxpayer.

Under the Maddox administration, personnel are recruited not on the basis of what they, who they know or where they're from, but solely on the basis of their qualifications for the job available. I have tried to operate state government just like you and others would operate your business.

In the area of mental health, our achievements are receiving nationwide attention. With the opening of new facilities, along with other innovations in the treatment of mental disease, which permitted the reduction of terribly overcrowded Central State facilities, it is now possible for a person with mental difficulty to get intensive treatment which often puts him back into a productive life as a taxpayer and supporter of his family.

This kind of treatment is more expensive, of course, but we simply cannot put a price tag on a person's life.

In the Department of Labor, a comprehensive manpower center has been established in Atlanta, the first of its kind in the United States. Its purpose is to provide one-stop service to both job seekers and employers.

To bring workers and jobs together quickly on a professional basis, a computerized job bank, the third such facility in the nation, has been established at the center and is now in full operation.

For the first time, a highly successful cooperative effort between the Corrections Board and Parole Board and the State Training and Employment Service, is bringing pre-release training, evaluation of inmates and jobs for them before or shortly after release.

Although sought for years without success, it was during this administration, too, that the greatest advancements were made in benefits for men and women of labor since the enactment of Workman's Compensation Laws.

Of course, virtually every adult in our state has had occasion to observe the new efficiency of the State Department of Revenue in handling the job of tax collection.

In spite of a greatly increased workload, the time required for an individual to get his income tax refund has been drastically reduced.

The Department of Agriculture has been modernized to better serve both the farmer and the consumer. Through more intensive programs of research, inspection and marketing, we have been able to not only help the farmer improve his lot and derive a fair profit from his investments, but we have also been able to provide the consumer—including the city housewife—with a better product at the lowest possible price.

And, my friends, we can all be proud of the job being done by the Department of Public Safety, even though we have not furnished this department with the number of men and cars to adequately patrol the highways.

Many previous unmarked cars are now identified properly as patrol cars when on Georgia highways, and these are helping us to keep down tragedies on our roads in spite of the fact that Georgia led the nation last year in the percentage of increases in both motor vehicle registrations and gasoline consumption.

With the help and cooperation of the Georgia General Assembly and the various state department heads, every state function has undergone some change for the better.

But, there is one area of state government that I have not mentioned thus far; and not because it is the least important, but because it is the most important. I am talking about public education.

You will recall that when we were in the midst of a serious teacher shortage in 1966, professional educators, public officials, political candidates, the news media and others predicted that this teacher shortage would become critical by the fall of 1967, and that education in Georgia would be crippled. I promised the people of Georgia that this would not happen. And, with the help of you in the General Assembly, we were able to increase salaries for teachers and professors more in two years than in any previous four-year period, and more than any other southeastern state during that period, thus averting a potential crisis.

We have also been able to make advances in our area vocation-technical education program which make this system second to no other in the nation. Not only do we have an outstanding system of area vocational-technical schools throughout the state, but we have also made tremendous increases in the number of high schools offering vocational-technical programs. We have expanded and improved our system of educational television to make it equal to the finest in the entire southeast. Expansions have been made in the educational programs for exceptional children, for those in our retardation centers, in our mental institutions and in many of our penal operations.

Education provides the heartbeat of our economy, of our culture and of our civilization. And, I know that you are proud of the great strides we have made in education and I believe you will agree with that these advances in the various areas of education contribute more than any other single factor to the industrial revolution we are now enjoying in America.

But, at this very moment, the heartbeat of Georgia, public education, is threatened—and with it the education, safety and liberty of our children throughout Georgia and America.

Public education in Georgia and elsewhere in America has fallen under the strong arm of a federal police state which demands that we surrender our children and grandchildren, their teachers and their schools and our communities, as outlined by the communist enemies of our children and America in their platform of 1928.

The communists have worked to implement this program for forty-two years and have met with great success because presidents, governors, congressmen, Supreme Court justices, state legislators and others, either knowingly or unwittingly, have fully supported their demands.

At this moment, public education in Georgia and America faces a crisis of unprecedented magnitude.

Children, teachers and parents are having their God-given and constitutionally granted liberty and freedom stolen from them by a national government that has gone mad and by governors, legislators, other elected public officials, top educators, and, yes, those who campaign for such offices who go along with the demands of cowards in our governments— the socialists and communists who demand the enslavement of our children, their teachers and the takeover of public education.

All during the past fifteen years, I predicted that our national government would follow the communists's demands to place education under a police state in America unless, parents , educators and public officials united to protect our children, preserve local control of education and defend the United States Constitution.

I stated many times the communist demands to close schools, bus students, transfer teachers and the resulting crime, immorality, chaos, disorder and down-grading of education in America would be our fate unless governors, legislators, congressmen, other elected officials and parents united and demanded that state and local governments and local systems of education be strengthened and preserved.

For having warned what would take place, I have been laughed at, ridiculed, ostracized and labeled a lunatic, a demagogue, an extremist and a redneck. And, not in all the history of Georgia has one man been so lied about, treated so dishonestly, unfairly and with such prejudice, hate and bitterness by major local news media. They have used rumors, analyses and views in their new stories and editorials to try to destroy Lester Maddox, even if in so doing so they hurt our wonderful state.

And the only thing I have done to warrant the hatred of the press that causes the most of the time to spread news that would reflect unfavorably against Lester Maddox, and pass by most that would reflect favorably, is to publicly and unashamedly profess my faith in God and love for my country, while taking a public stand for preservation of local control of education, the rights to private property and American private free enterprise.

Yes, mine was a lonely voice, but no more.

Georgians have now come face to face with the reality that everything I said would happen, relative to education and our children, is upon us.

Our schools are being destroyed, our children are being treated as animals and our teachers are being forced into involuntary servitude in violation of the United States Constitution. And they finally realize that unless we return to local control of education, freedom of choice is restored and our courts turn back to the United States Constitution, America, itself, will shortly go down the drain as a free republic.

Who brought on these conditions? Presidents, governors, congressmen, legislators, other elected officials and candidates for those offices who just plain don't have the guts and patriotism and love for our children needed for them to be Americans first and politicians later.

Sure, we have provided the dollars, bricks and mortar, which were made available by the people. I am here to tell you that politicians have generally placed the higher emphasis on dollars, material values and self and one another.

And, America has been forgotten.

Our children are being ignored.

And what is right and needed to preserve freedom and this great country has been sidetracked by too many public officials.

Even at this moment, the voices are few and faint from our own state house. Elected public officials in and our of the Georgia General Assembly seem to be afraid to be counted for local control of education and for our children—black and white—their safety and welfare.

I thank God for private education and I am thankful that so many are so blessed with the ability to send their children to private schools, thus protecting them from the intolerable conditions facing children in many public schools. But, when public officials and candidates for public office think so little of public schools as to flee with their children to exclusive private schools and then urge less fortunate parents and their children to surrender to the "police state" over public education, it is the most sickening, most disgusting and the most reprehensible brand of hypocrisy. Such politicians have no business being elected to, or serving in, any public office.

Any such man who demands for others and their children and grandchildren what he would not tolerate for his own is a coward and a hypocrite of the first order.

We see students marching, trying to save their schools, their education and their country, because of such hypocrites.

The fact that they are marching says that we, of our generation, have failed them.   We have provided the dollars and the bricks but not the guts, the patriotism, the courage and the leadership that we should have.

And by providing the dollars, the bricks, the buildings, the highways and all other material values will pale into insignificance if we fail our children in this present crisis.

I'm here to tell you, my fellow Georgians and my fellow public officials, that the people of this state, after seeing what is happening to their children, to their communities, to their schools and to their investments, are fed up.

They're sick and tired of seeing their liberty and their freedom go down the drain.

And they're disgusted with public officials, whoever they might be, who do not have the guts to speak up for their children, for their communities, for the survival of public education and for their rights as citizens of what is supposed to be a free country.

The people care about what happens to their children.

They want them protected so that they can grow up to be free citizens who love their county. And the citizens want your help. They are demanding it. They deserve it.

The people who elected us to public office care about what happens to their schools. They care about what happens to their communities. They love their liberty, and they want it defended and preserved—not surrendered by public officials. They care about what happens to their country and its constitution. They care. And they're fed up with public officials who don't care . They have a right to be fed up. And I am fed up, too.

It is time, my friends, for every elected public official, every educator, every teacher, every state house official, and, yes, for the Georgia General Assembly to say to the boys and girls in our schools and to their parents: "We, too, love our children, their schools and their communities, for they are our children, our schools and our communities."

We can tell them by sending a message to the president telling him to assume the position of leadership he said the president should in turning back federal control and the federal police state over education, rather than the position of leadership he now offers to those who strike down freedom of choice and local control of education.

And we must tell Georgia's boys and girls that we stand with them by calling upon Congress to cease action on all legislative matters until "freedom of choice" is restored and the federal police state is removed from public education.

I'm begging—I'm pleading with the members of this august body and with other state house officials to join in the effort by these children, by these teachers and by these parents, both black and white, to defend and protect their schools and their education. For, without freedom of choice for both students and teachers, there can be no freedom for any American.

Let us go from these great halls today and tell these boys and girls that we will no longer charge them with the responsibility of upholding the United States Constitution and defending the rights of all Americans, but that we will finally assume the responsibility that we have so long neglected.

I know this is an election year, but this crisis demands that we cast aside all political considerations and all personal considerations and that we consider only our responsibilities to our people.

We must take our stand in such a way that not only our fellow Georgians, but people throughout the nation, will look and listen and be filled with hope, with encouragement and inspiration. We must let them know that in Georgia, there has been a rebirth of commonsense government.

God help the members of this General Assembly rise to this challenge. May God help our children if you don't. Even though we are face to face with this most important of all issues—a threat to all we hold dear—things do look good in most other areas.

We have made progress; we have moved forward; we have kept the fire going. And, while I know that you are proud of these accomplishments and improvements in government, as I am proud, I cannot believe that you are satisfied. I know that Lester Maddox is not satisfied. I'm not satisfied, because I know that we could have done more, we should have done more, and now, we must do more.

With all the progress that we have already made, if we will now meet our responsibility to the Georgia people with courage, foresight and true statesmanship, this could be recorded as the greatest period of progress in Georgia's history. We could do that for the people who elected us to the high offices we hold.

I know that this is an election year, and decisions come more slowly when the weight of the electorate hangs heavy over our heads, but duty to the people demands that we put political considerations aside and base our decisions on one premise—what is best for the citizens of Georgia.

In my budget message on Thursday, I will outline to you a program which will test your courage, test your determination and test your statesmanship. I believe you will pass the test by passing most of this program for progress. I realize the awesome responsibility which you have and I wish you well. I want you to know that I will work with you in every way possible to better serve the people of Georgia. To accomplish that end, I will strive to keep an open door, an outstretched hand and an open mind. I am willing to give and take to get the job done.

As long as I am not required to compromise in my duty to my God, to the people of Georgia and to my family, I am willing to try new ways, re-examine old ways and seek a common ground. I ask and expect no more and no less of you.

Believing as I do that state government in Georgia belongs to all the people and does not belong just to Lester Maddox, nor any other individual, not just to Democrats, Republicans, Independents, whites or blacks, rich or poor, and not just to the young or the old…

And, believing that state government is duty-bound to serve equally, and without fear or favor, small cities and counties, as well as large cities and counties, the Maddox administration has been able to be fair with all of Georgia and with all Georgians.

This is so because no individual, no political party and no special interest group can come to the governor's office and force demands upon me which I believe not to be in the best interest of all citizens.

I am free to make my own decisions.

I am free to be fair.

And, with God's help, we will continue to do what is right for all Georgians.

And, because the question is often raised as to what makes Lester Maddox tick, there is something else I want you to know.

Ladies and gentlemen of the Georgia General Assembly, not only am I a Christian and proud of it, as I know those you of other faiths are proud of your religion, but I am also an American who loves his state and his country and who is proud to be a citizen of Georgia and of these United States.

My only regret is that I haven't done more to serve my God and my country.

I have never been the Christian, the citizen, the husband, the father nor the governor I want to be and ought to be.

But, just as I have in the past, and as I do now, I will keep praying to God that He give me wisdom, that He strengthen my faith, help me to follow His ways, and that He use me for His glory and forgive my sins.

And, I'll be praying that God do the same for my family and for you and your family.

To give you the basis of this faith, let me tell you something that happened just a few short years ago.

Without any knowledge as to how I got there, I found myself in a hospital bed in what appeared to be a very serious condition. The news from the doctor was not good. My family was saddened and disturbed, but it caused me no great alarm, because I was thankful for the many years we had had together, for it could have been only half as many years, or none at all.

So I pray, "Dear God, if You can use me better in death than in life, and if it be Your will that I die, then I m ready; but if Your will is that I live, that You can use me better in life than in death, and I leave this hospital bed again, then I will spend whatever additional life I am given doing my best for You and seeking Your way in my life."

And I prayed further, promising God that if I did leave that bed alive, I would also spend the rest of my life speaking loudly and standing strongly for liberty, America, constitutional government, the right to private property, private free enterprise and honesty and morality in life.

This is where I stand, and from this position I will not retreat.

I realize that some of the things which I say an do are not what you would ordinarily expect of a governor. But, you see, I place my faith in God and what I believe to be right ahead of politics and ahead of self.

And, I will be following this philosophy and this belief later this week when I outline my legislative program to you.

May God grant each of us the wisdom to give in when we are wrong and the courage to keep fighting when we are right.

Bibliography

Anderson, William. *The Wild Man From Sugar Creek*. Baton Rouge: Louisiana State University Press, 1975.

Arnall, Ellis. *The Shore Dimly Seen*. J. P. Lippincott Co. 1946.

Barone, Michael and Grant Ujifusa. *The Alamanac of Politics*. National Journal, 1987.

Bowles, Billy and Remer Tyson. *They Love a Man in the Country: Saints and Sinners in the South*. Atlanta: Peachtree Publishers, 1989.

Carter, Jimmy. *Turning Point: A Candidate, a State, and a Nation Come of Age*. New York: Random House, 1992.

———. *Why Not the Best?*. Broadman Press: Nashville TN, 1975.

Carter, Rosalynn. *First Lady from Plains*. New York: Ballantine Books, 1984.

Cleland, Max. *Strong at the Broken Places*. Atlanta GA: Cherokee Publishing Company, 1989.

Cook, James F. *Governors of Georgia*. Second Edition. Macon: Mercer University Press, 1994.

———. *Carl Sanders: Spokesman of the New South*. Macon: Mercer University Press, 1993.

Galphin, Bruce. *The Riddle of Lester Maddox*. Atlanta GA: Camelot Publishing Company, 1968.

Gulliver, Hal. *A Friendly Tongue*. Macon: Mercer University Press, 1984.

Henderson, Harold P. and Gary L. Roberts. *Georgia Governors in a Time of Change.* Athens: University of Georgia Press, 1988.

Maddox, Lester Garfield. *Speaking Out: The Autobiography of Lester Garfield Maddox.* Garden City NY: Doubleday and Company Inc, 1975.

————. Prelude to One of a Kind. 1994.

————. A Call to Duty. 1988.

————. Interview by John Allen. *An Oral History Interview with Governor Lester Maddox.* Georgia Government Documentation Project. Atlanta: Georgia State University Press, 1989.

————. "One of a Kind."

————. *Collected Speeches of Lester Maddox.* Georgia Department of Archives and History, 1971.

Miller, Zell. *The Mountains Within Me.* Toccoa GA: Commercial Printing Co., 1976.

Personal Diary of Charles Robert Short.

Talmadge, Herman, with Mark Royden Winchell. *Talmadge: A Political Legacy, a Politician's Life.* Atlanta: Peachtree Publishers, 1987.

The Politics of Change: A Political Biography of Ellis Arnall. Athens: University of Georgia Press, 1991.

White, William S. *The Professional: Lyndon B. Johnson.* New York: Crest Books, 1964.

Personal Interviews

Beasley, Mary. Governor Zell Miller's staff.

Blackmon, John. Former Georgia state revenue commissioner.

Broun, Paul. Georgia state senator.

Egan, Mike. Georgia state senator.

Eldridge, Frank. Georgia Secretary of the Senate.

Gillis, Hugh. Georgia state senator.

Irvin, Tommy. Georgia Commissioner of Agriculture.

Maddox, Lester. Former governor of Georgia.

McDonald, Lauren. Former Georgia state representative and candidate for governoR

Miller, Zell. Former governor of Georgia.

Murphy, Tom. Georgia Speaker of the House.

Partain, J. O. Former Pardon and Parole Boards member.

Rowan, Bobby. Former Georgia state senator.
Tysinger, Jim. Georgia state senator.

Newspapers
Atlanta (GA) *Constitution*
Atlanta (GA) *Journal*
Marietta (GA) *Daily Journal*
Columbus (GA) *Ledger-Enquirer*
Macon (GA) *Telegraph*
August (GA) *Chronicle*
Savannah (GA) *Morning News*
Brunswick (GA) *News*
Gainesville (GA) *Times*

Magazines
The Atlanta Historical Journal
Georgia History Journal
Georgia Trend
Atlanta Magazine
Time Magazine

Index

www.ingramcontent.com/pod-product-compliance
Lightning Source LLC
Chambersburg PA
CBHW030531100426
42813CB00001B/214